# GAMBLING
## WHAT'S AT STAKE?

ISSN 1543-4915

# GAMBLING
## WHAT'S AT STAKE?

Melissa J. Doak

**INFORMATION PLUS® REFERENCE SERIES**
Formerly Published by Information Plus, Wylie, Texas

GALE
CENGAGE Learning™

Detroit • New York • San Francisco • New Haven, Conn • Waterville, Maine • London

**Gambling: What's at Stake?**

Melissa J. Doak

Paula Kepos, Series Editor

Project Editors: Elizabeth Manar, Kathleen J. Edgar

Rights Acquisition and Management: Barbara McNeil, Tracie Richardson

Composition: Evi Abou-El-Seoud, Mary Beth Trimper

Manufacturing: Cynde Bishop

Product Management: Carol Nagel

For product information and technology assistance, contact us at **Gale Customer Support, 1-800-877-4253.**
For permission to use material from this text or product, submit all requests online at **www.cengage.com/permissions.**
Further permissions questions can be e-mailed to **permissionrequest@cengage.com**

Gale
27500 Drake Rd.
Farmington Hills, MI 48331-3535

ISBN-13: 978-0-7876-5103-9 (set)     ISBN-10: 0-7876-5103-6 (set)
ISBN-13: 978-1-4144-3374-5           ISBN-10: 1-4144-3374-3

ISSN 1543-4915

This title is also available as an e-book.
ISBN-13: 978-1-4144-5756-7 (set)
ISBN-10: 1-4144-5756-1 (set)
Contact your Gale sales representative for ordering information.

Printed in the United States of America
1 2 3 4 5 6 7 13 12 11 10 09

# TABLE OF CONTENTS

# PREFACE

*Gambling: What's at Stake?* is part of the *Information Plus Reference Series*. The purpose of each volume of the series is to present the latest facts on a topic of pressing concern in modern American life. These topics include today's most controversial and studied social issues: abortion, capital punishment, care for the elderly, crime, the environment, gambling, health care, immigration, minorities, national security, social welfare, women, youth, and many more. Even though this series is written especially for high school and undergraduate students, it is an excellent resource for anyone in need of factual information on current affairs.

By presenting the facts, it is the intention of Gale, a part of Cengage Learning, to provide its readers with everything they need to reach an informed opinion on current issues. To that end, there is a particular emphasis in this series on the presentation of scientific studies, surveys, and statistics. These data are generally presented in the form of tables, charts, and other graphics placed within the text of each book. Every graphic is directly referred to and carefully explained in the text. The source of each graphic is presented within the graphic itself. The data used in these graphics are drawn from the most reputable and reliable sources, in particular from the various branches of the U.S. government and from major independent polling organizations. Every effort has been made to secure the most recent information available. Readers should bear in mind that many major studies take years to conduct, and that additional years often pass before the data from these studies are made available to the public. Therefore, in many cases the most recent information available in 2009 is dated from 2006 or 2007. Older statistics are sometimes presented as well, if they are of particular interest and no more-recent information exists.

Even though statistics are a major focus of the *Information Plus Reference Series*, they are by no means its only content. Each book also presents the widely held positions and important ideas that shape how the book's subject is discussed in the United States. These positions are explained in detail and, where possible, in the words of their proponents. Some of the other material to be found in these books includes historical background, descriptions of major events related to the subject, relevant laws and court cases, and examples of how these issues play out in American life. Some books also feature primary documents, or have pro and con debate sections giving the words and opinions of prominent Americans on both sides of a controversial topic. All material is presented in an even-handed and unbiased manner; readers will never be encouraged to accept one view of an issue over another.

## HOW TO USE THIS BOOK

Gambling has long been a favorite pastime worldwide, and its history in the United States dates back to the founding of the nation. It has been estimated that Americans spend more than $1 trillion per year on charitable gambling, betting on horse and greyhound races, lottery purchases, casino wagering, and other legal and illegal gambling activities. Much controversy surrounds the gambling industry. While pro-gambling elements argue that the economic benefits of gambling far outweigh any potential risks, some individuals oppose gambling on moral grounds or argue that it can cause an increase in various types of social problems. This book presents in-depth information on how casino gambling, sports gambling, lotteries, and Internet gambling work, provides up-to-date financial data for each, and discusses the effects of these and other gambling activities on the communities in which they take place. Also discussed are American attitudes toward gambling.

*Gambling: What's at Stake?* consists of nine chapters and three appendixes. Each chapter is devoted to a particular aspect of gambling in the United States. For a summary of the information covered in each chapter, please see the synopsis provided in the Table of Contents at the front of the book. Chapters generally begin with an overview of the basic facts and background information on the chapter's topic, then proceed to examine subtopics of particular interest. For example, Chapter 5: Native American Tribal Casinos begins with a brief historical look at the growth of tribal casinos in the United States. Next, the chapter explains why the Indian Gaming Regulatory Act of 1988 came about and how it established a regulatory system and three classes of gambling activities. Tribal casinos are regulated at the federal, state, and local levels, and the chapter explains the types of government and tribal organizations and tribal-state compacts that oversee this regulation. Before a tribe opens a casino, it has to be federally recognized as a tribe. The chapter details the criteria that have to be met for a group of Native Americans to receive federal recognition as a tribe. The chapter also examines the revenue that tribes make and discusses how it is used, such as to fund the tribal government and the members of the tribe and to support the operations of local government agencies. Then the chapter examines the pros and cons of tribal-commercial casino ventures and tribal casinos being located off the reservation. The chapter concludes by discussing the development of tribal casinos in Connecticut and California and how these casinos have affected their respective state. Readers can find their way through a chapter by looking for the section and subsection headings, which are clearly set off from the text. Or, they can refer to the book's extensive index, if they already know what they are looking for.

**Statistical Information**

The tables and figures featured throughout *Gambling: What's at Stake?* will be of particular use to readers in learning about this topic. These tables and figures represent an extensive collection of the most recent and valuable statistics on gambling, as well as related issues—for example, graphics cover how much consumers spend on casino gambling as compared to other recreational pursuits, public opinion on the economic benefits of casinos, types of modern lottery games, horse racing purses paid out by state, and participation in gambling by college student-athletes. Gale, a part of Cengage Learning, believes that making this information available to readers is the most important way to fulfill the goal of this book: to help readers understand the issues and controversies surrounding gambling in the United States and reach their own conclusions.

Each table or figure has a unique identifier appearing above it, for ease of identification and reference. Titles for the tables and figures explain their purpose. At the end of each table or figure, the original source of the data is provided.

To help readers understand these often complicated statistics, all tables and figures are explained in the text.

References in the text direct readers to the relevant statistics. Furthermore, the contents of all tables and figures are fully indexed. Please see the opening section of the index at the back of this volume for a description of how to find tables and figures within it.

**Appendixes**

Besides the main body text and images, *Gambling: What's at Stake?* has three appendixes. The first is the Important Names and Addresses directory. Here, readers will find contact information for a number of government and private organizations that can provide further information on different aspects of gambling. The second appendix is the Resources section, which can also assist readers in conducting their own research. In this section, the author and editors of *Gambling: What's at Stake?* describe some of the sources that were most useful during the compilation of this book. The final appendix is the index.

**ADVISORY BOARD CONTRIBUTIONS**

The staff of Information Plus would like to extend its heartfelt appreciation to the Information Plus Advisory Board. This dedicated group of media professionals provides feedback on the series on an ongoing basis. Their comments allow the editorial staff who work on the project to continually make the series better and more user-friendly. The staff's top priorities are to produce the highest-quality and most useful books possible, and the Advisory Board's contributions to this process are invaluable.

The members of the Information Plus Advisory Board are:

- Kathleen R. Bonn, Librarian, Newbury Park High School, Newbury Park, California

- Madelyn Garner, Librarian, San Jacinto College–North Campus, Houston, Texas

- Anne Oxenrider, Media Specialist, Dundee High School, Dundee, Michigan

- Charles R. Rodgers, Director of Libraries, Pasco-Hernando Community College, Dade City, Florida

- James N. Zitzelsberger, Library Media Department Chairman, Oshkosh West High School, Oshkosh, Wisconsin

**COMMENTS AND SUGGESTIONS**

The editors of the *Information Plus Reference Series* welcome your feedback on *Gambling: What's at Stake?* Please direct all correspondence to:

Editors
*Information Plus Reference Series*
27500 Drake Rd.
Farmington Hills, MI 48331-3535

# CHAPTER 1
# GAMBLING IN THE UNITED STATES: AN OVERVIEW

Gambling is an activity in which something of value is risked on the chance that something of greater value might be obtained, based on the uncertain outcome of a particular event. Organized gambling has become an industry because so many people are willing and even eager to risk their money in exchange for a chance at something bigger and better. The elements of risk and uncertainty actually add to gambling's appeal—and to its danger. Throughout history, various cultures have considered gambling alternately harmless and sinful, respectable and corrupt, legal and illegal. Societal attitudes are dependent on customs, traditions, religion, morals, and the context in which gambling occurs.

Lawmakers have struggled to define gambling and determine which activities should be legal and which should not. For example, betting activities with an element of skill involved (such as picking a horse in a race or playing a card game) might be more acceptable than those based entirely on chance (such as spinning a roulette wheel or playing slot machines). Acceptability also depends on who profits from the gambling. Bingo games held for charity and lotteries that fund state programs are more commonly legal than casinos run for corporate profit.

Dan Seligman estimates in "In Defense of Gambling" (*Forbes*, June 23, 2003) that Americans legally gamble $900 billion per year. However, why do people gamble at all? Common sense suggests that risking something of value on an event with an uncertain outcome is irrational. Scientists postulate a variety of reasons for gambling, including the lure of money, the excitement and fun of the activity, and the influence from peers. At its deepest level, gambling may represent a human desire to control the randomness that seems to permeate life. Whatever the drive may be, it must be strong. An entire gambling culture has developed in the United States in which entrepreneurs (legal and otherwise) offer people opportunities to gamble, and business is booming.

## THE HISTORY OF GAMBLING
### Ancient Times

Archaeologists have discovered evidence that people in Egypt, China, Japan, and Greece played games of chance with dice and other devices as far back as 2000 BC. According to *Encyclopedia Britannica*, loaded dice—which are weighted to make a particular number come up more often than others—have been found in ancient tombs in Egypt, the Far East, and even North and South America.

Dice are probably the oldest gambling implements known. They were often carved from sheep bones and known as knucklebones. They are mentioned in several historical documents, including the *Mahabharata*, the epic poem and philosophy text written in India approximately twenty-five hundred years ago. A story in the New Testament of the Bible describes Roman soldiers throwing dice to determine who would get the robe of Jesus (4? BC–AD 29?). Roman bone dice have been found dating from the first to the third centuries AD. The Romans also gambled on chariot races, animal fights, and gladiator contests.

### The Medieval Period

During medieval times (approximately 500 to 1500) gambling was legalized by some governments, particularly in areas of modern-day Spain, Italy, Germany, and the Netherlands. England and France were much less permissive, at times outlawing all forms of gambling. King Louis IX (1215–1270) of France prohibited gambling during his reign for religious reasons. Still, illegal gambling continued to thrive.

During this period Christian powers in Europe launched the Crusades (military expeditions against Muslim powers that controlled lands considered holy by Christians). They also permitted gambling, but only by knights and people of higher rank. Violators were subject to severe whippings. Even among the titled gamblers, there was a legal limit on how much money could be lost, a concept that later would come to be known as limited-stakes gambling.

English knights returned from the Crusades with long-legged Arabian stallions, which they bred with sturdy English mares to produce Thoroughbred racehorses. Betting on private horse races became a popular pastime among the nobility. Card games also became popular in Europe around the end of the fourteenth century. According to the International Playing-Card Society, in "History of Playing-Cards" (June 2000, http://i-p-c-s.org/history .html), one of the earliest known references to playing cards in Europe dates from 1377. During the late 1400s and early 1500s lotteries began to be used in Europe to raise money for public projects. In "Lottery History" (2008, http://www.naspl.org/index.cfm?fuseaction=content&Page ID=12&PageCategory=11), the North American Association of State and Provincial Lotteries states that Queen Elizabeth I (1533–1603) established the first English state lottery in 1567.

## Precolonial America and the Colonial Era

Native Americans played games of chance as part of tribal ceremonies and celebrations hundreds of years before North America was colonized. One of the most common was a dice and bowl game in which five plum stones or bones carved with different markings were tossed into a bowl or basket. Wagers were placed before the game began, and scoring was based on the combination of markings that appeared after a throw. The Cheyenne called the game *monshimout*. A similar game was called *hubbub* by the Arapaho and by New England tribes.

European colonists brought gambling traditions with them to the New World. Historical accounts report that people in parts of New England gambled on horse racing, cockfighting, and bull baiting. Bull baiting was a blood sport in which a bull was tethered in a ring or pit into which dogs were thrown. The dogs were trained to torment the bull, which responded by goring the dogs. Spectators gambled on how many of the dogs the bull would kill.

In 1612 King James I (1566–1625) of England created a lottery to provide funds for Jamestown, Virginia, the first permanent British settlement in North America. Lotteries were later held throughout the colonies to finance the building of towns, roads, hospitals, and schools and to provide other public services.

Many colonists, though, disapproved of gambling. The Pilgrims and Puritans fled to North America during the 1620s and 1630s to escape persecution in Europe for their religious beliefs. They believed in a strong work ethic that considered labor morally redeeming and viewed gambling as sinful because it wasted time that might have been spent in productive endeavors.

Cockfighting, bear and bull baiting, wrestling matches, and footraces were popular gambling sports throughout Europe during the sixteenth and seventeenth centuries. The predecessors of many modern casino games were also developed and popularized during this period. For example, the roulette wheel is often attributed to French mathematician Blaise Pascal (1623–1662).

Gambling among British aristocrats became so customary during the early years of the eighteenth century that it presented a financial problem for the country. Gentlemen gambled away their belongings, their country estates, and even their titles. Cuthbert William Johnson noted in *The Law of Bills of Exchange, Promissory Notes, Checks, &c* (1839) that large transfers of land and titles were disruptive to the nation's economy and stability, so the reigning monarch, Queen Anne (1665–1714), responded in 1710 with the Statute of Anne, which made large gambling debts "utterly void, frustrate, and of none effect, to all intents and purposes whatsoever." In other words, large gambling debts could not be legally enforced. This prohibition has prevailed in common law for centuries and is still cited in U.S. court cases. Queen Anne is also known for her love of horse racing, which became a popular betting sport (along with boxing) during her reign.

A surge of evangelical Christianity swept through England, Scotland, Germany, and the North American colonies during the mid- to late 1700s. Many historians refer to this as the Great Awakening, a time when conservative moral values became more prevalent and widespread. Evangelical Christians considered gambling to be a sin and dangerous to society, and religion became a powerful tool for bringing about social change.

In October 1774 the Continental Congress of the North American colonies issued the Articles of Association (September 28, 2008, http://www.yale.edu/lawweb/ avalon/contcong/10–20–74.htm), which stated in part that the colonists "will discountenance and discourage every species of extravagance and dissipation, especially all horse racing, and all kinds of games, cock fighting, exhibitions of shews [*sic*], plays, and other expensive diversions and entertainments." The purpose of the directive was to "encourage frugality, economy, and industry."

## The Nineteenth Century

In general, gambling was tolerated as long as it did not upset the social order. According to James R. Westphal et al., in "Gambling in the South: Implications for Physicians" (*Southern Medical Journal*, vol. 93, no. 9, 2000), Georgia, Virginia, and South Carolina passed versions of the Statute of Anne during the colonial period to prevent gambling from getting out of hand. New Orleans became a gambling mecca during the 1700s and 1800s, even though gambling was outlawed during much of that time. In the 1830s almost all southern states outlawed gambling in public places; however, some exceptions were made for "respectable gentlemen."

In 1823, eleven years after becoming a state, Louisiana legalized several forms of gambling and licensed several gambling halls in New Orleans. Even though the licensing act was repealed in 1835, casino-type gambling continued to prosper and spread to riverboats traveling the Mississippi River. Professional riverboat gamblers soon developed an unsavory reputation as cheats and scoundrels. Several historians trace the popularization of poker and craps in the United States to Louisiana gamblers of that period. Riverboat gambling continued to thrive until the outbreak of the Civil War (1861–1865).

Andrew Jackson (1767–1845) was president of the United States from 1829 to 1837. The Jacksonian era was associated with a new attention to social problems and a focus on morality. A new wave of evangelical Christianity swept the country. According to I. Nelson Rose of Whittier Law School, in "The Rise and Fall of the Third Wave: Gambling Will be Outlawed in Forty Years" (William R. Eadington and Judy A. Cornelius, eds., *Gambling and Public Policy: International Perspectives*, 1991), gambling scandals and the spread of a conservative view of morality led to an end to most legal gambling in the United States by the mid-1800s.

Across the country, private and public lotteries were plagued by fraud and scandal and fell into disfavor. Objectionable to many southern legislators on moral grounds, lotteries had been banned in most southern states by the 1840s. By 1862 only two states, Missouri and Kentucky, had legal lotteries. However, lotteries were reinstated after the Civil War to raise badly needed funds. In 1868 Louisiana implemented a lottery known as "the Great Serpent." Even though it was extremely popular, the lottery was plagued with fraud and was eventually outlawed by the state in 1895. Casino gambling, which had been legalized again in Louisiana in 1869, was outlawed at the same time as the lottery.

Frontier gambling in the Old West, both legal and illegal, peaked during the mid- to late nineteenth century. Saloons and other gambling houses were common in towns catering to cowboys, traders, and miners. Infamous gamblers of the time included Doc Holliday (1851–1887), Bat Masterson (1853–1921), Poker Alice (1851–1930), and Wild Bill Hickok (1837–1876). Hickok was shot while playing poker in 1876. At the time, he held a hand of two black aces and two black eights, which came to be known as the "dead man's hand."

Gambling in general fell into disfavor as the nineteenth century ended. In England, Queen Victoria (1819–1901) ruled from 1837 to 1901; her rule was characterized by concern for morality and by the spread of conservative values. These attitudes permeated American society as well. Gambling fell out of favor as a pastime for respectable people. Many eastern racetracks and western casinos were pressured to close for moral and ethical reasons. As new states entered the Union, many included provisions against gambling in their constitutions. By federal law, all state lotteries were shut down by 1900.

## GAMBLING IN THE UNITED STATES SINCE 1900

As the twentieth century began, there were forty-five states in the Union. The territories of Oklahoma, New Mexico, and Arizona gained statehood between 1907 and 1912. According to Rose, the closure of casinos in New Mexico and Arizona was a precondition for statehood. In 1910 Nevada outlawed casino gambling. That same year, horse racing was outlawed in New York, and almost all gambling was prohibited in the United States. The only legal gambling options at the time were horse races in Maryland and Kentucky and a few isolated card clubs.

### Legalized Casinos in Nevada

The 1930s were a time of reawakening for legal gambling interests. Many states legalized horse racing and charitable gambling. Nevada went even further. In 1931 its legislature made casino gambling legal again. It seemed like a logical step: frontier gambling was widely tolerated in the state, even though gambling was officially illegal. More important, Nevada, like the rest of the country, was suffering from a deep recession, and it sought to cash in on two events. The state's divorce laws were changed in the early 1930s to allow the granting of a divorce after only six weeks of residency, so people from other states temporarily moved into small motels and inns to satisfy the residency requirement. At the same time, construction began on the massive Hoover Dam, only thirty miles from Las Vegas. Thousands of construction workers—like the people waiting for their divorces to become final—were all potential gamblers.

Small legal gambling halls opened in Reno (in the northern part of the state), but they catered mostly to cowboys and local residents and had a reputation for being raunchy and wild. In April 1931, however, the first gambling licenses were issued in Las Vegas. The first big casino, El Rancho Vegas, was opened in 1941 on what would later be known as the Strip.

Many in the business world doubted that casino gambling in Nevada would be successful. Most of the casino hotels were small establishments operated by local families or small private companies (some were dude ranches—western-style resorts that offered horseback riding). They were located in hot and dusty desert towns far from major cities, had no air conditioning, and offered few amenities to travelers. There was little or no state and local oversight of gambling activities.

However, the end of Prohibition—which had made it illegal to import or sell alcoholic beverages in the United States—brought another element to Las Vegas. During the Prohibition Era (1920–1933) organized crime syndicates operated massive bootlegging rings and became very powerful and wealthy. When Prohibition ended, they switched their focus to gambling. Organized criminals in New York and Chicago were among the first to see the potential of Nevada. Meyer Lansky (1902–1983) and Frank Costello (1891–1973) sent fellow gangster Benjamin "Bugsy" Siegel (1906–1947) west to develop new criminal enterprises. Siegel invested millions of dollars of the mob's money in a big and lavish casino in Las Vegas that he was convinced would attract top-name entertainers and big-spending gamblers. The Flamingo, a hotel and casino, opened in 1946. It was a failure at first, and Siegel was soon killed by his fellow mobsters.

POST–WORLD WAR II. Nevada's casinos grew slowly until after World War II (1939–1945). Postwar Americans were full of optimism and had spending money. Tourism began to grow in Nevada. Las Vegas casino resorts attracted Hollywood celebrities and famous entertainers. The state began collecting gaming taxes during the 1940s. The growing casinos in Las Vegas provided good-paying jobs to workers who brought their families with them, building a middle-class presence. In 1955 the state legislature created the Nevada Gaming Control Board within the Nevada Tax Commission. Four years later, the Nevada Gaming Commission was established.

CORPORATE GROWTH: THE 1960S. During the 1960s the Las Vegas casinos continued to grow. By that time, organized crime syndicates used respectable front men in top management positions while they manipulated the businesses from behind the scenes. Publicly held corporations had been largely kept out of the casino business by a provision in Nevada law that required every individual stockholder to be licensed to operate a casino.

One corporation that was able to get into the casino business was the Summa Corporation, a spin-off of the Hughes Tool Company, with only one stockholder: Howard Hughes (1905–1976). Hughes was a wealthy and eccentric businessman who owned the very profitable Hughes Aircraft Company. He spent a lot of his time in Las Vegas during the 1940s and 1950s and later moved there. In 1966 he bought the Desert Inn, a casino hotel on the Strip in Las Vegas. Later, he bought the nearby Sands, Frontier, Castaways, and Silver Slipper casinos.

Legend has it that mobsters threatened Hughes to drive him out of the casino business in Las Vegas, but he refused to leave. He invested hundreds of millions of

dollars in Las Vegas properties and predicted that the city would be an entertainment center by the end of the century. In 1967 the Nevada legislature changed the law to make it easier for corporations to own casinos.

To combat organized crime, federal statutes against racketeering (the act extorting money or favors from businesses through the use of intimidating tactics or by other illegal means) were enacted in 1971, and Nevada officials overhauled the casino regulatory system, making it more difficult for organized crime figures to be involved. Corporations and legitimate financiers began to invest heavily in casino hotels in Las Vegas and other parts of the state.

## The Development of Gambling beyond Nevada

During the early 1970s the U.S. Commission on the Review of the National Policy toward Gambling studied Americans' attitudes about gambling and their gambling behavior. The commission found that 80% of Americans approved of gambling and 67% engaged in gambling activities. In its final report, *Gambling in America* (1976), the commission made recommendations to state governments that were considering the legalization of gambling and concluded that states should set gambling policy without interference from the federal government, unless problems developed from the infiltration of organized crime or from conflicts between states.

In 1978 the first legal casino outside of Nevada opened in Atlantic City, New Jersey. By the mid-1990s nine additional states had legalized casino gambling: Colorado (1990), Illinois (1990), Indiana (1993), Iowa (1989), Louisiana (1991), Michigan (1996), Mississippi (1990), Missouri (1993), and South Dakota (1989).

STATE-SPONSORED LOTTERIES. In 1964 New Hampshire was the first state to make a lottery legal again. Called the New Hampshire Sweepstakes, it was tied to horse-race results to avoid laws prohibiting lotteries. New York established a lottery in 1967. Twelve other states followed suit during the 1970s. These legal lottery states were concentrated in the Northeast: Connecticut (1972), Delaware (1975), Illinois (1974), Maine (1974), Maryland (1973), Massachusetts (1972), Michigan (1972), New Jersey (1970), Ohio (1974), Pennsylvania (1971), Rhode Island (1974), and Vermont (1977).

An additional twenty-three states and the District of Columbia legalized lotteries during the 1980s and 1990s. The first multistate lottery game began operating in 1988 and included Iowa, Kansas, Oregon, Rhode Island, West Virginia and the District of Columbia. It went through several incarnations before becoming the Powerball game in 1992.

South Carolina began operating a lottery in January 2002, following voter approval in a 2000 referendum. In

November 2002 voters in Tennessee and North Dakota approved referendums allowing lotteries in their states. Both began operating in early 2004. Oklahoma started a state-controlled, institutionalized lottery in 2005, followed by North Carolina in 2006. Lotteries are examined in detail in Chapter 7.

**NATIVE AMERICAN GAMBLING ENTERPRISES.** Native American tribes established bingo halls to raise funds for tribal operations, and these became highly popular during the 1970s. Some of the most successful were high-stakes operations in Maine and Florida, where most other forms of gambling were prohibited. However, as the stakes were raised, the tribes began to face legal opposition from state governments. The tribes argued that their status as sovereign (independent) nations made them exempt from state laws against gambling. Tribes in various states sued, and the issue was debated in court for years. Finally, the U.S. Supreme Court's landmark ruling in *California v. Cabazon Band of Mission Indians* (480 U.S. 202 [1987]) opened the door to tribal gaming when it found that gambling activities conducted on tribal lands did not fall within the legal jurisdiction of the state. The Indian Gaming Regulatory Act, passed by Congress in 1988, allowed federally recognized Native American tribes to open gambling establishments on their reservations if the states in which they were located already permitted legalized gambling.

In 2000 California voters passed Proposition 1A, which amended the state constitution to permit Native American tribes to operate lottery games, slot machines, and banking and percentage card games on tribal lands. Previously, the tribes were largely restricted to operating bingo halls. The National Indian Gaming Association states in "Indian Gaming Facts" (2008, http://www.indian gaming.org/library/indian-gaming-facts/index.shtml) that 225 tribes were engaged in Class II or III gaming in 28 states in 2008. Class II and III gaming includes bingo, lotto, card and table games, slot machines, and pari-mutuel gambling (gambling in which those who bet on the top competitors share the total amount bet and the house gets a percentage). Native American Tribal Casinos are examined in detail in Chapter 5.

**INTERNET GAMBLING.** During the mid-1990s Internet gambling sites began operating, most of them based in the Caribbean. By the end of the decade, between six hundred and seven hundred Internet gambling sites were available. Christiansen Capital Advisors (January 9, 2006, http://www.cca-i.com/Primary%20Navigation/Online%20Data%20Store/internet_gambling_data.htm), which provides analysis and management for the gaming industry, indicates that the Internet segment of the gambling industry was estimated to generate $21 billion worldwide in 2008 and was poised for growth as cellular technologies and other innovations made it easier for patrons to log into gambling sites.

However, even though some countries, such as Great Britain, embraced Internet gambling and began to regulate the industry, the United States took action to interrupt online gambling activity by U.S. gamblers. Passage of the Unlawful Internet Gambling Enforcement Act of 2006 made it illegal for banks and credit card companies to process payments from U.S. customers to online gambling Web sites. Many sites immediately stopped accepting customers in the United States. In the press release "After Months of Steady Growth, U.S. Online Gambling Shows Decline in October" (October 2006, http://www.netratings.com/pr/pr_061114.pdf), Nielsen/NetRatings reports a 67% drop in traffic at PartyPoker.com, the most popular online gambling Web site, between September 2006 and October 2006, the month in which the U.S. law was passed. Overall, Nielsen/NetRatings states that the top-ten online gaming sites experienced a 56% decline in traffic between September 2006 and October 2006. However, Jessica M. Gulash explains in "The Unlawful Internet Gambling Enforcement Act's Effects on the Online Gambling Industry" (*Journal of Technology Law and Policy*, April 2007) that within months many U.S. gamblers were finding ways to circumvent the act. Internet gambling is examined in depth in Chapter 9.

## THE MODERN INDUSTRY

Industry analysts believe many sectors of the American gambling market are reaching maturity. In other words, the growth spurt of the past few decades is likely over. Commercial casino gambling has not spread beyond the eleven states in which it operated in 1996. In November 2004 voters in Maine rejected a referendum that would have allowed tribal casinos in their state, and in 2004 the Alaskan legislature failed to pass a bill that would have paved the way for casinos in Anchorage. In 2005 Oklahoma installed its first slot machines at racetracks, and facilities for slot machines at racetracks opened in 2006 for the first time in Pennsylvania and Florida. Allowing machine gambling at existing gambling venues such as racetracks is generally more acceptable to voters and politicians than full-fledged casino gambling. However, this is not true in all states. Kentucky and Maryland legislators have continually rejected bills that expand gambling at the state's racetracks.

Charitable gambling was the most common type of gaming allowed in 2008, operating in forty-seven states and the District of Columbia. Gambling on horse races was also prevalent, both at live venues and at off-track betting sites. Lotteries operated in forty-two states and the District of Columbia during 2006. Even though tribal casinos were less common, the National Indian Gaming Association indicates in "Indian Gaming Facts" that in 2008, 423 operations existed in 28 states. Gambling on greyhound races occurred in a handful of states. A number of states that did not allow commercial casinos allowed card rooms instead, and a few states allowed slot machines at businesses other than casinos. Only Florida offered wagering on jai alai, a fast-paced ball game played on a walled court.

## GAMBLING ISSUES AND SOCIAL IMPACT

In 1957 two men addicted to gambling decided to meet regularly to discuss the problems gambling had caused them and the changes they needed to make in their life to overcome it. After meeting for several months, each realized that the moral support offered by the other was allowing them to control their desire to gamble. They started an organization based on the spiritual principles used by Alcoholics Anonymous and similar groups to control addictions. The first group meeting of Gamblers Anonymous was held on September 13, 1957, in Los Angeles, California.

As gambling became more widespread throughout the country, efforts were undertaken to help those whose lives had been negatively affected by gambling. In recognition of the wide social impact of the industry, the American Psychiatric Association officially recognized pathological gambling as a mental health disorder in 1980. Pathological gambling was listed under disorders of impulse control and described as a "chronic and progressive failure to resist impulses to gamble." During the 1980s many states began setting up programs to offer assistance to compulsive gamblers. Harrah's Entertainment became the first commercial casino company to officially address problem gambling when it instituted the educational campaigns Operation Bet Smart and Project 21 to promote responsible gaming and raise awareness about problems associated with underage gambling.

In 1996 Congress authorized the National Gambling Impact Study Commission to investigate the social and economic consequences of gambling in the country. The federally funded group included nine commissioners representing pro- and antigambling positions. Existing literature was reviewed, and new studies were ordered. The commission held hearings around the country at which a variety of people involved in and affected by the gambling industry testified. In *Final Report* (June 1999, http://govinfo .library.unt.edu/ngisc/reports/fullrpt.html), the National Gambling Impact Study Commission concluded in 1999 that, except for Internet gambling, gambling policy decisions were best left up to state, tribal, and local governments. The commission also recommended that legalized gambling not be expanded further until all related costs and benefits were identified and reviewed.

Also during 1999, *Pathological Gambling: A Critical Review*, published by the National Academies Press, identified and analyzed all available scientific research studies dealing with pathological and problem gambling. The researchers estimated that about 1.5% of American adults had been pathological gamblers at some point in their life, with about 1.8 million compulsive gamblers actively gambling during a given year. Even though the researchers were able to draw some general conclusions about the prevalence of pathological gambling in the United States, they cited a lack of scientific evidence as a limiting factor in their ability to draw more specific conclusions. For example, they found that men were more likely than women to be pathological gamblers, but they lacked data to estimate the prevalence of problem gambling among demographic subgroups such as the elderly or those with low incomes.

## PUBLIC OPINION

In May 2008 the Gallup Organization conducted a nationwide poll to determine the moral acceptability of a variety of social issues. Overall, gambling was considered morally acceptable by 63% of those asked. (See Table 1.1.) Roughly the same percentage of people believed the death penalty (62%), medical research using stem cells obtained from human embryos (62%), and sex between an unmarried man and woman (61%) were morally acceptable. Joseph Carroll of the Gallup Organization reports in *Republicans, Democrats Differ on What Is Morally Acceptable* (May 24, 2006, http://www.gallup .com/poll/22915/Republicans-Democrats-Differ-What-Morally-Acceptable.aspx) that in May 2006 Democrats and Republicans were found to differ on the moral acceptability of gambling. Nearly two-thirds (65%) of Democrats found gambling acceptable, compared to only 54% of Republicans.

**TABLE 1.1**

Public opinion on the moral acceptability of sixteen issues, May 2008

| | Morally acceptable % | Morally wrong % |
|---|---|---|
| Divorce | 70 | 22 |
| Gambling | 63 | 32 |
| The death penalty | 62 | 30 |
| Medical research using stem cells obtained from human embryos | 62 | 30 |
| Sex between an unmarried man and woman | 61 | 36 |
| Medical testing on animals | 56 | 38 |
| Having a baby outside of marriage | 55 | 41 |
| Buying and wearing clothing made of animal fur | 54 | 39 |
| Doctor-assisted suicide | 51 | 44 |
| Homosexual relations | 48 | 48 |
| Abortion | 40 | 48 |
| Cloning animals | 33 | 61 |
| Suicide | 15 | 78 |
| Cloning humans | 11 | 85 |
| Polygamy—one husband has more than one wife at the same time | 8 | 90 |
| Married men and women having an affair | 7 | 91 |

SOURCE: Adapted from *Moral Issues*, The Gallup Organization, 2008, http://www.gallup.com/poll/1681/Moral-Issues.aspx (accessed July 15, 2008). Copyright © 2008 by The Gallup Organization. Reproduced by permission of The Gallup Organization.

FIGURE 1.1

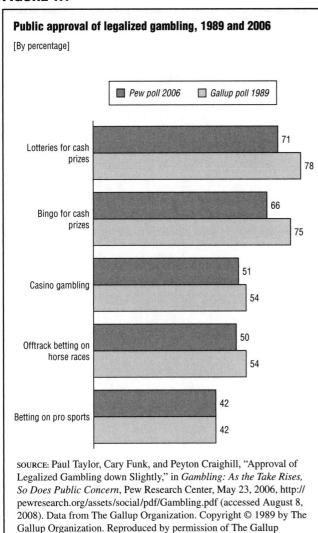

**Public approval of legalized gambling, 1989 and 2006**

[By percentage]

■ *Pew poll 2006*  □ *Gallup poll 1989*

Lotteries for cash prizes — 71 / 78

Bingo for cash prizes — 66 / 75

Casino gambling — 51 / 54

Offtrack betting on horse races — 50 / 54

Betting on pro sports — 42 / 42

SOURCE: Paul Taylor, Cary Funk, and Peyton Craighill, "Approval of Legalized Gambling down Slightly," in *Gambling: As the Take Rises, So Does Public Concern*, Pew Research Center, May 23, 2006, http://pewresearch.org/assets/social/pdf/Gambling.pdf (accessed August 8, 2008). Data from The Gallup Organization. Copyright © 1989 by The Gallup Organization. Reproduced by permission of The Gallup Organization.

FIGURE 1.2

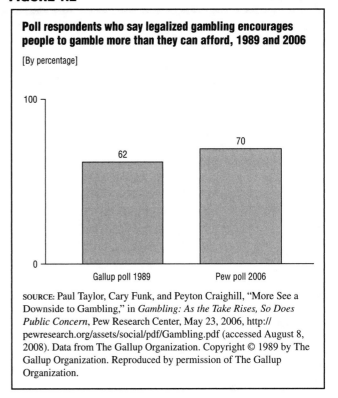

**Poll respondents who say legalized gambling encourages people to gamble more than they can afford, 1989 and 2006**

[By percentage]

Gallup poll 1989 — 62

Pew poll 2006 — 70

SOURCE: Paul Taylor, Cary Funk, and Peyton Craighill, "More See a Downside to Gambling," in *Gambling: As the Take Rises, So Does Public Concern*, Pew Research Center, May 23, 2006, http://pewresearch.org/assets/social/pdf/Gambling.pdf (accessed August 8, 2008). Data from The Gallup Organization. Copyright © 1989 by The Gallup Organization. Reproduced by permission of The Gallup Organization.

Between February and March 2006 Pew Research Center polled 2,250 adults and asked them about their attitude toward legalized gambling. The results were published by Paul Taylor, Cary Funk, and Peyton Craighill in *Gambling: As the Take Rises, So Does Public Concern* (May 23, 2006, http://pewresearch.org/assets/social/pdf/Gambling.pdf). In 2006, 71% of adults approved of cash lotteries and 66% approved of bingo for cash prizes. (See Figure 1.1.) Casino gambling and off-track betting on horse races received less support. Legalized betting on professional sports received the lowest approval rating.

Overall, a smaller percentage of Americans approved of gambling in the 2006 Pew poll than did in a similar survey conducted by the Gallup Organization in April 1989 cited by the report. (See Figure 1.1.) Approval of legalized lotteries and bingo dropped the most between 1989 and 2006. Taylor, Funk, and Craighill suggest that the change in Americans' attitudes about gambling has less to do with moral values and more to do with economic values. Less than one-third (28%) of respondents to the 2006 Pew poll thought gambling was immoral, but 70% of respondents believed legalized gambling caused people to spend more money than they can afford. (See Figure 1.2.) This represented a 13% increase from the 62% of respondents who felt the same way in 1989.

The Pew Research Center took a closer look in 2006 at the demographics of those who believed gambling is morally wrong, morally acceptable, or not a moral issue. Women were more likely than men to believe gambling was morally wrong (38% and 33%, respectively), and more than half (52%) of senior citizens aged sixty-five and older condemned gambling on moral grounds, compared to 30% of adults aged eighteen to forty-nine. (See Table 1.2.)

Income, education, and church attendance were also associated with how people thought about gambling. On the whole, people who are better educated, wealthier, and seldom attend church tended to view gambling as not a moral issue. (See Table 1.2.) By contrast, people with a high school education or less (46%), with family incomes of less than $30,000 (43%), who attend church at least once a week (50%), or who are white, evangelical Protestants (57%) tended to view gambling as morally wrong.

**TABLE 1.2**

## Views of gambling by demographic characteristics, 2006

PERCENT WHO BELIEVE THIS BEHAVIOR IS. . .

| | Morally wrong | Morally acceptable | Not a moral issue | (Vol.) Depends | Don't know | N |
|---|---|---|---|---|---|---|
| | % | % | % | % | % | |
| **All adults** | 35 | 17 | 42 | 3 | 3=100 | 745 |
| **Gender** | | | | | | |
| Men | 33 | 20 | 42 | 3 | 2=100 | 359 |
| Women | 38 | 13 | 43 | 3 | 3=100 | 336 |
| **Age** | | | | | | |
| 13–49 | 30 | 19 | 45 | 3 | 3=100 | 357 |
| 50–61 | 33 | 13 | 43 | 3 | 3=100 | 230 |
| 65+ | 52 | 15 | 27 | 3 | 3=100 | 147 |
| **Education** | | | | | | |
| College grad | 24 | 17 | 53 | 3 | 3=100 | 304 |
| Some college | 26 | 17 | 50 | 5 | 2=100 | 188 |
| High school or less | 46 | 17 | 33 | 1 | 3=100 | 249 |
| **Family income** | | | | | | |
| $75,000 or more | 23 | 19 | 53 | 2 | 3=100 | 234 |
| $30,000 to $75,000 | 37 | 16 | 43 | 3 | 1=100 | 254 |
| Less than $30,000 | 43 | 16 | 34 | 4 | 3=100 | 180 |
| **Marital status** | | | | | | |
| Married | 39 | 16 | 39 | 4 | 2=100 | 447 |
| Not married | 30 | 19 | 47 | 2 | 2=100 | 292 |
| **Church attendance** | | | | | | |
| Weekly or more | 50 | 13 | 31 | 3 | 3=100 | 290 |
| Monthly or less | 29 | 21 | 46 | 3 | 1=100 | 246 |
| Seldom or never | 21 | 17 | 56 | 2 | 4=100 | 193 |
| **Religion** | | | | | | |
| White Evangelical Protestant | 57 | 7 | 29 | 4 | 3=100 | 173 |
| White mainline Protestant | 30 | 20 | 46 | 2 | 2=100 | 172 |
| Catholic | 24 | 24 | 48 | 3 | 1=100 | 173 |
| **Ideology** | | | | | | |
| Conservative | 47 | 14 | 35 | 2 | 2=100 | 301 |
| Moderate | 30 | 18 | 45 | 4 | 3=100 | 291 |
| Liberal | 19 | 17 | 58 | 4 | 2=100 | 126 |
| **Party identification** | | | | | | |
| Republican | 43 | 16 | 37 | 3 | 1=100 | 242 |
| Democrat | 34 | 22 | 38 | 2 | 4=100 | 239 |
| Independent | 27 | 11 | 55 | 4 | 3=100 | 228 |
| **Region** | | | | | | |
| Northeast | 23 | 19 | 52 | 4 | 2=100 | 128 |
| Midwest | 35 | 14 | 46 | 2 | 3=100 | 177 |
| South | 49 | 17 | 30 | 2 | 2=100 | 254 |
| West | 26 | 17 | 49 | 4 | 4=100 | 186 |

N = Population.

SOURCE: Paul Taylor, Cary Funk, and Peyton Craighill, "Gambling," in *A Barometer of Modern Morals: Sex, Drugs, and the 1040*, Pew Research Center, March 28, 2006, http://pewsocialtrends.org/pubs/?chartid=77 (accessed July 18, 2008)

# CHAPTER 2
# SUPPLY AND DEMAND: WHO OFFERS GAMBLING?
# WHO GAMBLES?

Like any business in a capitalist society, the gambling industry is driven by the principles of supply and demand. Gambling proponents argue that demand drives supply. In other words, the industry grows and spreads into new markets because the public is eager to gamble. Illegal gambling has always flourished, and opinion polls show that most Americans support legal gambling opportunities, particularly lotteries and casinos.

Gambling is one of the most popular leisure activities in the country. Commercial casinos took in over $34.1 billion in 2007 (see Figure 2.1), and tribal casinos took in $26 billion, according to the National Indian Gaming Commission, in *National Indian Gaming Commission Newsletter* (summer 2008, http://www.nigc.gov/LinkClick .aspx?link=NIGC+Uploads%2fNewsletters%2fSummer .2008.pdf&tabid=140&mid=760). These numbers dwarf, for example, box office sales of the U.S. motion picture industry, which the Motion Picture Association of America indicates in "Research & Statistics" (2008, http://www .mpaa.org/researchStatistics.asp) earned $9.6 billion in the domestic market and $26.7 billion worldwide in 2007.

However, gambling opponents argue that supply drives demand. They surmise that people would not be tempted to gamble or to gamble as often if opportunities were not so prevalent and widespread. They see gambling as an irresistible temptation with potentially dangerous consequences. It bothers them that gambling opportunities are presented, promoted, and supported not only by the business world but also by government leaders and politicians—people who are supposed to represent the best interests of the public they serve.

Whatever the driving reason, gambling has become a big business and a popular pastime for many Americans.

## SUPPLY: GAMBLING OPPORTUNITIES AND OPPORTUNISTS

A variety of gambling opportunities are available in the United States, both legal and illegal. Gambling is a moneymaking activity for corporations, small businesses, charities, governments, and in some cases, criminals. The legal gambling industry employs hundreds of thousands of people across the country. In addition, it generates business in a variety of related industries, including manufacturing companies that provide slot machines and other supplies, travel and tourism operators that provide transportation, food, and lodging for gamblers, advertising agencies that promote gambling enterprises, breeders that raise and train racehorses, and many more.

The American Gaming Association (AGA) explains in the fact sheet "Gaming Revenue: 10-Year Trends" (April 2008, http://www.americangaming.org/Industry/fact sheets/statistics_detail.cfv?id=8) that the legal gambling industry's gross revenue increased from $45.1 billion in 1995 to $90.9 billion in 2006. A significant portion of this growth took place after 2000. Gross gambling revenue is the money taken in by the industry minus the winnings paid out. In other words, it is equivalent to sales. From this number, then, operating expenses such as wages, benefits, and taxes must be subtracted to gauge the profits realized by the industry. In *2008 State of the States: The AGA Survey of Casino Entertainment* (2008, http://www.americangaming.org/assets/files/aga_2008_sos .pdf), the AGA estimates that the gross revenue for the commercial casino industry was about $34.1 billion in 2007; of that, $13.8 billion was paid out in wages and $5.8 billion was paid in taxes.

### Casino Owners and Operators

Corporations have profited the most from legalized gambling since they took over the small casinos of Las Vegas during the late 1960s. Organized crime had been pushed out by the government, so the corporations could bring their management practices to an increasingly profitable business. They invested money in new and bigger properties in Las Vegas and throughout the state of

FIGURE 2.1

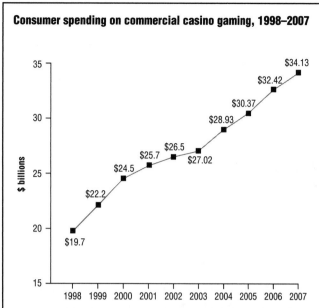

**Consumer spending on commercial casino gaming, 1998–2007**

SOURCE: "U.S. Consumer Spending on Commercial Casino Gaming, 1998–2007," in *2008 State of the States: The AGA Survey of Casino Entertainment*, American Gaming Association, 2008, http://www.americangaming.org/assets/files/aga_2008_sos.pdf (accessed August 1, 2008). Data for 1998–99 from Christiansen Capital Advisors. Reprinted with permission of the American Gaming Association. All rights reserved.

Nevada and then, in 1978, opened the first casino hotel in Atlantic City, New Jersey. As of 2008, most corporations in the industry owned or operated several commercial casinos. Casino City estimates in "United States Gaming Industry Overview" (2005, http://casinocitypress.com/Advertising/PocketDirectory/PGD2006_IndustryOverview Pages.pdf) that in 2005 commercial casinos and card rooms controlled 39% of the legal gambling revenue pie, compared to 28% controlled by lotteries and 25% by tribal casinos. Some companies, such as Harrah's Entertainment, also manage casinos for Native American tribes. The tribes are increasingly partnering with large, well-known corporations to take advantage of their name recognition and corporate experience.

Many of the nation's gambling properties are controlled by five well-known corporations: Harrah's Entertainment, MGM Mirage, Boyd Gaming Corporation, Penn National Gaming, and Station Casinos.

**HARRAH'S ENTERTAINMENT.** According to Harrah's Entertainment, in *Annual Report of Harrah's Entertainment, Inc., to the United States Securities and Exchange Commission* (December 31, 2007, http://www.sec.gov/Archives/edgar/data/858339/000119312508043934/d10k.htm), in 2007 the company owned or managed fifty casinos in six countries, primarily in the United States and United Kingdom. Its casinos were operated primarily under the Harrah's, Caesars, and Horseshoe brand names. The company also owned the World Series of Poker

tournament. It employed approximately eighty-seven thousand people and had a net revenue of $10.8 billion in 2007, up from $4.4 billion in 2004.

In Las Vegas the company owned Harrah's Las Vegas, Rio All-Suite Hotel & Casino, Caesars Palace, Bally's Las Vegas, Flamingo Las Vegas, Paris Las Vegas, Imperial Palace Hotel & Casino, and Bill's Gamblin' Hall & Saloon. Elsewhere in Nevada, the company owned Harrah's Reno, Harrah's Laughlin, Harrah's Lake Tahoe, Harveys Resort and Casino, and Bill's Casino. In Atlantic City, Harrah's owned Harrah's Atlantic City, Showboat Atlantic City, Caesars Atlantic City, and Bally's Atlantic City. The company also owned casinos in Illinois, Indiana, Iowa, Mississippi, Missouri, Louisiana, Pennsylvania, Arizona, North Carolina, and California, and in Uruguay, Canada, the United Kingdom, Egypt, and South Africa.

Harrah's was acquired by TPG Capital and Apollo Global Management in January 2008. The private acquisition meant that Harrah's stock would no longer be publicly traded.

**MGM MIRAGE.** MGM Mirage notes in *Vision: MGM Mirage 2007 Annual Report* (2007, http://library.corporate-ir.net/library/10/101/101502/items/287871/MGMM_2007_AR.pdf) that on December 31, 2007, it owned seventeen casino resorts and had 50% investments in four others. These establishments included the Bellagio, MGM Grand Las Vegas, Mandalay Bay, The Mirage, Luxor, Treasure Island, New York–New York, Excalibur, Monte Carlo, Circus Circus Las Vegas, and Slots-A-Fun, all in Las Vegas. The company also owned or partially owned casinos in Michigan, Mississippi, New Jersey, and Illinois. The company also owned several golf courses. In 2007 the company closed or sold several casino operations. In 2007 MGM Mirage employed sixty-seven thousand people and had a revenue of $7.7 billion, up from just $4 billion in 2004, an increase of 92% in that three-year period.

**BOYD GAMING CORPORATION.** In *Boyd Gaming Annual Report 2007* (2007, http://216.139.227.101/interactive/byd2007/?zz=144), the Boyd Gaming Corporation notes that in December 2007 it owned fifteen casinos, including California Hotel and Casino, Fremont Hotel and Casino, Main Street Station Casino, Gold Coast Hotel and Casino, The Orleans Hotel and Casino, Sam's Town Hotel and Gambling Hall, Suncoast Hotel and Casino, Eldorado Casino, and Jokers Wild Casino, all in Las Vegas. The corporation also owned hotels in Indiana, Illinois, Louisiana, and New Jersey. In 2007 the company began construction on an 87-acre (35 ha) resort on the Las Vegas Strip, Echelon.

Boyd Gaming Corporation employed approximately 16,900 people in 2007. The company had a net corporate revenue of $2 billion in 2007, down from a high of $2.2 billion in 2006.

**PENN NATIONAL GAMING.** According to Penn National Gaming, in *Annual Report of Penn National Gaming, Inc., to the United States Securities and Exchange Commission* (December 31, 2007, http://www.sec.gov/Archives/edgar/data/921738/000104746908002032/a2182949z10-k.htm), in 2007 it owned eighteen gaming properties in the United States and ran one additional property in Canada. It acquired several of those establishments from Argosy Gaming Corporation in October 2005 for $2.3 billion. It owned nine riverboat casinos, including the Boomtown in Biloxi, Mississippi; Argosy Casino Alton in Illinois; Argosy Casino Riverside near Kansas City, Missouri; Hollywood Casino in Baton Rouge, Louisiana; Argosy Casino Sioux City in Iowa; Hollywood Casino Aurora in Indiana; and the Empress Casino in Joliet, Illinois. The company's land-based casinos included Bullwhackers Casino in Black Hawk, Colorado; Hollywood Slots in Bangor, Maine; Charles Town Entertainment Complex in Charles Town, West Virginia; and Hollywood Casino Bay in St. Louis, Missouri. The company also owned several racetracks.

In 2007 Penn National Gaming employed 15,289 people. The company had a net revenue of $2.4 billion in 2007, up 78% from $1.4 billion in 2005. In 2008 a merger with Fortress Investment Group and Centerbridge Partners was pending.

**STATION CASINOS.** Station Casinos reports in *Annual Report to the Security Exchange Commission* (March 5, 2008, http://phx.corporate-ir.net/phoenix.zhtml?c=103083&p=irol-sec&secCat01.1_rs=21&secCat01.1_rc=10) that in 2007 it owned at least a 50% share in nine major hotel/casino properties under the Station and Fiesta brand names, and eight smaller casino properties in the Las Vegas area. Properties owned included Palace Station Hotel & Casino, Boulder Station Hotel & Casino, Texas Station Gambling Hall & Hotel, Sunset Station Hotel & Casino, Santa Fe Station Hotel & Casino, Red Rock Casino Resort Spa, Fiesta Rancho Casino Hotel, Fiesta Henderson Casino Hotel, Wild Wild West Gambling Hall & Hotel, Wildfire Casino, Magic Star Casino, Gold Rush Casino, and Lake Mead Casino. The company also managed the Thunder Valley Casino for the United Auburn Indian Community in Lincoln, California.

On January 31, 2008, Station Casinos employed approximately 14,500 people. The company had been named as one of *Fortune* magazine's top one hundred companies to work for the previous four years. In November 2007 a merger was completed with FCP Acquisition Sub, with Station Casinos continuing as the surviving corporation. Following this acquisition, the company became a privately owned company. The company had a net revenue of $1.2 billion between January 1, 2007, and November 7, 2007, and an additional revenue of $210 million during the period between November 8, 2007, and December 31, 2007.

**OTHER GAMBLING CORPORATIONS.** Different companies play important roles in other realms of the gambling industry. Two publicly traded companies, Churchill Downs and Magna Entertainment, are major organizations in the Thoroughbred horse racing business. Churchill Downs notes in *2007 Annual Report* (2008, http://www.churchilldownsincorporated.com/sites/churchilldownsincorporated.com/files/Annual%20Report%202007.pdf) that it operates tracks in Florida, Illinois, Louisiana, and Kentucky—including the famed track where the Kentucky Derby is run annually. In 2007 it had a revenue of $411 million. In *2007 Annual Report* (2008, http://library.corporate-ir.net/library/98/986/98631/items/285705/MEC.2007AnnualReport.pdf), Magna Entertainment, a Canadian-based corporation, states that it operates ten racetracks throughout North America. It notes that in 2007 it had a revenue of $617.2 million.

Many corporations directly support the gambling industry by providing equipment, goods, supplies, and services. They may be members of the Gaming Standards Association, an international organization devoted to the development of uniform standards for communication and computer technology used in gambling machines. Some examples of these corporations are:

- GTECH Corporation, which introduced the first lottery terminal in 1982 and now provides technology services to lotteries in twenty-five states

- Bally Technology, which introduced its first slot machine in 1936 and is now a successful machine manufacturer and distributor

- Konami Gaming, a leading producer of high-tech video slot machines and multisite casino management systems

- WMS Gaming, which is engaged entirely in the manufacture, sale, leasing, and licensing of gambling machines

**GAMBLING AS AN INVESTMENT.** The investment firm MUTUALS.com sells shares in the Vice Fund, a mutual fund composed entirely of companies in the alcohol, tobacco, gambling, and defense industries. The fact sheet "Vice Fund—VICEX" (August 31, 2008, http://vicefund.com/docs/fact_sheet_august_08_vicex_web.pdf) states that as of June 2008 the fund's returns were down 20.68%.

## Small Businesses

Many small casinos and racetracks, minicasinos, and card rooms around the country are owned or operated by small companies, families, and entrepreneurs. Other ways in which small businesses are engaged in or serve the gambling industry include:

- Selling lottery tickets and operating electronic gaming devices at independently owned convenience stores, markets, service stations, bars, restaurants, bowling alleys, and newsstands

- Manufacturing and distributing equipment such as slot machines, roulette wheels, lottery tickets, dice, and cards

- Providing services such as advertising, marketing, public relations, accounting, information technology, and food

- Breeding, training, and caring for horses and greyhounds

Most small businesses that offer gambling do so through lottery ticket sales or electronic gaming devices, such as slot machines. These are considered forms of convenience gambling, because patrons do not have to travel to special destinations, such as casinos and race-tracks. Convenience gambling has been more controversial than destination gambling. Critics argue that allowing gambling in stores and restaurants and other places that people visit as part of their everyday routine makes it too easy for them to gamble. The same criticism is leveled against Internet gambling, which patrons can do at home.

INTERNET GAMBLING BUSINESSES. Internet gambling is illegal in the United States, so most Internet gambling sites are operated by small companies located offshore, many in the Caribbean. Little is known about these companies, which operate without regulatory oversight. However, David O. Stewart estimates in *An Analysis of Internet Gambling and Its Policy Implications* (2006, http://www.americangaming.org/assets/files/studies/wpaper_internet_0531.pdf) that more than twenty-five hundred Internet gambling sites operated around the world in 2005. In the fact sheet "Internet Gambling" (2007, http://www.americangaming.org/Industry/factsheets/issues_detail.cfv?id=17), the AGA reports that approximately eight million Internet gamblers in the United States generated $5.9 billion in 2005.

## Criminals

Gambling has had a checkered legal history in the United States. At various times it has been legal, illegal but tolerated, or illegal and actively prosecuted. During times when gambling opportunities have been outlawed, entrepreneurs have stepped in to offer them anyway. These entrepreneurs range from mobsters running million-dollar betting rings to grandmothers running neighborhood bingo games. Either way, the illegal nature of the activity makes these entrepreneurs criminals.

Organized crime groups have often been associated with gambling, a cash business with high demand and good profits. Crime syndicates on the East Coast were among the first to see the potential of Las Vegas, invest in it, and profit from it. At times, they have infiltrated other segments of the legal gambling industry, such as horse racing. Strict regulations and crackdowns by law enforcement have been put into place to push them out. The federal Racketeer Influenced and Corrupt Organizations (RICO) Act of 1970 was designed to combat infiltration by organized crime into legitimate businesses, including gambling enterprises. Most analysts believe RICO has been largely successful at keeping mobsters from establishing or taking over legal gambling businesses.

However, even though they have been denied casino ownership and management roles, some organized crime figures have infiltrated casinos in other ways, such as through labor unions and maintenance or food services. Law enforcement officials also believe organized crime families have been involved in bribing state officials who were considering the extension or expansion of gambling options, particularly relating to electronic gambling machines.

The Nevada Gaming Commission and State Gaming Control Board maintain a list of people who are prohibited from gambling in Nevada. The List of Excluded Persons, more commonly known as "Nevada's Black Book," includes known cheaters, crime family bosses, mob associates, and others linked in some way to organized crime. These people are considered so dangerous to the integrity of legal gambling that they are not allowed to set foot in Nevada casinos. In "GCB Excluded Person List" (June 22, 2006, http://gaming.nv.gov/loep_main.htm), the Nevada Gaming Commission and State Gaming Control Board provide photographs of these excluded people.

The most lucrative sector of the gambling industry for organized crime has been and continues to be illegal bookmaking and numbers games. Bookmaking is a gambling activity in which a bookmaker takes bets on the odds that a particular event will occur or that an event will have a particular outcome. The vast majority of bookmaking revolves around sporting events, such as college and professional football and basketball games. Such wagering is extremely popular in the United States. Because sports bookmaking is legal only in Nevada, there is a large illegal market for it across the country. Michael McCarthy reports in "Football Bettors Put Billions on the Line" (*USA Today*, September 7, 2005) that gaming industry and sports analysts estimate gamblers illegally wager between $100 billion and $300 billion each year on sports in the United States.

Illegal numbers games are similar to lottery games in that players wager money on particular numbers to be selected in a drawing or by other means. Illegal numbers operators thrive in many parts of the country, especially large cities—even those where legal lotteries are offered.

Not all bookmaking is done through mobsters. Many enterprising entrepreneurs run small-time illegal gambling books, mostly related to sporting events. Office pools, in which coworkers pool small wagers on sports or office events—for example, when a baby is going to be born—are common. Even though society does not generally consider private wagers and small-stakes office pools to be illegal gambling, the laws in most states do.

Despite widespread illegal gambling, few people are actually arrested for engaging in it. According to the

**TABLE 2.1**

**Estimated arrests by type of crime, 2006**

United States, 2006

| | |
|---|---:|
| Total[a] | 14,380,370 |
| Murder and nonnegligent manslaughter | 13,435 |
| Forcible rape | 24,535 |
| Robbery | 125,605 |
| Aggravated assault | 447,948 |
| Burglary | 304,801 |
| Larceny-theft | 1,081,157 |
| Motor vehicle theft | 137,757 |
| Arson | 16,582 |
|     Violent crime[b] | 611,523 |
|     Property crime[b] | 1,540,297 |
| Other assaults | 1,305,757 |
| Forgery and counterfeiting | 108,823 |
| Fraud | 280,693 |
| Embezzlement | 20,012 |
| Stolen property; buying, receiving, possessing | 122,722 |
| Vandalism | 300,679 |
| Weapons; carrying, possessing, etc. | 200,782 |
| Prostitution and commercialized vice | 79,673 |
| Sex offenses (except forcible rape and prostitution) | 87,252 |
| Drug abuse violations | 1,889,810 |
| Gambling | 12,307 |
| Offenses against the family and children | 131,491 |
| Driving under the influence | 1,460,498 |
| Liquor laws | 645,734 |
| Drunkenness | 553,188 |
| Disorderly conduct | 703,504 |
| Vagrancy | 36,471 |
| All other offenses | 4,022,068 |
| Suspicion | 2,482 |
| Curfew and loitering law violations | 152,907 |
| Runaways | 114,179 |

[a]Does not include suspicion.
[b]Violent crimes are offenses of murder, forcible rape, robbery, and aggravated assault. Property crimes are offenses of burglary, larceny-theft, motor vehicle theft, and arson.

SOURCE: "Table 29. Estimated Number of Arrests, United States, 2006," in *Crime in the United States, 2006*, U.S. Department of Justice, Federal Bureau of Investigation, September 2007, http://www.fbi.gov/ucr/cius2006/data/table_29.html (accessed July 18, 2008)

Federal Bureau of Investigation, in *Crime in the United States 2006*, authorities made only 12,307 arrests for gambling out of nearly 14.4 million total arrests in 2006. (See Table 2.1.)

**Charities**

Charitable gambling is the most widely practiced form of gambling in the United States. In 2008 it was legal in forty-seven states and the District of Columbia (prohibited only in Arkansas, Hawaii, and Utah). In charitable gambling, a specified portion of the money raised (minus prizes, expenses, and any state fees and taxes) goes to qualified charitable organizations. Such organizations include religious groups, fraternal organizations, veterans groups, volunteer fire departments, parent-teacher organizations, civic and cultural groups, booster clubs, and other nonprofit organizations.

Generally, a charitable organization has to have been in existence for several years and has to obtain a state license for the gambling activity. Most states will only

issue licenses to organizations that have been recognized by the Internal Revenue Service as exempt from federal income tax under Tax Code section 501(c). Thousands of charitable organizations are registered to conduct gambling throughout the country.

Most charitable gambling is regulated by state governments, although not uniformly by the same department—it may be the department of revenue, the state police, the alcohol control board, or the lottery, gaming, or racing commission. Administrative fees and taxes are levied in most states. In some states charitable gambling activity is unregulated.

Typical games allowed include bingo (the most common), pull tabs (lottery tickets with tabs that gamblers pull open to reveal cash prizes), raffles, and card games such as poker or blackjack. Slot machines and table games such as roulette and craps are generally not permitted. Limits are usually placed on the size of cash prizes that can be awarded. States allow different games for charity fundraising. For example, California only allows bingo games.

Because of the inconsistencies in state oversight, it is difficult to determine the complete extent of charitable gambling in the United States. The AGA estimates in the fact sheet "Gaming Revenue: Current-Year Data" (October 2007, http://www.americangaming.org/Industry/factsheets/statistics_detail.cfv?id=7) that revenues from charitable gaming totaled $2.2 billion in 2006.

In *Charity Gaming in North America Annual Report 2006* (2007, http://www.naftm.org/vertical/Sites/%7B10B16680-A509-4D78-B468-8A1901FC0CF7%7D/uploads/%7BD4D77A5E-A85D-4F9D-A720-DAABDBE1A572%7D.PDF), the National Association of Fundraising Ticket Manufacturers (NAFTM), a trade association representing companies that manufacture bingo paper, pull tabs, and other supplies used in the charitable gambling industry, notes that in 2006 nearly $7.2 billion was wagered on charitable gaming in the thirty-five states for which it compiled statistics and the District of Columbia. The top-five states were Minnesota ($1.3 billion), Washington ($787 million), Texas ($662 million), Kentucky ($527 million), and Indiana ($526 million). (See Table 2.2.) On average, about 73% of gross receipts went to prize payouts, 14% to expenses, and 3% to taxes and fees. (See Figure 2.2.) The remaining 10% was net profit for the charitable organizations.

According to the NAFTM, nearly all states charge licensing fees to conduct charitable gambling events. For example, South Carolina charges a onetime fee of $1,000. Other states charge a fee per event or set weekly, monthly, or yearly fees, which generally run from $10 to $100. A handful of states base licensing fees on the amount of gross receipts, so the fees can be thousands of dollars. Most states also impose a gaming tax on the

TABLE 2.2

**Gross receipts and proceeds from charitable gaming in top ten participation states, 2006**

| Top ten states by gross receipts | | Top ten states by net proceeds | |
| --- | --- | --- | --- |
| **State** | **Gross receipts** | **State** | **Net proceeds** |
| Minnesota | $1,288,115,000 | Minnesota | $113,210,000 |
| Washington | $787,078,392 | Michigan | $72,149,010 |
| Texas | $662,254,915 | Indiana | $67,343,989 |
| Kentucky | $527,262,973 | New York | $57,273,043 |
| Indiana | $525,748,892 | Kentucky | $53,332,248 |
| Michigan | $413,131,952 | Virginia | $43,050,000 |
| New York | $353,149,354 | Wisconsin | $39,866,015 |
| Alaska | $349,429,648 | Alaska | $35,732,844 |
| Virginia | $321,261,000 | Texas | $33,814,326 |
| North Dakota | $261,675,261 | New Jersey | $31,384,133 |

SOURCE: "Top Ten States by Gross Receipts/Top Ten States by Net Proceeds," in *Charity Gaming in North America: Annual Report 2006*, National Association of Fundraising Ticket Manufacturers, 2007, http://www.naftm.org/vertical/Sites/%7B10B16680-A509-4D78-B468-8A1901FC0CF7%7D/uploads/%7BD4D77A5E-A85D-4F9D-A720-DAABDBE1A572%7D.PDF (accessed July 18, 2008)

**FIGURE 2.2**

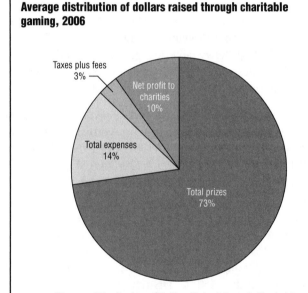

**Average distribution of dollars raised through charitable gaming, 2006**

Taxes plus fees 3%

Net profit to charities 10%

Total expenses 14%

Total prizes 73%

SOURCE: "Average Distribution of Dollars Raised through Charitable Gaming in the U.S.," in *Charity Gaming in North America: Annual Report 2006*, National Association of Fundraising Ticket Manufacturers, 2007, http://www.naftm.org/vertical/Sites/%7B10B16680-A509-4D78-B468-8A1901FC0CF7%7D/uploads/%7BD4D77A5E-A85D-4F9D-A720-DAABDBE1A572%7D.PDF (accessed July 18, 2008)

proceeds from charitable gambling and/or collect administrative fees. A majority of states allocate all or a portion of these revenues to their general funds or to the agencies that oversee charitable gambling. A few states split the money with local law enforcement agencies.

Minnesota is believed to have the highest gross receipts from charitable gambling of any state—probably half of all money wagered in the United States for this purpose. According to the Minnesota Gambling Control Board, in *Annual Report of the Minnesota Gambling Control Board: Fiscal Year 2007* (2008, http://www.gcb.state.mn.us/PDF_Files/FY07.pdf), charity gambling brought in gross receipts of almost $1.3 billion during fiscal year (FY) 2007, down slightly from FY 2006. Total prizes paid out amounted to $1 billion in FY 2007, or 81.7% of gross receipts.

## The Government

Federal, state, tribal, and local agencies collect money from gambling operations through the assessment of taxes and fees and, in some cases, by directly supplying gambling opportunities. Because the money raised is spent on public programs, many Americans are ultimately affected by the government's involvement in gambling. In states facing budget deficits, the expansion of gambling often seems an attractive solution. Mandy Rafool reports in "Gambling on Gaming" (*State Legislatures*, January 2005) that John Rogers (1940–), a representative of the Alabama House of Representatives, said, "Given the choice, people will take gambling over tax increases any day."

THE FEDERAL GOVERNMENT. The primary means by which the federal government makes money from the gambling industry is by taxing winning gamblers and gambling operators. Gamblers must declare gambling earnings when they file their personal income taxes. They get to subtract their gambling losses, but they must keep thorough records and have receipts, if possible, to prove their losses. For racetrack gamblers, this means saving losing betting slips and keeping a gambling diary of dates, events, and amounts. Casino gamblers who join "slot clubs" can get a detailed printout of their gambling history from the casino.

Gambling operators, like all companies, are subject to corporate taxes. They are required to report winnings that meet certain criteria to the Internal Revenue Service. (See Table 2.3.) The gambling operator must withhold income tax from winnings of more than $5,000, usually at a withholding rate of 25%. However, 28% is withheld from the winnings of gamblers who do not provide the gambling operator with their Social Security number or if the winnings are from bingo, keno, or slots. Gamblers who win noncash prizes, such as cars or other merchandise, have to pay taxes on the fair market value of the item.

The federal government is also in the gambling business. Diana B. Henriques reports in "Temptation to Gamble Is Near for Troops Overseas" (*New York Times*, October 19, 2005) that the U.S. armed forces operated 4,150 modern video slot machines at U.S. military bases in 9 overseas countries in 2005. Revenues from the machines totaled about $120 million. Based on an average payout of 94%, the total amount wagered in military

**TABLE 2.3**

**Gambling winnings that must be reported to the Internal Revenue Service (IRS), 2008**

| Type of game | Amount of prize paid is equal to or greater than |
|---|---|
| Lotteries sweepstakes, horse races, dog races, instant bingo game prizes, and other wagering transactions | $600 and prize is at least 300 times wager |
| Bingo | $1,200 |
| Slot machines | $1,200 |
| Keno | $1,500 |
| Poker tournaments | $5,000 |

SOURCE: Adapted from *2008 Instructions for Forms W-2G and 5754*, U.S. Department of the Treasury, Internal Revenue Service, March 2008, http://www.irs.gov/pub/irs-pdf/iw2g.pdf (accessed July 18, 2008)

slot machines was around $2 billion per year. In addition, the U.S. Army ran bingo games at military bases. Its revenue totaled $7 million.

**STATE GOVERNMENTS.** State governments make money from legal gambling enterprises operated within their borders, including lotteries, commercial casinos, horse and dog races, jai alai games, card rooms, charitable gambling, and video machine gambling. Only lotteries are operated by state governments. All other gambling options are operated by other parties. As of October 2008, there were no state-owned casinos in the United States; proposals for such establishments have been offered in several states, but all have failed to become law.

According to the North American Association of State and Provincial Lotteries, in "Sales and Profits" (2008, http://www.naspl.org/index.cfm?fuseaction=content&PageID=3&PageCategory=3), forty-two states and the District of Columbia operated lotteries in 2008; Alabama, Alaska, Arkansas, Hawaii, Mississippi, Nevada, Utah, and Wyoming did not. State lotteries had approximately $57.4 billion in sales for FY 2006 and a profit of $17.1 billion. Generally, after paying expenses and the winners and retailers who sell the tickets, states have a 30% to 40% profit to spend on government programs, such as education.

**TRIBAL GOVERNMENTS.** Native American tribes that have been officially recognized by the U.S. government are considered sovereign nations, which means that, to a certain extent, they govern themselves. In 1988 Congress passed the Indian Gaming Regulatory Act, which allows federally recognized tribes to open gambling establishments if the state in which they are located already permits certain types of legalized gambling.

The National Indian Gaming Commission indicates in "Indian Gaming Facts" (2008, http://www.indiagaming.org/library/indian-gaming-facts/index.shtml) that in 2006 Native American tribes operated 423 gambling locations and made $25.7 billion. Net revenues fund tribal government operations or programs, provisions for the general welfare of the tribe and its members, tribal economic development, charitable contributions, and operations of local government agencies. Tribal governments have used gambling revenues to build health clinics, schools, houses, and community centers and to provide educational scholarships and social services for their members. Tribal gaming employed 670,000 people in 2008.

**LOCAL GOVERNMENTS.** Local governments in some states collect taxes and fees from gambling activities operated within their jurisdictions. This is particularly true for casinos and racetracks.

New York City is particularly active in the gambling industry. The New York City Off-Track Betting Corporation was founded in 1970 to provide a legal alternative to the widespread off-track wagering that was offered by organized crime syndicates. Even though the corporation is a government entity, it operates as a private enterprise that turns profits over to state and local governments. According to the article "Off-Track Betting" (*New York Times*, September 30, 2008), in FY 2006 the corporation handled nearly $1.1 billion in off-track wagers.

## DEMAND: THE GAMBLERS

Gambling is a leisure activity—people gamble because they enjoy it. Proponents say there is no difference between spending money at a theme park and spending it at a casino: the money is exchanged for a good time in either case. However, gambling has a powerful allure besides fun: the dream of wealth, which is a strong motivator. Some options, such as lotteries, offer the chance to risk a small investment for an enormous payoff. This potential is too appealing for many people to pass up.

### Adults

In *One in Six Americans Gamble on Sports* (February 1, 2008, http://www.gallup.com/poll/104086/One-Six-Americans-Gamble-Sports.aspx), Jeffrey M. Jones of the Gallup Organization finds that 65% of Americans had taken part in the past year in one or more forms of eleven types of gambling mentioned in a December 2007 poll. (See Table 2.4.) Lottery play was the most popular gambling activity—nearly half (46%) of those asked had engaged in it—whereas 24% had visited a casino, 14% had participated in an office pool on a sporting event, and 12% had played a video poker machine.

Paul Taylor, Cary Funk, and Peyton Craighill of the Pew Research Center note in *Gambling: As the Take Rises, So Does Public Concern* (May 23, 2006, http://pewresearch.org/assets/social/pdf/Gambling.pdf) that the popularity of gambling has dropped since the Gallup Organization conducted a similar survey in 1989. Seventy-one percent of people in the Gallup survey reported gambling in 1989. However, some forms of gambling were more popular in 2008 than in 1989, including visiting a casino and playing a video poker game. (See Table 2.5.) A higher percentage of people bet on professional sports and horse racing in 1989 than in 2008.

According to Taylor, Funk, and Craighill, in 2006 about seven out of ten (72%) men had gambled in the past year, whereas six out of ten (62%) women had. (See Table 2.6.) Those with a college education were slightly less likely to have gambled than those with only some college or with a high school degree or less. The participation rate for people with higher incomes (greater than $100,000 per year) was higher than for other income groups. Only 59% of those making less than $30,000 per year reported gambling during the previous twelve months, compared to 79% of those making more than $100,000 per year.

## TABLE 2.4

**Gambling in past year, by type of bet, December 2007**

|  | Yes | No |
|---|---|---|
|  | % | % |
| Bought a state lottery ticket | 46 | 54 |
| Visited a casino | 24 | 76 |
| Participated in an office pool on the World Series, Super Bowl, or other game | 14 | 86 |
| Played a video poker machine | 12 | 88 |
| Done any other kind of gambling not mentioned here | 9 | 91 |
| Bet on a professional sports event such as baseball, basketball, or football | 7 | 93 |
| Played bingo for money | 7 | 93 |
| Bet on a horse race | 5 | 95 |
| Bet on a college sports event such as basketball or football | 4 | 96 |
| Bet on a boxing match | 3 | 97 |
| Gambled for money on the Internet | 2 | 98 |

SOURCE: Jeffrey M. Jones, "Most Common Forms of Gambling," in *One in Six Americans Gamble on Sports*, The Gallup Organization, February 1, 2008, http://www.gallup.com/poll/104086/One-Six-Americans-Gamble-Sports.aspx (accessed July 15, 2008). Copyright © 2008 by The Gallup Organization. Reproduced by permission of The Gallup Organization.

Taylor, Funk, and Craighill indicate that gambling participation rates vary with religion as well. Protestants (61%) reported less gambling activity in 2006 than Catholics (77%) or those who were identified as secular (72%). (See Table 2.6.) Among Protestants, members of mainline denominations, such as Methodists, gambled far more than those who identified with evangelical denominations. Northeasterners were more active gamblers than those living in other regions of the country. A larger percentage of white people (68%) than African-Americans (62%) or Hispanics (62%) reported gambling during the previous year. Differences in participation by age were minor, although poll participants over age sixty-five were less likely to gamble than were younger people.

**SENIOR CITIZENS.** According to Taylor, Funk, and Craighill, 58% of people aged sixty-five and older reported gambling during 2006. Other studies show similar, or even higher rates, of participation. For example, Suzi Levens et al. reveal in "Gambling among Older, Primary-Care Patients" (*American Journal of Geriatric Psychiatry*, vol. 13, no. 1, January 2005) that in 2005 nearly 70% of Americans older than sixty-five reported gambling in the previous twelve months. This study, which was based on a survey of 843 elderly patients, also finds that nearly 11% of those questioned were "at risk" for problem gambling.

For older adults not at risk for gambling problems, the activity may have a positive impact. In "Health Correlates of Recreational Gambling in Older Adults" (*American Journal of Psychiatry*, vol. 161, no. 9, 2004), Rani A. Desai et al. indicate that a correlation exists between gambling and good health among people older than age sixty-five. The researchers do not find a similar correlation in those aged eighteen to sixty-four. The study, which is based on interviews with 2,417 older adults, focuses only on recreational gamers and does not include subjects who exhibited gambling addiction.

## TABLE 2.5

**Gambling trends by type of game, selected years 1989–2008**

|  | Bought a state lottery ticket | Visited a casino | Played a video poker game | Bet on pro sports | Bet on a horse race | Gambled on the internet |
|---|---|---|---|---|---|---|
| 1989 | 54 | 20 | 11 | 22 | 9 | * |
| 1990 | * | * | * | 21 | 9 | * |
| 1992 | 56 | 21 | 11 | 12 | 12 | * |
| 1996 | 57 | 27 | 17 | 10 | 6 | 1 |
| 1999 | 57 | * | 20 | 13 | * | * |
| 2003 | 49 | 30 | 14 | 10 | 4 | 1 |
| 2006 | 52 | 29 | 8 | 14 | 5 | 2 |
| 2008 | 46 | 24 | 12 | 7 | 5 | 2 |

SOURCE: Adapted from Jeffrey M. Jones, *Gambling a Common Activity for Americans*, The Gallup Organization, March 24, 2004, http://www.gallup.com/poll/11098/Gambling-Common-Activity-Americans.aspx (accessed July 18, 2008). Copyright © 2008 by The Gallup Organization. Reproduced by permission of The Gallup Organization; Paul Taylor, Cary Funk, and Peyton Craighill, "What Kind of Bet Did You Place This Year?" in *Gambling: As the Take Rises, So Does Public Concern*, Pew Research Center, May 23, 2006, http://pewresearch.org/assets/social/pdf/Gambling.pdf (accessed July 18, 2008); Jeffrey M. Jones, "Most Common Forms of Gambling," in *One in Six Americans Gamble on Sports*, The Gallup Organization, February 1, 2008, http://www.gallup.com/poll/104086/One-Six-Americans-Gamble-Sports.aspx (accessed July 15, 2008). Copyright © 2008 by The Gallup Organization. Reproduced by permission of The Gallup Organization.

**TABLE 2.6**

**Gamblers by demographic characteristics, March 2005–March 2006**

| | Any type of gambling | Bought lottery ticket | Visited casino | Bet[a] on sports | Played cards for money |
|---|---|---|---|---|---|
| | % | % | % | % | % |
| **All adults** | 67 | 52 | 29 | 23 | 17 |
| **Gender** | | | | | |
| Men | 72 | 56 | 31 | 32 | 25 |
| Women | 62 | 48 | 27 | 15 | 10 |
| **Race/ethnicity** | | | | | |
| White | 68 | 53 | 30 | 23 | 18 |
| Black | 62 | 45 | 24 | 24 | 14 |
| Hispanic[b] | 62 | 47 | 22 | 16 | 12 |
| **Age** | | | | | |
| 18–29 | 71 | 48 | 30 | 30 | 32 |
| 30–49 | 69 | 56 | 30 | 25 | 17 |
| 50–64 | 68 | 55 | 31 | 22 | 11 |
| 65+ | 58 | 43 | 22 | 13 | 10 |
| **Education** | | | | | |
| College grad | 65 | 48 | 31 | 25 | 15 |
| Some college | 71 | 55 | 32 | 23 | 21 |
| H.S. grad or less | 66 | 52 | 27 | 22 | 17 |
| **Family income** | | | | | |
| $100,000+ | 79 | 57 | 40 | 39 | 24 |
| $50K–$99K | 74 | 60 | 37 | 27 | 22 |
| $30K–$49K | 67 | 54 | 27 | 22 | 21 |
| Less than $30K | 59 | 44 | 21 | 16 | 11 |
| **Region** | | | | | |
| Northeast | 77 | 63 | 31 | 26 | 20 |
| Midwest | 64 | 52 | 26 | 23 | 18 |
| South | 62 | 48 | 24 | 21 | 15 |
| West | 68 | 47 | 38 | 23 | 17 |
| **Religion** | | | | | |
| Protestant | 61 | 48 | 24 | 19 | 13 |
| Catholic | 77 | 62 | 39 | 30 | 23 |
| Secular | 72 | 52 | 29 | 24 | 23 |
| **White Protestants** | | | | | |
| Evangelical | 50 | 40 | 19 | 14 | 11 |
| Mainline | 73 | 58 | 29 | 24 | 17 |

[a]Betting on sports includes professional sports, college sports or an office pool.
[b]Hispanics are of any race.

SOURCE: Paul Taylor, Cary Funk, and Peyton Craighill, "Profile of Gamblers," in *Gambling: As the Take Rises, So Does Public Concern*, Pew Research Center, May 23, 2006, http://pewresearch.org/assets/social/pdf/Gambling.pdf (accessed August 8, 2008)

## Young People

The minimum legal age for placing a legal bet ranges from eighteen to twenty-one, depending on the state and the activity. For example, most states limit the sale of lottery tickets to those eighteen or older, although most allow minors to receive lottery tickets as gifts. All commercial casinos have a minimum gambling age of twenty-one as set by state law. Tribal casinos are allowed to set their own minimum gambling age as long as it is at least eighteen. The minimum age to participate in charitable gambling activities, such as bingo games, is eighteen in most states. A few states allow people as young as sixteen to participate.

Each year the Annenberg Public Policy Center at the University of Pennsylvania releases the National Annenberg Risk Survey of Youth. In "Card Playing Down among College-Age Youth; Internet Gambling Also Declines" (October 18, 2007, http://www.annenbergpublic policycenter.org/Downloads/Releases/CardPlayingDeclines oct18version.pdf), the center notes that card playing for money among youth aged eighteen to twenty-two had declined in 2007. The overall percentage of males of that age who reported playing cards for money each week dropped from 16.3% in 2006 to 4.4% in 2007, about the same rate reported by male high school students (5.5%). Internet gambling also declined among male eighteen- to twenty-two-year-olds: 5.8% of these youth reported gambling at least once a week on the Internet in 2006, whereas only 1.5% reported doing so in 2007.

### Problem Gamblers

Problem gambling is a broad term that covers all gambling behaviors that are harmful to people in some way—financially, emotionally, socially, and/or legally. The harmful effects of problem gambling include:

- Financial difficulties, such as unpaid bills, loss of employment, large debts, and even bankruptcy

- Emotional problems, such as depression, anxiety, addictions, and thoughts of suicide

- Social problems, as evidenced by strained or broken relationships with spouses, family, friends, and coworkers

- Legal problems related to neglect of children or commission of criminal acts to obtain money

Taylor, Funk, and Craighill indicate that in 2006, 6% of those asked said gambling had been a source of problems for their family. (See Table 2.7.) This percentage was up slightly from those reported by the Gallup polling organization in 1989, 1992, and 1996, but down slightly from the percentage reported in 1999. The researchers note that there is a marked difference in answers by age. Only 5% of those aged fifty and older said gambling had been a problem for their family, compared to 12% of adults younger than fifty.

In general, scientists characterize gambling behavior by the level of harm that it causes. People who experience no harmful effects are called "nonproblem gamblers," or social, casual, or recreational gamblers. Those who gamble regularly and may be prone to a gambling problem are called "at-risk gamblers," and those who experience minor to moderate harm from their gambling behavior are called "problem gamblers." Pathological gamblers are severely harmed by their gambling activities.

Scientists use a screening process to determine which category fits a particular gambler. One of the most common is the South Oaks Gambling Screen (SOGS), a sixteen-item questionnaire developed in the 1980s by

## TABLE 2.7

**Poll respondents who have experienced family problems related to gambling, selected years 1989–2006**

DO YOU SOMETIMES GAMBLE MORE THAN YOU THINK YOU SHOULD?

|  | Yes | No | Don't know |
|---|---|---|---|
| **All gamblers** | % | % | % |
| March 2006 | 9 | 90 | 1=100 |
| December 2003 | 10 | 90 | 0=100 |
| May 1999 | 11 | 88 | 1=100 |
| June 1996 | 7 | 93 | =100 |
| November 1992 | 9 | 91 | 0=100 |
| April 1989 | 10 | 90 | 0=100 |

HAS GAMBLING EVER BEEN A SOURCE OF PROBLEMS WITHIN YOUR FAMILY?

| **All adults** |  |  |  |
|---|---|---|---|
| March 2006 | 6 | 93 | 1=100 |
| December 2003 | 6 | 94 | =100 |
| May 1999 | 9 | 91 | =100 |
| June 1996 | 5 | 95 | =100 |
| November 1992 | 5 | 94 | 1=100 |
| April 1989 | 4 | 96 | =100 |

Note: Based on people who gambled in past year. March 2006 figures are from Pew Research Center; data from all other years are from the Gallup Organization.

SOURCE: Paul Taylor, Cary Funk, and Peyton Craighill, "Gamble Too Much? Has Gambling Ever Been a Source of Problems within Your Family?" in *Gambling: As the Take Rises, So Does Public Concern*, Pew Research Center, May 23, 2006, http://pewresearch.org/assets/social/pdf/Gambling.pdf (accessed August 8, 2008). Data from The Gallup Organization. Copyright © 1989–2003 by The Gallup Organization. Reproduced by permission of The Gallup Organization.

## TABLE 2.8

**Twenty questions designed to determine whether a person is a compulsive gambler**

1. Did you ever lose time from work or school due to gambling?
2. Has gambling ever made your home life unhappy?
3. Did gambling affect your reputation?
4. Have you ever felt remorse after gambling?
5. Did you ever gamble to get money with which to pay debts or otherwise solve financial difficulties?
6. Did gambling cause a decrease in your ambition or efficiency?
7. After losing did you feel you must return as soon as possible and win back your losses?
8. After a win did you have a strong urge to return and win more?
9. Did you often gamble until your last dollar was gone?
10. Did you ever borrow to finance your gambling?
11. Have you ever sold anything to finance gambling?
12. Were you reluctant to use "gambling money" for normal expenditures?
13. Did gambling make you careless of the welfare of yourself or your family?
14. Did you ever gamble longer than you had planned?
15. Have you ever gambled to escape worry, trouble, boredom or loneliness?
16. Have you ever committed, or considered committing, an illegal act to finance gambling?
17. Did gambling cause you to have difficulty in sleeping?
18. Do arguments, disappointments or frustrations create within you an urge to gamble?
19. Did you ever have an urge to celebrate any good fortune by a few hours of gambling?
20. Have you ever considered self-destruction or suicide as a result of your gambling?

SOURCE: "Twenty Questions," Gamblers Anonymous, 2008, http://www.gamblersanonymous.org/20questions.html (accessed August 8, 2008)

Henry Lesieur and Sheila Blume. A detailed description of the questionnaire and its development was first presented by Lesieur and Blume in "SOGS: A New Instrument for the Identification of Pathological Gamblers" (*American Journal of Psychiatry*, vol. 144, no. 9, 1987). The researchers used information from 1,616 subjects to develop the SOGS, including patients with substance abuse and pathological gambling problems, members of Gamblers Anonymous, university students, and hospital employees. Because the questionnaires are filled out by potential problem gamblers themselves, scores depend entirely on the truthfulness of the people answering the questions.

Another means of defining problem gamblers was created by Gamblers Anonymous, the self-help organization, which prefers the term *compulsive gambling*. In "Questions and Answers: About the Problem of Compulsive Gambling and the G.A. Recovery Program" (November 9, 2007, http://www.gamblersanonymous.org/qna .html), the organization explains that compulsive gamblers exhibit certain characteristic behaviors:

- An "inability and unwillingness to accept reality"
- A belief that they have a "system" that will eventually pay off
- A lot of time spent daydreaming about what they will do when they finally make a big win

- Feelings of emotional insecurity when they are not gambling
- Immaturity and a desire to escape from responsibility
- Wanting all the good things in life without expending much effort for them
- Desire to be a "big shot" in the eyes of other people

Gamblers Anonymous has a list of twenty questions that gamblers can use to determine if they have a gambling problem. (See Table 2.8.) The organization indicates that compulsive gamblers are likely to answer yes to at least seven of the questions.

**PATHOLOGICAL GAMBLERS.** In general, pathological gambling is a disorder characterized by irrational thinking in which people continuously (or periodically) lose control over their gambling behavior. Pathological gamblers become preoccupied with gambling, constantly thinking about their next bet or how to raise more money with which they can gamble. This behavior continues even if the gambler suffers adverse consequences, such as financial difficulties or strained relationships with family and friends.

The American Psychiatric Association (APA) officially recognized pathological gambling as a mental health disorder in 1980 and listed it in its publication *Diagnostic and Statistical Manual of Mental Disorders*. The SOGS questionnaire was designed to correlate with criteria provided by the APA.

In 1996 the National Center for Responsible Gaming provided a grant to researchers at Harvard Medical School to perform a large-scale study of the prevalence of problem gambling. The results were published by Howard J. Shaffer, Matthew N. Hall, and Joni Vander Bilt in *Estimating the Prevalence of Disordered Gambling in the U.S. and Canada: A Meta-Analysis* (1997). A meta-analysis is an analysis of previously collected data. After examining hundreds of scientific studies on gambling in the United States and Canada, the researchers developed a ranking system for problem gambling:

- Level 0—nongamblers
- Level 1—social gamblers with no gambling problems
- Level 2—problem gamblers
- Level 3—pathological gamblers

Shaffer, Hall, and Vander Bilt calculate the lifetime prevalence rate of Level 3 gambling in the adult North American population to be 1.6%.

*Pathological Gambling: A Critical Review* was published in 1999 by the National Academies Press. The book identifies and analyzes all available scientific research studies dealing with pathological and problem gambling. The studies are reviewed by dozens of researchers on behalf of the National Research Council, an organization administered by the National Academy of Sciences, the National Academy of Engineering, and the Institute of Medicine. The researchers estimate that 1.5% of U.S. adults are pathological gamblers at some point in their life. In any given year, 0.9% of U.S. adults (approximately 1.8 million people) and 1.1 million adolescents aged twelve to eighteen are pathological gamblers. The following general conclusions are drawn:

- Men are more likely than women to be pathological gamblers.

- Pathological gambling often occurs concurrently with other behavioral problems, such as drug and alcohol abuse and mood and personality disorders.

- The earlier in life a person starts to gamble, the more likely he or she is to become a pathological gambler.

- Pathological gamblers are more likely than those without a gambling problem to have pathological gamblers as parents.

- Pathological gamblers who seek treatment generally get better.

However, the researchers are unable to determine from available studies whether any particular treatment technique is more effective than most others or even if some pathological gamblers are able to recover on their own. They are also unable to determine whether particular groups, such as the elderly and the poor, have dispropor-

tionately high rates of pathological gambling. The researchers conclude that further studies are needed to provide a detailed understanding of pathological gambling.

**TREATMENT ORGANIZATIONS.** A variety of treatment methods are available to problem gamblers through organizations and private counselors. For example, Gamblers Anonymous is open to all people who want to stop gambling. At its meetings, which are held throughout the United States, gamblers remain anonymous by using only their first name. The group method offers compulsive gamblers moral support and an accepting environment where they can talk about their past experiences and the problems that gambling creates in their life. Gambling is not treated as a vice but as a progressive illness.

Peter Ferentzy, Wayne Skinner, and Paul Antze explain in "Recovery in Gamblers Anonymous" (*Journal of Gambling Issues*, vol. 17, August 2006) that Gamblers Anonymous regards compulsive gamblers as people with an illness who can recover by following the organization's twelve-step recovery program. (See Table 2.9.) These steps are similar to those employed by support groups such as Alcoholics Anonymous. Even though the steps have a spiritual aspect, Gamblers Anonymous is not affiliated with any religious group or institution, and the organization is funded by donations. The premise of Gamblers Anonymous is that a recovering compulsive gambler cannot gamble at all without succumbing to the gambling compulsion, so it advocates a "cold turkey" approach to quitting (the gambler just stops gambling) rather than a gradual reduction in gambling activity.

The National Council on Problem Gambling is a nonprofit organization founded to increase public awareness about pathological gambling and to encourage the

**TABLE 2.9**

**Gamblers Anonymous 12-Step Recovery Program**

1. We admitted we were powerless over gambling—that our lives had become unmanageable.
2. Came to believe that a power greater than ourselves could restore us to a normal way of thinking and living.
3. Made a decision to turn our will and our lives over to the care of this power of our own understanding.
4. Made a searching and fearless moral and financial inventory of ourselves.
5. Admitted to ourselves and to another human being the exact nature of our wrongs.
6. Were entirely ready to have these defects of character removed.
7. Humbly asked God (of our understanding) to remove our shortcomings.
8. Made a list of all persons we had harmed and became willing to make amends to them all.
9. Make direct amends to such people wherever possible, except when to do so would injure them or others.
10. Continued to take personal inventory and when we were wrong, promptly admitted it.
11. Sought through prayer and meditation to improve our conscious contact with God as we understood Him, praying only for knowledge of His will for us and the power to carry that out.
12. Having made an effort to practice these principles in all our affairs, we tried to carry this message to other compulsive gamblers.

SOURCE: "The Recovery Program," Gamblers Anonymous, 2008, http://www.gamblersanonymous.org/recovery.html (accessed August 8, 2008) development of educational, research, and treatment programs. It sponsors the *Journal of Gambling Studies*, an academic journal dedicated to scientific research. It has thirty-five state affiliate chapters and operates a confidential hotline (1-800-522-4700) for problem gamblers who need help.

The council also operates the National Certified Gambling Counselor program and offers a database of counselors throughout the United States who have completed its certification program. Other organizations that certify gambling counselors include the American Compulsive Gambling Certification Board and the American Academy of Health Care Providers in the Addictive Disorders.

**TREATMENT METHODS.** Many problem gamblers seek professional counseling. The most common treatment method, in both group and individual counseling sessions, is cognitive behavior therapy. The cognitive portion of the therapy focuses attention on the person's thoughts, beliefs, and assumptions about gambling. The primary goal is recognizing and changing faulty thinking patterns, such as a belief that gambling can lead to great riches. Behavior therapy focuses on changing harmful behaviors. Most counselors favor complete abstinence from gambling during treatment. For those with mild to moderate gambling problems, treatment usually involves weekly meetings with a support group and/or individual counseling sessions. Nicki Dowling, David Smith, and Trang Thomas find in "A Comparison of Individual and Group Cognitive-Behavioural Treatment for Female Pathological Gambling" (*Behaviour Research and Therapy*, vol. 45, no. 9, September 2007) that individual treatment seems to be more effective than group treatment at least among some gamblers, although Tony Toneatto and Rosa Dragonetti indicate in "Effectiveness of Community-Based Treatment for Problem Gambling: A Quasi-experimental Evaluation of Cognitive-Behavioral vs. Twelve-Step Therapy" (*American Journal on Addictions*, vol. 17, no. 4, July 2008) that twelve-step programs are also effective. Those with severe gambling problems usually check into addiction treatment centers to curb their addiction. Such treatment centers isolate patients from the outside world so they can focus on overcoming their addiction. Some treatment centers even forbid patients from keeping cash on them or from using laptops, phones, or any device that could allow them to gamble.

More and more, mental health professionals and gambling treatment centers are using antidepressants along with cognitive therapy to treat compulsive gambling. Researchers speculate that some compulsive gamblers experience highly elevated levels of euphoria-causing chemicals, such as dopamine, in the brain when they gamble. A number of antidepressant drugs have been proven to prevent such chemicals from interacting with the brain.

For example, in "Multicenter Investigation of the Opiod Antagonist Nalmefene in the Treatment of Pathological Gambling" (*American Journal of Psychiatry*, vol. 163, no. 2, 2006), Jon E. Grant et al. report that the antidepressant nalmefene significantly lowers the need to gamble among people diagnosed with compulsive gambling. Donald W. Black, Martha C. Shaw, and Jeff Allen of the University of Iowa find in "Extended Release Carbamazepine in the Treatment of Pathological Gambling: An Open-Label Study" (*Progress in Neuro-Psychopharmacology and Biological Psychiatry*, vol. 32, no. 5, July 1, 2008) that carbamazepine, an antiseizure drug sometimes used to treat bipolar disorder, appears to be effective in treating pathological gambling. In 2008 a number of studies were under way to test the ability of other antidepressants, such as sertraline, to suppress gambling urges.

# CHAPTER 3
# AN INTRODUCTION TO CASINOS

When most people picture a casino, they will probably imagine one of the megaresorts in Las Vegas—a massive hotel and entertainment complex, blazing with neon lights, games, and fun—however, casinos come in all sizes. Some casinos are huge, whereas others are small businesses defined more by the types of gambling they offer than by glitz and glamour.

The federal government classifies all businesses and industries operated within the United States with a six-digit code called the North American Industry Classification System code. According to the U.S. Census Bureau, in *2002 NAICS Definitions: 713 Amusement, Gambling, and Recreation Industries* (May 6, 2003, http://www.census.gov/epcd/naics02/def/NDEF713.HTM), the code for casinos, 713210, is defined as follows: "This industry comprises establishments primarily engaged in operating gambling facilities that offer table wagering games along with other gambling activities, such as slot machines and sports betting. These establishments often provide food and beverage services. Included in this industry are floating casinos (i.e., gambling cruises, riverboat casinos)." Casino hotels—that is, hotels with a casino on the premises—fall under code 721120. They typically offer a variety of amenities, including dining, entertainment, swimming pools, and conference and convention rooms.

For practical purposes, casino gambling encompasses games of chance and skill played at tables and machines. Therefore, casino games take place in massive resorts as well as in small card rooms. There are also floating casinos operating on boats and barges on waterways across the country. Casino game machines have been introduced at racetracks to create racinos. In some states, casino-type game machines are also allowed in truck stops, bars, grocery stores, and other small businesses.

Successful casinos take in billions of dollars each year for the companies, corporations, investors, and Native American tribes that own and operate them. State and local governments also reap casino revenues in the form of taxes, fees, and other payments.

## THE HISTORICAL AND CURRENT STATUS OF CASINOS

Gambling was illegal for most of the nation's history. This did not keep casino games from occurring, sometimes openly and with the complicity of local law enforcement, but it did keep them from developing into a legitimate industry. Even after casino gambling was legalized in Nevada in 1931, its growth outside that state was stifled for decades. It took forty-seven years before a second state, New Jersey, decided to allow casino gambling within its borders.

As Atlantic City, New Jersey, opened casinos during the late 1970s, a shift occurred in the legality of gambling elsewhere in the country, much of it due to the efforts of some Native American tribes. A string of legal victories allowed the tribes to convert the small-time bingo halls they had been operating into full-scale casinos. Other states also wanted to profit from casino gambling. Between 1989 and 1996 nine states authorized commercial casino gambling: Colorado, Illinois, Indiana, Iowa, Louisiana, Michigan, Mississippi, Missouri, and South Dakota.

The American Gaming Association (AGA) estimates in *2008 State of the States: The AGA Survey of Casino Entertainment* (2008, http://www.americangaming.org/assets/files/aga_2008_sos.pdf) that commercial casinos had revenues of $34.1 billion in 2007, up from $32.4 billion in 2006, and the National Indian Gaming Commission reports in *National Indian Gaming Commission Newsletter* (Summer 2008, http://www.nigc.gov/LinkClick.aspx?link=NIGC+Uploads%2fNewsletters%2fSummer.2008.pdf&tabid=140&mid=760) that tribal casino revenue totaled $26 billion in 2007. According to the AGA, 467 commercial casinos, 424 tribal casinos, and 41 racetrack casinos operated nationwide in 2007.

**FIGURE 3.1**

**Casino locations by category, 2007**

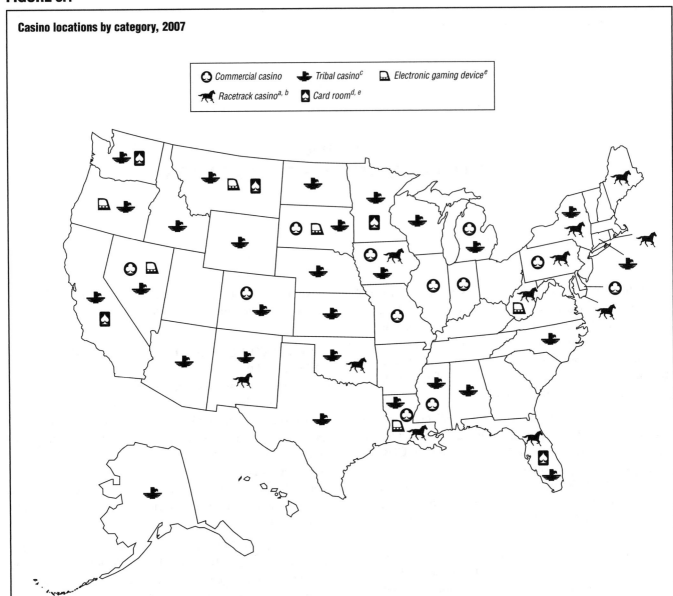

[a]In Rhode Island, there are video lottery terminals operating at a closed jai alai fronton, not considered a racetrack casino, but a pari-mutuel facility.
[b]The states with racetrack casinos operate class III gaming machines. There are two racinos in Alabama—not indicated on this map—that have class II machines only, which are legal only in the counties where they operate.
[c]Native American casinos noted here include both class II and class III facilities. States with class II gaming only are Alabama, Alaska, Florida, Nebraska and Texas.
[d]The States with card rooms indicated here do not include states that have commercial casinos with poker facilities.
[e]The card rooms in Washington operate blackjack and other house- or player-banked card games in addition to poker.
[f]The electronic gaming devices operating in the states indicated on this map are recognized as legal operations. There are some states with similar facilities, but the machines may not be authorized.

SOURCE: "Casino Locations by Category," in *2008 State of the States: The AGA Survey of Casino Entertainment*, American Gaming Association, 2008, http://www.americangaming.org/assets/files/aga_2008_sos.pdf (accessed August 1, 2008). Reprinted with permission of the American Gaming Association. All rights reserved.

Another 707 card rooms operated in 5 states. (See Figure 3.1 and Table 3.1.)

By the end of 2007, commercial casinos operated in Colorado, Illinois, Indiana, Iowa, Louisiana, Michigan, Mississippi, Missouri, Nevada, New Jersey, Pennsylvania, and South Dakota, and Native American casinos operated in twenty-nine states. Besides the full-scale casinos, racetrack casinos existed in eleven states: Delaware, Florida, Iowa, Louisiana, Maine, New Mexico, New York, Oklahoma, Pennsylvania, Rhode Island, and West Virginia. These facilities are racetracks that also offer slot machines.

**CASINO ACCEPTABILITY**

Each year the AGA releases results of a survey on the attitudes of Americans toward casino gambling. Most peo-

TABLE 3.1

**Number of casinos by state and category, 2007**

| State | ♣ | 🐎 | 🦅 | ♠ | 🚃[a] |
|---|---|---|---|---|---|
| Alabama | | | 3* | | |
| Alaska | | | 3* | | |
| Arizona | | | 25 | | |
| California | | | 61 | 91 | |
| Colorado | 45° | | 2 | | |
| Connecticut | | | 2 | | |
| Delaware | | 3■ | | | |
| Florida | | 3 | 8* | 18 | |
| Idaho | | | 6 | | |
| Illinois | 9 | | | | |
| Indiana | 11 | | | | |
| Iowa | 17 | 3 | 1 | | |
| Kansas | | | 6 | | |
| Louisiana | 18 | 4 | 3 | | 2,351 |
| Maine | | 1 | | | |
| Michigan | 3 | | 19 | | |
| Minnesota | | | 34 | 1 | |
| Mississippi | 29 | | 2 | | |
| Missouri | 12 | | 1 | | |
| Montana | | | 23 | 494 | 1,686 |
| Nebraska | | | 6* | | |
| Nevada | 270[b] | | 3 | | 2,216[c] |
| New Jersey | 11 | | | | |
| New Mexico | | 5 | 21 | | |
| New York | | 8■ | 8 | | |
| North Carolina | | | 2 | | |
| North Dakota | | | 6 | | |
| Oklahoma | | 3 | 95 | | |
| Oregon | | | 10 | | 2,263 |
| Pennsylvania | 6 | 5 | | | |
| Rhode Island | | 2■ | | | |
| South Dakota | 36° | | 10 | | 1,477■ |
| Texas | | | 1* | | |
| Washington | | | 33 | 103 | |
| West Virginia | | 4■ | | | 1,663■ |
| Wisconsin | | | 28 | | |
| Wyoming | | | 2 | | |
| **Total** | **467** | **41** | **424** | **707** | **11,656** |
| **Number of states** | **12** | **11** | **29** | **5** | **6** |

*Class II games only.
°Limited-stakes gaming.
■Video lottery terminals.
[a]Refers to number of non-casino locations in state where electronic gaming devices are present.
[b]Includes only locations with gross gaming revenue of at least $1 million.
[c]Locations have 15 or fewer machines.

SOURCE: "Casinos per State," in *2008 State of the States: The AGA Survey of Casino Entertainment*, American Gaming Association, 2008, http://www.americangaming.org/assets/files/aga_2008_sos.pdf (accessed August 1, 2008). Reprinted with permission of the American Gaming Association. All rights reserved.

FIGURE 3.2

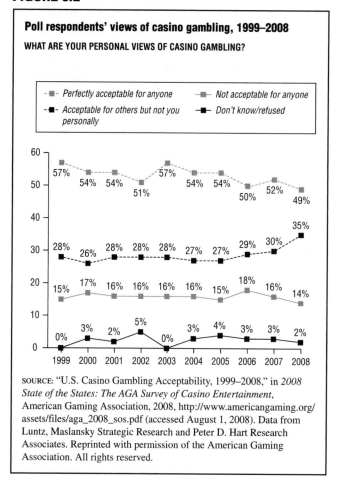

**Poll respondents' views of casino gambling, 1999–2008**

WHAT ARE YOUR PERSONAL VIEWS OF CASINO GAMBLING?

SOURCE: "U.S. Casino Gambling Acceptability, 1999–2008," in *2008 State of the States: The AGA Survey of Casino Entertainment*, American Gaming Association, 2008, http://www.americangaming.org/assets/files/aga_2008_sos.pdf (accessed August 1, 2008). Data from Luntz, Maslansky Strategic Research and Peter D. Hart Research Associates. Reprinted with permission of the American Gaming Association. All rights reserved.

ple surveyed in 2008 considered casino gambling acceptable: 49% of respondents found casino gambling to be acceptable for anyone, and 35% considered it acceptable for others, but not for themselves. (See Figure 3.2.) Only 14% of respondents thought casino gambling was not acceptable for anyone. Since 2003, the percentage of those who believed casino gambling was acceptable for anyone had dropped from 57%, whereas the percent of those who said it was acceptable for others but not themselves had risen from 28%. In other words, even though the percent of those who thought gambling was acceptable for others had not changed, a slight shift had occurred in views of the personal acceptability of gambling.

## CASINO GAMES

Casinos offer a variety of games, including card games, dice games, domino games, slot machines, and gambling devices (such as the roulette wheel). Some games are banked games, meaning that the house has a stake in the outcome of the game and bets against the players. Banked games include blackjack, craps, keno, roulette, and traditional slot machines. A nonbanked game is one in which the payout and the house's cut depend on the number of players or the amount that is bet, not the outcome of the game. In percentage games, the house collects a share of the amount wagered.

For example, in traditional poker players bank their own games. Each player puts money into the "pot" and competes against the other players to win the pot. A portion of the pot is taken by the house. In house-banked games the players compete against the house rather than each other. Another type of house-banked game is one in which there is a posted payout schedule for winning hands rather than a pot.

Gaming machines are by far the most popular type of casino activity. They are simple to operate and can offer large payouts for small wagers. The first commercial gambling machines, introduced in 1896, were called slot machines because the gambler inserted a coin into a slot to begin play. Each slot machine consisted of a metal box housing three reels, each of which was decorated all around with symbols (usually types of fruit or spades, hearts, diamonds, and clubs). When the player moved the handle on the machine, the reels spun randomly until they were slowed by stoppers within the machine. If a matching sequence of symbols appeared when the reels stopped, the player won. Each reel had many symbols, so literally thousands of outcomes were possible. Because of their construction, ease of play, and low odds, slot machines came to be known as "one-armed bandits."

Some casinos still offer old-fashioned slot machines, but most gaming machines in the twenty-first century are electronic and computer controlled. They are manufactured to strict technical specifications and use a computer programming technique called random number generation. A computer chip in each machine determines the percentage of payout. The machines are similar to high-tech video games, offering sophisticated graphics and sound. Some are even designed to mimic the look and feel of reel-type machines. Patrons may have a choice of a modern push button or an old-fashioned handle to activate play.

Electronic slot machines offer many different games (poker is one of the most popular) and are called by a variety of names: electronic gaming devices, video gaming terminals, video gaming devices, video poker machines, or just slots. Harrah's Entertainment explains in *Profile of the American Casino Gambler: Harrah's Survey 2006* (June 2006, http://www.harrahs.com/images/PDFs/Profile_Survey _2006.pdf) that slot machines can be played for a variety of denominations—from a penny up to more than $5. The quarter and fifty-cent slot machines are the most popular.

Some casinos have slot machines with progressive jackpots—in other words, the jackpot grows with continued play. Most progressive jackpot machines are connected to others in a computerized network. Play on any one machine within the group causes the jackpot to increase. On March 21, 2003, a man playing a progressive slot machine at the Excalibur Hotel and Casino in Las Vegas won $38.7 million, the largest slot machine payout in U.S. history (as of October 2008).

### Odds against Gamblers

Because casinos are businesses and must make money to survive, the mathematical odds are always against players in casino games. For example, in "Easy Money!" (June 10, 1997, http://www.pbs.org/wgbh/pages/frontline/ shows/gamble/), *Frontline* explains that a person betting $100 an hour on roulette will lose an average of $5.26 per hour in the long run. The "long run" is a concept often overlooked by gamblers. This is especially true of gamblers who play games of chance such as roulette.

Most roulette wheels have two colors: red and black. On each spin of the wheel, the odds of red or black coming up are fifty-fifty. Many people believe this means the number of black results will equal the number of red results over the course of time they are playing the game. Thus, when several consecutive spins have come up red, they feel that black is overdue, so they bet on that color.

This belief is false, and is known as the gambler's fallacy. Each spin of the roulette wheel is independent of the spins that came before and has the same fifty-fifty chance of being red or black. The fact that four or five results in a row have been red does not change the odds for the next spin. Therefore, even though it is true that over the long run the number of red and black results will be roughly equal, during that long run there may be many periods in which large numbers of spins come up red or black.

The same holds true for slot machines. Many gamblers believe that if they have bet on a slot machine many times in a row and lost, this increases the odds of the next bet being a winner. This is not the case. The Colorado Division of Gaming explains slot machines in the brochure *Understanding How a Slot Machine Works* (January 11, 2005, http://www.revenue.state.co.us/Gaming/ Documents/slotbrochure.pdf). The brochure notes that a slot machine with a 97% payout would theoretically be expected to pay back 97% of all money taken in over the lifetime of the machine, which is typically seven years. Therefore, a gambler who gambled on that machine continuously for seven years could expect to attain a 97% payout. However, during those seven years there will likely be periods in which he wins frequently, and periods in which he loses frequently, with no way to predict when they will occur.

### THE CASINO GAMBLER

In 2008, 24% of Americans had visited a casino in the past year. (See Table 2.5 in Chapter 2.) This rate was up substantially from 20% in 1989.

### Demographics

According to the AGA, in *2008 State of the States*, casino customers are slightly older and have a higher income than the U.S. population as a whole. In 2007 U.S. casino customers had a median age of forty-seven years, whereas the U.S. population had a median age of forty-six years. (See Figure 3.3.) The median household income of casino gamblers in 2007 was $59,735, 16% higher than the median household income of the U.S. population as a whole, which was $51,653. (See Figure 3.4.) About 18% of casino gamblers in 2007 had college degrees and 9% had

**FIGURE 3.3**

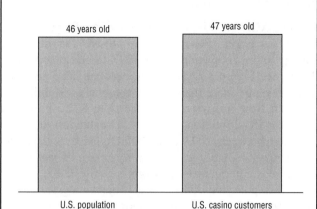

**Median age of U.S. population age 21 and older and U.S. casino customers, 2007**

46 years old 47 years old

U.S. population U.S. casino customers

**FIGURE 3.4**

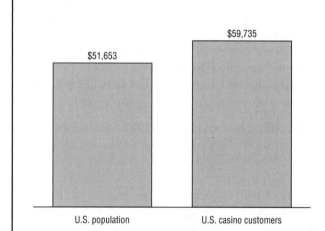

**Median household income of U.S. population and U.S. casino customers, 2007**

$51,653 $59,735

U.S. population U.S. casino customers

**FIGURE 3.5**

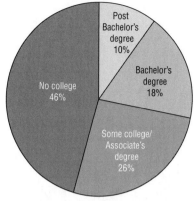

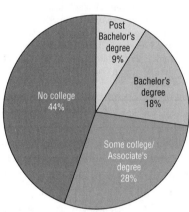

**Education level of casino gamblers vs. national average, 2007**

Post Bachelor's degree 10%

Bachelor's degree 18%

No college 46%

Some college/ Associate's degree 26%

**U.S. population**

Post Bachelor's degree 9%

Bachelor's degree 18%

No college 44%

Some college/ Associate's degree 28%

**U.S. casino customer**

a graduate degree. (See Figure 3.5.) About 28% had some college credits or an associate's degree. Nearly half (44%) had not attended college. This compares roughly with education levels on a national basis.

Harrah's Entertainment explains that *Profile of the American Casino Gambler* is based on two studies:

the National Profile Study by Roper Reports GfK NOP and the U.S. Gaming Panel by TNS. The National Profile Study included face-to-face interviews with 2,000 American adults, and the U.S. Gaming Panel had a questionnaire mailed to 100,000 adults (57,205 responded). Harrah's Entertainment finds that in 2005 the typical casino gambler was a forty-six-year-old female from a household with an above-average income. Older parents over the age of forty-five, who often have more vacation time and available spending money than younger adults, made up the largest group—23%—of casino gamblers in 2005. Harrah's Entertainment also finds that participation in casino gambling dropped with decreasing income—31% of Americans with annual household incomes more than $95,000 were casino gamblers, whereas only 20% of Americans with incomes of less than $35,000 per year participated.

**FIGURE 3.6**

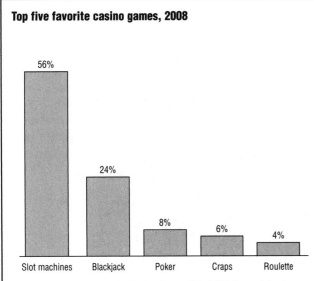

Top five favorite casino games, 2008

Slot machines were the most popular casino game among casino gamblers in 2008. (See Figure 3.6.) Over half (56%) of casino gamblers indicated they preferred to play slot machines and other electronic gaming devices. Nearly a quarter (24%) of survey respondents preferred blackjack, 8% preferred poker, 6% preferred craps, and 4% preferred roulette.

Harrah's Entertainment finds that in 2005 female casino gamblers showed a marked preference for electronic gaming, with 79% of those surveyed indicating that it was their favorite type of game, compared to 63% for men. Forty-one percent of women preferred machines in the $0.25- to $0.50-per-play range. Men (21%) were more likely to participate in table games than were women (9%). Game preference also varied by age; younger gamblers were more likely to prefer table games than were older gamblers.

**The Popularity of Poker**

With the advent of computer-simulated card games and Internet card rooms, poker surged in popularity in the early 2000s. Gamblers were no longer required to play experienced poker players to gain experience themselves. By 2003 a particular type of poker known as Texas Hold 'Em emerged as the game of choice. In Texas Hold 'Em players attempt to make a winning hand from a combination of cards dealt to them face down and community cards revealed to all players. Individuals who had never visited a commercial poker table began spending their weekends at local casinos or in online poker rooms, trying to wrest money from each other. Cable networks such as ESPN and the Travel Channel broadcast games from the World Series of Poker and the World Poker Tour—once obscure competitions reserved primarily for hard-core poker players.

The AGA includes in *2008 State of the States* a special report on poker. Poker revenue in Nevada decreased slightly from $60.9 million in 1997 to $57.5 million in 2002. (See Figure 3.7.) However, between 2003 and 2007 poker revenue more than tripled, totaling $168 million in 2007. In New Jersey revenue rose from $32.5 million in 2002 to $84.2 million in 2007. The biggest increases occurred between 2003 and 2005. In *2006 State of the States: The AGA Survey of Casino Entertainment* (2006, http://www.americangaming.org/assets/files/2006_Survey_for_Web.pdf), the AGA reveals that young to middle-aged men visited poker rooms more than any other demographic group. Some 25% of males and 13% of females reported playing poker in 2005, which was up from 15% of males and 10% of females in 2003. Poker playing increased across all age groups.

**HOW DO CASINOS PERSUADE PEOPLE TO GAMBLE?**

Casino gambling is different from other forms of gambling, such as lotteries and Internet gambling, because of its social aspect. Players are either directly interacting with others, as in craps or poker, or surrounded by other people as they play the slot machines. Players often shout out encouragement. Alcoholic drinks are easily accessible and delivered directly to gamblers by waiters circulating throughout the casino. Nonalcoholic drinks and snacks are sometimes provided free of charge. The casino atmosphere is designed around noise, light, and excitement.

According to the AGA, in *2002 State of the States: The AGA Survey of Casino Entertainment* (2002, http://www.americangaming.org/assets/files/AGA_survey_2002.pdf), 92% of survey respondents went to casinos in the company of their spouses, families, and friends or as part of organized groups in 2002. The AGA notes in *2007 State of the States: The AGA Survey of Casino Entertainment* (2007, http://www.americangaming.org/assets/files/aga_2007_sos.pdf) that survey respondents were asked in 2007 to rate which was more fun for them: the gambling itself or the food, shows, and entertainment offered at casinos. Nearly half (49%) said it was the food, shows, and entertainment, and a quarter (23%) said it was the gambling itself.

Casinos use sophisticated marketing and design to get gamblers into their facilities and keep them gambling as long and as happily as possible. Most of them invest millions of dollars to determine which colors, sounds, and scents are most appealing to patrons. The legend that oxygen is pumped into casinos to keep customers alert is

**FIGURE 3.7**

**Consumer spending on poker in Nevada and New Jersey, 1997–2007**

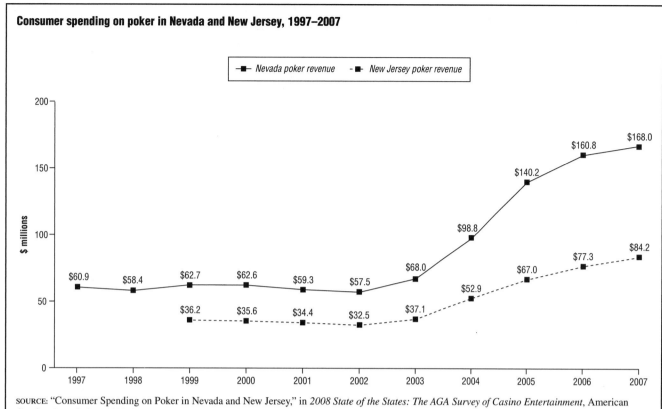

not true—it would be an extreme fire hazard. However, casinos do use bright and sometimes gaudy floor and wall coverings that have a stimulating and cheering effect. Red is a popular decorating color because it is thought to make people lose track of time. Also, there are no clocks on casino walls.

According to *The Tech of a Casino* (TechTV, June 2002), casinos use a variety of tricks to attract gamblers. Slot machines and gaming tables are arranged in a maze-like fashion so that wandering patrons are continuously enticed by more gambling options. Slot machines are designed to be appealing to the senses of sight, touch, and sound—the noises of the machines are electronically tuned to the musical key of C to be pleasing to the ear. Bells, lights, whistles, and the clang of dropping coins are constant. Humans are attracted to bright lights, so more than 15,000 miles (24,100 km) of neon tubing are used to light the casinos along the Las Vegas Strip.

Casinos also focus on customer service. For example, they provide perks designed to encourage gamblers to spend more and to reward those who do. Most casinos offer "comps," which is short for "complimentaries" (free items). During the 1970s Las Vegas casinos were famous for their deeply discounted travel packages, cheap buffets,

and free show tickets. The strategy at that time was to maximize the volume of people going to Las Vegas. Gambling revenue was driven by filling hotel rooms and the casino floor with as many people as possible.

In the twenty-first century, casinos are choosier. They concentrate their investments on the "high rollers" (gamblers who spend much more than average). Such people often gamble in special rooms, separate from the main casino floor, where the stakes (i.e., the amount bet) can be in the tens of thousands of dollars. Casinos make much of their profit from these high-stakes gamblers. Therefore, the high rollers receive comps worth a great deal of money, such as free luxury suites, as well as lavish personal attention.

Less expensive comps are available to smaller spenders. Most casinos offer clubs that are similar to airline frequent-flyer programs. Gamblers who join receive a card that can be swiped electronically before they play a game. Casino computers track their usage and spending habits and tally up points that can be exchanged for coupons for free slot play or for free or discounted meals, drinks, or shows. The comp programs serve as a valuable marketing tool for the casinos, as well: they develop a patron database that can be used for advertising and to track trends in game preference and spending.

# CHAPTER 4
# COMMERCIAL CASINOS

## THE MARKET

Commercial casinos are profit-making businesses owned by individuals, private companies, or large public corporations. The term *commercial casino* is used in the United States to indicate a gaming facility that is not owned and operated on Native American lands by a tribal government. (See Chapter 5.) Casinos are closely regulated by state governments. Some states allow land-based casinos, whereas others restrict casino games to floating gambling halls on barges or riverboats. A handful of states allow casino games such as slot machines at other locations, including horse and dog racetracks or other commercial establishments. Some states allow only limited-stakes gambling, in which a limit is placed on the amount that can be wagered.

In *2008 State of the States: The AGA Survey of Casino Entertainment* (2008, http://www.americangaming.org/assets/files/aga_2008_sos.pdf), the American Gaming Association (AGA) states that in 2007 there were 467 commercial casinos operating in 12 states: Colorado, Illinois, Indiana, Iowa, Louisiana, Michigan, Mississippi, Missouri, Nevada, New Jersey, Pennsylvania, and South Dakota. These included both land-based and floating casinos. Major markets for floating casinos included Chicago; Tunica, Mississippi; the Mississippi Gulf Coast; and Bossier City, Shreveport, and Lake Charles, Louisiana. Some of the largest gaming companies, including Harrah's Entertainment, MGM Mirage, and Penn National Gaming, operated floating casinos. Nearly one-third (32%) of casino patrons visit casinos in the West, about a quarter visit casinos in the north-central part of the country (25%) or the South (24%), and 19% visit casinos in the Northeast. (See Figure 4.1.)

The casino industry measures its revenue by consumer spending, that is, the money gamblers spend while gambling. According to the AGA, consumer spending on gambling in 2007 totaled $34.1 billion. In gambling terminology, the handle is the gross amount of money wagered by gamblers. The money that the gamblers win is called the payout, and the money that the casinos keep is called the gross gaming revenue or the casino win.

## NEVADA

Gambling has a long history in Nevada. It was common in the frontier towns of the Old West but was outlawed around the end of the nineteenth century, a time when conservative values predominated. However, illegal gambling was widely tolerated throughout the state. In 1931 gambling was legalized again in Nevada. The country was in a deep economic depression at the time, and gambling was seen as a source of needed revenue.

Casino development was slow at first. Many business people were not convinced that the desert towns of Nevada could attract sufficient tourists to make the operations profitable. In 1941 El Rancho Vegas opened in Las Vegas. Five years later the mobster Benjamin "Bugsy" Siegel (1906–1947) opened the Flamingo Hotel and Casino, also in Las Vegas. (Siegel was eventually murdered by his business partners because of cost overruns.) Organized crime's relationship with Las Vegas continued for thirty years and tainted casino gambling in many people's minds.

Even though the state of Nevada began collecting gaming taxes during the 1940s, regulation of the casinos was lax until the 1970s. Organized crime figures were pushed out of the casino business after Congress passed the Racketeer Influenced and Corrupt Organizations Act in 1970. Corporations moved in to take their place. In 1975 gaming revenues in the state reached $1 billion, according to the Las Vegas Convention and Visitors Authority (LVCVA), in "Stats & Facts: History of Las Vegas" (2008, http://www.lvcva.com/press/statistics-facts/vegas-history.jsp). The AGA notes in *2008 State of the States* that by 2007 the gambling industry employed 201,953 people in Nevada and contributed $1 billion in tax revenue into the state's general fund.

**FIGURE 4.1**

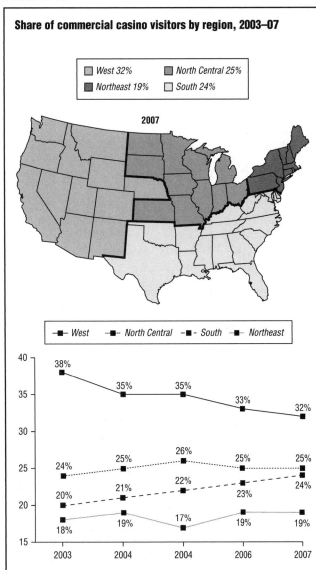

Share of commercial casino visitors by region, 2003–07

Legend:
- West 32%
- North Central 25%
- Northeast 19%
- South 24%

2007

West · North Central · South · Northeast

SOURCE: "Share of Commercial Casino Visitors by Region," in *2008 State of the States: The AGA Survey of Casino Entertainment*, American Gaming Association, 2008, http://www.americangaming.org/assets/files/aga_2008_sos.pdf (accessed August 1, 2008). Data from Harrah's Entertainment, Inc./TNS. Reprinted with permission of the American Gaming Association. All rights reserved.

**FIGURE 4.2**

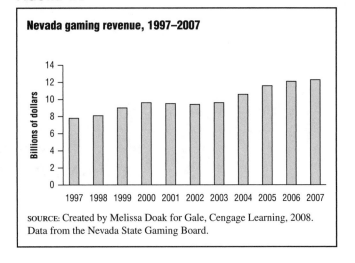

Nevada gaming revenue, 1997–2007

SOURCE: Created by Melissa Doak for Gale, Cengage Learning, 2008. Data from the Nevada State Gaming Board.

**TABLE 4.1**

Consumer spending on casino gaming, by selected states, 2006 and 2007

| State | 2006 | 2007 | Change |
|---|---|---|---|
| Colorado | $782.098 million | $816.130 million | +4.4% |
| Illinois | $1.924 billion | $1.983 billion | +3.1% |
| Indiana | $2.577 billion | $2.625 billion | +1.8% |
| Iowa | $1.173 billion | $1.363 billion | +16.2% |
| Louisiana | $2.567 billion | $2.566 billion | 0.0% |
| Michigan | $1.303 billion | $1.335 billion | +2.4% |
| Mississippi | $2.570 billion | $2.891 billion | +12.5% |
| Missouri | $1.592 billion | $1.592 billion | 0.0% |
| Nevada | $12.622 billion | $12.849 billion | +1.8% |
| New Jersey | $5.219 billion | $4.921 billion | −5.7% |
| Pennsylvania | —* | $1.090 billion | N/A |
| South Dakota | $89.828 million | $98.223 million | +9.3% |

*There are no 2006 statistics for Pennsylvania because stand-alone casinos there only became operational in 2007.

SOURCE: "State-by-State Consumer Spending on Commercial Casino Gaming, 2006 vs. 2007," in *2008 State of the States: The AGA Survey of Casino Entertainment*, American Gaming Association, 2008, http://www.americangaming.org/assets/files/aga_2008_sos.pdf (accessed August 1, 2008). Reprinted with permission of the American Gaming Association. All rights reserved.

Many different forms of legal gambling are available in Nevada, including live bingo, keno, and horse racing; card rooms; casino games; and off-track and phone betting on sports events and horse races. Establishments such as bars, restaurants, and stores are restricted to fewer than fifteen slot machines. Casinos are allowed to have more than fifteen machines; many have hundreds of slot machines.

According to the AGA, in 2007 there were 270 non-tribal, commercial casinos operating in Nevada—by far the most of any state. According to the Nevada State Gaming Control Board, the state's commercial casinos generated $12.3 billion in revenue from gambling operations during 2007, up from $12.1 billion in 2006. (See Figure 4.2.) Casino revenues have been increasing stead-ily since 1997, although they leveled off for a brief period following the terrorist attacks of September 11, 2001, and then again between 2006 and 2007 in response to economic recession. Consumers spend by far more money on commercial casino gaming in Nevada than in any other state. (See Table 4.1.)

Nevada casino revenue, or casino win, for 2007 is broken down by gambling category in Table 4.2. Slot machines accounted for $8.5 billion (66%) of the casinos' gaming revenue of $12.8 billion. Table games brought in $4.2 billion in revenue in that year. According to the Nevada State Gaming Control Board, in *State of Nevada Gaming Revenue Report: Year Ended December 31, 1989* (1999, http://gaming.nv.gov/documents/pdf/1g_98dec.pdf), gross gaming revenue jumped from

**TABLE 4.2**

**Nevada gaming revenue, selected statistics, 2007**

[Win amounts are in thousands]

| Games and tables: | Win amount | % Change | Win percent |
|---|---|---|---|
| Twenty-one | 1,420,549 | 2.80 | 12.40 |
| Craps | 478,151 | 3.18 | 13.56 |
| Roulette | 374,964 | 8.01 | 17.92 |
| 3-Card Poker | 175,236 | −2.75 | 26.27 |
| Baccarat | 907,951 | 3.72 | 12.74 |
| Mini-Baccarat | 156,023 | −19.26 | 12.25 |
| Keno | 50,384 | −9.81 | 27.04 |
| Bingo | 5,391 | 325.04 | 2.69 |
| Caribbean Stud | 14,114 | −25.37 | 29.43 |
| Let It Ride | 63,834 | 7.46 | 22.36 |
| Pai Gow | 28,780 | −15.38 | 17.21 |
| Pai Gow Poker | 141,329 | 10.09 | 22.17 |
| Race Book[1] | 94,256 | −2.30 | 15.80 |
| Sports Pool[2] | 168,363 | −12.10 | 6.49 |
| Other games | 150,929 | 18.29 | 24.65 |
| **Total games** | **4,230,254** | **1.82** | **13.44** |
| **Card games** | **167,975** | **4.38** | |
| | | | |
| **Slot machines:** | | | |
| 1 Cent | 1,631,069 | 24.87 | 10.10 |
| 5 Cent | 491,506 | −14.40 | 8.48 |
| 25 Cent | 1,076,963 | −15.46 | 6.43 |
| 1 Dollar | 994,269 | −4.18 | 5.52 |
| Megabucks | 88,858 | −11.88 | 12.72 |
| 5 Dollar | 284,589 | 7.95 | 5.62 |
| 25 Dollar | 65,889 | −6.93 | 3.69 |
| 100 Dollar | 46,767 | −6.49 | 3.95 |
| Multi denomination | 3,609,346 | 4.32 | 5.21 |
| Other slot machines | 161,653 | −3.92 | |
| **Total slot machines** | **8,450,908** | **1.75** | **6.13** |
| **Total gaming win** | **12,849,137** | **1.81** | |
| [1]Race Pari-Mutuel | 93,854 | −3.18 | 17.03 |
| [2]Sports pool details | | | |
| Football | 73,532 | −19.32 | 6.25 |
| Basketball | 37,452 | −18.92 | 5.45 |
| Baseball | 25,382 | 14.62 | 4.80 |
| Sports Parlay Cards | 20,283 | −3.81 | 29.56 |
| Sports Pari-Mutuel | −78 | −6623.44 | −25.80 |
| Other | 11,792 | 7.42 | 8.80 |

SOURCE: Adapted from "Statewide, All Nonrestricted Locations, Twelve-Month Summary—01/01/07 to 12/31/07," in *State of Nevada Gaming Revenue Report: Year Ended December 31, 2007*, Nevada State Gaming Control Board, 2008, http://gaming.nv.gov/documents/pdf/1g_07dec.pdf (accessed July 18, 2008)

$8.1 billion in 1998 to $12.8 billion in 2007 (see Table 4.2), an increase of 58%.

Multidenomination slot machines made the most money of any game in Nevada's casinos in 2007 ($3.6 billion), followed by one-cent slot machines ($1.6 billion). The table game with the highest revenue was twenty-one, bringing in $1.4 billion, followed by baccarat ($908 million).

Even though casinos are located throughout the state, the major gambling markets in Nevada are in the southern part of the state in Clark County (which encompasses Las Vegas and Laughlin) and along the California border in Washoe County (which encompasses Reno) and the Lake Tahoe resort area.

## Las Vegas

Perhaps no other city is more associated with casinos than Las Vegas. According to the LVCVA, in "Stats & Facts: Visitor Statistics" (2008, http://www.lvcva.com/getfile/ES-YTD2007%20Final.pdf?fileID=350), the city had 39.2 million visitors in 2007, up 0.7% from 2006. The city's hotel and motel rooms had an occupancy rate of 90.4%. In *Las Vegas Visitor Profile, Calendar Year 2007* (December 2007, http://www.lvcva.com/getfile/VPS-2007 %20Las%20Vegas.pdf?fileID=107), the LVCVA indicates that most visitors were married (79%) and had a household income of at least $40,000 (79%). The average age of visitors was forty-nine, and 26% of visitors were retired. Visitors stayed an average of 3.5 nights in the city. The LVCVA indicates in "Stats & Facts: Visitor Statistics" that in 2007, 23,847 conventions were held in Las Vegas, attracting 6.2 million attendees with an estimated economic impact of $8.4 billion.

In *Las Vegas Visitor Profile, Calendar Year 2007*, the LVCVA notes that in 2007, 19% of visitors to Las Vegas were first-time visitors. Eleven percent of visitors stated that their primary purpose in visiting the city was to gamble, up significantly from 2004, when only 4% stated gambling was their primary purpose. However, 84% of all visitors to Las Vegas gambled during their visit, spending an average of 3.4 hours per day gambling, with an average gambling budget of $555.64.

The casinos on the 4-mile (6.4-km) stretch of Las Vegas Boulevard known as the Strip made up the top commercial casino market in the country in 2007. (See Table 4.3.) Nearly forty hotel-casinos line the Strip, a

**TABLE 4.3**

**Top 20 casino markets, 2007**

| | Location | Revenue |
|---|---|---|
| 1 | Las Vegas Strip, Nev. | $6.750 billion |
| 2 | Atlantic City, N.J. | $4.921 billion |
| 3 | Chicagoland, Ill./Ind. | $2.602 billion |
| 4 | Connecticut | $1.685 billion |
| 5 | Detroit, Mich. | $1.335 billion |
| 6 | Tunica/Lula, Miss. | $1.243 billion |
| 7 | Biloxi, Miss. | $1.007 billion |
| 8 | St. Louis, Mo./Ill. | $999.37 million |
| 9 | Boulder Strip, Nev. | $927.70 million |
| 10 | Reno/Sparks, Nev. | $927.60 million |
| 11 | Shreveport, La. | $844.13 million |
| 12 | Lawrenceburg/Rising Sun/ Belterra, Ind. | $791.10 million |
| 13 | Kansas City, Mo. (includes St. Joseph) | $758.18 million |
| 14 | New Orleans, La. | $703.59 million |
| 15 | Lake Charles, La. | $640.63 million |
| 16 | Downtown Las Vegas, Nev. | $632.93 million |
| 17 | Laughlin, Nev. | $630.92 million |
| 18 | Black Hawk, Co. | $581.39 million |
| 19 | Council Bluffs, Iowa | $470.86 million |
| 20 | Charles Town, W.Va. | $463.37 million |

SOURCE: "Top 20 U.S. Casino Markets, 2007," in *2008 State of the States: The AGA Survey of Casino Entertainment*, American Gaming Association, 2008, http://www.americangaming.org/assets/files/aga_2008_sos.pdf (accessed August 1, 2008). Data from The Innovation Group. Reprinted with permission of the American Gaming Association. All rights reserved.

number of which are among the largest hotels in the United States. These lavishly decorated megaresorts offer amenities such as spas, pools, top-quality restaurants, and top-notch entertainment. The companies operating these establishments generate a substantial amount of their revenue from nongambling sources, including lodging, dining, and entertainment.

Besides those on the Strip, casinos are located throughout Las Vegas and in other parts of Clark County, including Mesquite, Primm, and Laughlin. The Nevada State Gaming Control Board reports in *State of Nevada Gaming Revenue Report: Year Ended December 31, 2007* (2008, http://gaming.nv.gov/documents/pdf/1g_07dec .pdf) that in total, the 182 casinos in Clark County, both on the Strip and off, had gaming revenue of $10.9 billion during 2007. This amounted to 85% of the state's total casino gambling revenues for that year.

## NEW JERSEY

In June 1976 New Jersey voters legalized casino gambling in Atlantic City, making it the second state to do so. In 2007 it was the second-largest gambling market in the country. (See Table 4.3.)

### Atlantic City

Atlantic City was an immensely popular resort destination throughout the late 1800s and early 1900s. It was easily accessible by rail, and people visited the beautiful beaches and elegant hotels along the boardwalk, which stretches nearly 5 miles (8 km). During the 1960s the city lost most of its tourist trade to beaches farther south, mainly in Florida and the Caribbean, and the city fell into an economic slump. Casinos were seen as a way to revitalize the city and attract tourists again. The first casino, Resorts International, opened in 1978, followed by Caesars Atlantic and Bally's Park Place in 1979. By 1991 casino gambling was permitted twenty-four hours per day.

The city's eleven casinos had gross revenue of $4.9 billion in 2007, down from $5.2 billion in 2006, a 6% decrease. (See Table 4.4.) The New Jersey Casino Control Commission theorized that revenues were down for the first time in the history of casino gambling in Atlantic City due to a confluence of factors. Slot machines were introduced at racetracks in New York and Pennsylvania, a partial ban on smoking was imposed on the casino floor, and a downturn in the overall U.S. economy left consumers with less money for travel and gambling.

All Atlantic City casinos are land based. According to the New Jersey Casino Control Commission, in *New Jersey Casino Control Commission 2007 Annual Report* (2008, http://www.state.nj.us/casinos/about/commrepo/docs/2007/2007_annual_report.pdf), as of December 31, 2007, they offered 1,600 table games, 16 keno windows,

and 35,615 slot machines. Atlantic City casinos employed 40,788 people in 2007 and paid wages of $1.1 billion. They paid another $394 million in taxes.

Atlantic City differs from Las Vegas in many ways. There are far fewer hotel rooms (only 14,575) with fewer amenities. Atlantic City is considered a "day-tripper market," attracting people within driving or train distance who visit for the day (many of them from New York City and Philadelphia). Casino development was sluggish in Atlantic City during the 1990s; no new casinos were built. However, in July 2003 the Boyd Gaming Corp. and MGM Mirage collaborated to open Borgata, the city's newest casino and hotel, and approximately twenty-five hundred new hotel rooms were scheduled to open due to hotel expansions in 2008, and a new casino hotel owned by Revel Entertainment was scheduled to open in 2010.

In Atlantic City each casino is assessed an 8% tax on its gross revenue (i.e., casino revenue after all winners are paid but before other expenses are paid). The tax payments go into a fund that is distributed among various state programs. The New Jersey Casino Control Commission states that in fiscal year (FY) 2007, $410 million from the gross revenue tax was dispersed to funds such as the Department of Health and Senior Services, the Department of Human Services, the Department of Transportation, the Department of Labor and Workforce Development, and the Department of Law and Public Safety. Most of these taxes funded programs to benefit senior citizens and disabled people living in the state.

The casinos of Atlantic City have not changed the town into a trendy tourist destination as was originally hoped. In fact, Atlantic City has the reputation of being a slum with casinos. Industry experts point to two primary factors for this perception: the town relies on day-trippers rather than on long-term vacationers, and casino tax revenues have largely funded physical and mental health programs throughout the state rather than being invested in local infrastructure and economic development.

## MISSISSIPPI

In 1989 Mississippi became the first state to permit gambling on cruise ships that were in state waters on their way to or from international waters, but gambling in Mississippi had a long history. Gambling along the Mississippi River and its connecting waterways was widespread during the early 1800s. The rivers were the equivalent of the modern-day interstate highway system, carrying cash-laden farmers, merchants, and tourists to bustling towns along the riverbank. Gambling halls became notorious establishments that attracted professional gamblers, especially cardsharps, who employed various methods of cheating to earn a living at cards.

**TABLE 4.4**

**New Jersey casino revenue, selected statistics, 2006 and 2007**

[$ in thousands]

| Casino hotel | Casino win | Daily average casino win | Adjustments | Gross revenue | Tax | Market share of casino win |
|---|---|---|---|---|---|---|
| AC Hilton | | | | | | |
| 2007 | $ 304,898 | $ 835 | $ — | $ 304,898 | $ 24,392 | 6.2% |
| 2006 | $ 330,083 | $ 904 | — | $ 330,083 | $ 26,407 | 6.3% |
| Bally's Atlantic City | | | | | | |
| 2007 | 641,418 | 1,757 | — | 641,418 | 51,314 | 13.0% |
| 2006 | 677,290 | 1,856 | — | 677,290 | 54,183 | 13.0% |
| Borgata | | | | | | |
| 2007 | 750,967 | 2,057 | — | 750,967 | 60,077 | 15.3% |
| 2006 | 739,289 | 2,025 | — | 739,2B9 | 59,143 | 14 2% |
| Caesars | | | | | | |
| 2007 | 583,338 | 1,598 | (93) | 583,431 | 46,675 | 11.9% |
| 2006 | 555,243 | 1,521 | (0,6) | 555,329 | 44,426 | 10.7% |
| Harrah's Marina | | | | | | |
| 2007 | 519,497 | 1,423 | (19) | 519,516 | 41,561 | 10.5% |
| 2006 | 508,980 | 1,394 | — | 508,980 | 40,718 | 9.8% |
| Resorts | | | | | | |
| 2007 | 278,731 | 764 | (18) | 278,749 | 22,300 | 5.7% |
| 2006 | 282,896 | 775 | (9) | 282,905 | 22,632 | 5.4% |
| Sands* | | | | | | |
| 2007 | — | — | — | — | — | n/a |
| 2006 | 147,976 | 471 | (1,045) | 149,021 | 11,922 | 2.8% |
| Showboat | | | | | | |
| 2007 | 407,421 | 1,116 | (27) | 407,448 | 32,596 | 8.3% |
| 2006 | 429,514 | 1,177 | (20) | 429,534 | 34,363 | 8.2% |
| Tropicana | | | | | | |
| 2007 | 403,667 | 1,106 | — | 403,667 | 32,293 | 8.2% |
| 2006 | 459,150 | 1,258 | — | 459,150 | 36,732 | 8.8% |
| Trump Marina | | | | | | |
| 2007 | 241,939 | 663 | 15 | 241,924 | 19,354 | 4.9% |
| 2006 | 257,166 | 705 | (7) | 257,173 | 20,574 | 4.9% |
| Trump Plaza | | | | | | |
| 2007 | 280,343 | 768 | (171) | 280,514 | 22,441 | 5.7% |
| 2006 | 300,894 | 824 | (62) | 300,956 | 24,077 | 5.8% |
| Trump Taj Mahal | | | | | | |
| 2007 | 508,568 | 1,393 | (237) | 508,805 | 40,704 | 10.3% |
| 2006 | 529,233 | 1,450 | (256) | 529,489 | 42,359 | 10.1% |
| Totals | | | | | | |
| 2007 | $4,920,787 | $13,482 | $(550) | $4,921,337 | $393,707 | 100.0% |
| 2006 | $5,217,714 | $14,295 | $(1,485) | $5,219,199 | $417,536 | 100.0% |

*Sands ceased operations on November 10, 2006. Daily average win adjusted for closing date.

SOURCE: "The New Jersey Casino Industry Gross Revenue Statistics for the Years Ended December 31, 2007 and 2006," in *2007 Annual Report*, State of New Jersey Casino Control Commission, 2008, http://www.state.nj.us/casinos/about/commrepo/docs/2007/2007_annual_report.pdf (accessed August 1, 2008)

By the 1830s the cardsharps had worn out their welcome. According to Richard Dunstan, in *Gambling in California* (1997), five cardsharps were lynched in Mississippi in 1835, and the professional gamblers moved to the riverboats cruising up and down the rivers. Gambling was a popular pastime for riverboat passengers during the 1840s and 1850s. The onset of the Civil War (1861–1865) and then the antigambling movement around the turn of the twentieth century dampened, but did not destroy, open gambling in the state.

During and after World War II (1939–1945), the Mississippi coast experienced a resurgence in illegal casino gambling, particularly in Harrison County, which is where the Keesler Air Force Base is located. The officers' club at the base reportedly operated slot machines. During the 1960s the Alcohol Beverage Control Board began refusing licenses to public facilities that allowed gambling. A few

private clubs and lodges continued to offer card games and slot machines, but they were shut down by the mid-1980s.

In 1987 the ship *Europa Star* and several other ships from Biloxi ports began taking gamblers on "cruises to nowhere"—cruises to international waters in the Gulf of Mexico, where passengers could gamble legally. Even though the cruises were supported by the city of Biloxi, the state initially opposed them until it became apparent that they were reviving tourism in port towns. The state was in desperate economic times—the 1980 census revealed it was the poorest state in the country.

The Mississippi legislature legalized casino gambling in 1990, although each county was allowed to decide whether it would permit gambling within its borders. Fourteen counties along the Gulf Coast and the Mississippi River held referenda to allow dockside casinos, and all voted them down. The next year a city-by-city vote was held, and voters in Biloxi, which was nearly bankrupt at the time, approved the referendum. In 1992 nine dockside casinos opened in Biloxi.

Casinos are grouped in three parts of the state: the northern region centered in Tunica; the central region based in Vicksburg and Natchez; and the coastal region centered in Biloxi, Gulfport, and Bay St. Louis. Tunica was the sixth-largest casino market and Biloxi the seventh-largest in 2007. (See Table 4.3.)

Mississippi has set no limit on the number of casinos that can be built in the state. Instead, it allows competition to determine the market size. Before Hurricane Katrina hit the state in August 2005 and devastated the area around Biloxi, casinos were required to be permanently docked in the water along the Mississippi River and the Mississippi Gulf Coast. The gambling halls of the casinos actually sat on the water, while their associated lodging, dining, and entertainment facilities were on land. After the hurricane partially or completely destroyed all twelve casinos along the Gulf Coast, the legislature passed a law allowing casino operators who had establishments on the coast in Biloxi, Gulfport, and Bay St. Louis to relocate their casinos 800 feet (244 m) inland so they would be safe from any future storm surges. Along the Mississippi River, the gambling halls sit in slips cut into the riverbank. The Mississippi Band of Choctaw Indians operates the only land-based casinos, which are located in Neshoba County.

As of March 2006, there were twenty-nine commercial casinos licensed to operate in Mississippi. (See Table 4.5.) In total, they employed 26,388 people and offered nearly 1.4 million square feet (130,000 sq m) of gaming space, 34,485 slot machines, 934 table games, and 153 poker games. Table games offered included blackjack, craps, roulette, baccarat, and keno. The state allows round-the-clock gambling with no bet limits.

Gross casino revenue for the state was $2.9 billion in 2007, the first year when revenues exceeded pre–Hurricane Katrina revenues. (See Figure 4.3.) The newest property to open was the Hard Rock Casino and Hotel, which opened in July 2007.

According to the Mississippi Gaming Commission, in "Mississippi Tax Revenues from Gaming" (September 8, 2008, http://www.mstc.state.ms.us/taxareas/misc/gaming/stats/gamtax.pdf), the casino industry produces a substantial percentage of the state's annual budget. For FY 2008 (July 2007–June 2008), casinos paid $344.6 million in taxes. Approximately $194 million (56%) was paid into the state's general fund, $114.5 million (33%) went to local governments, and the remainder went to retire debt. In total, $4.3 billion had been collected in casino taxes in Mississippi between July 1992 and June 2008.

## LOUISIANA

Like Mississippi, Louisiana has a long gambling history. In 1823, eleven years after Louisiana became a state, its legislature legalized several forms of gambling and licensed six "temples of chance" in the city of New Orleans. Each was to pay $5,000 per year to fund the Charity Hospital and the College of Orleans. The casinos attracted many patrons, including professional gamblers, swindlers, and thieves. In 1835 the legislature repealed the licensing act and passed laws making gambling hall owners subject to prison terms or large fines.

However, casino-type gambling continued and even prospered throughout the southern part of the state. By 1840 New Orleans had an estimated five hundred gambling halls that employed more than four thousand people but paid no revenue to the city. Riverboat casinos frequented by hundreds of professional gamblers plied the Mississippi River between New Orleans and St. Louis. When the Civil War broke out, the riverboats were pressed into military service. In 1869 the legislature legalized casino gambling once again, requiring each casino to again pay the state a tax of $5,000.

In *Bad Bet on the Bayou: The Rise of Gambling in Louisiana and the Fall of Governor Edwin Edwards* (2001), Tyler Bridges credits Louisiana gamblers for popularizing craps and poker in the United States during the nineteenth century. Both were games of chance that had originated in Europe. The Louisiana state lottery began in 1868 but was outlawed in 1892, along with other forms of gambling, after massive fraud was uncovered. Casino gambling went underground and continued to flourish well into the 1960s, thanks to mobsters and political corruption. Two of the state's governors, Earl Kemp Long (1895–1960) and Edwin Edwards (1927–), were well-known gamblers. Edwards reportedly hosted high-stakes gambling games at the governor's mansion; he also went to prison in 2001 for extorting money from people who sought riverboat casino licenses.

During the early 1990s the state legalized gambling again, authorizing a lottery, casinos, and the operation of video poker machines in restaurants, bars, and truck stops. In 1991 the legislature authorized operation of up to fifteen riverboat casinos in the state; all but those along the Red River were required to make regularly scheduled cruises. The riverboat casinos were required to be at least 150 feet (46 m) long and decorated to look like nineteenth-century paddleboats. The first riverboat casino, the *Showboat Star*, began operating in 1993.

New Orleans received special permission from the legislature in 1993 to allow a limited number of land-based casinos. In January 1995 Harrah's began construction of one in the heart of the city. By November 1995 the casino had declared bankruptcy. Following years of negotiations with the state and the city, it reopened in

# TABLE 4.5

## Mississippi casino statistics, January–March 2008

| Coastal region | Number of employees | Hotel employees | Gaming sq. footage | Other sq. footage | Total sq. footage | # Slot games | # Table games | # Poker games | Activities in addition to gaming |
|---|---|---|---|---|---|---|---|---|---|
| Beau Rivage - Biloxi | 2,863 | 726 | 76,715 | 2,150,000 | 2,226,715 | 2,048 | 93 | 16 | 8 Restaurants, retail promenade, convention center, showroom, spa, and hotel. |
| Boomtown - Biloxi | 637 | N/A | 51,665 | 15,435 | 67,100 | 1,219 | 22 | 7 | Buffet, restaurant and fun center. |
| Grand Casino - Biloxi | 956 | 89 | 26,480 | 453,520 | 480,000 | 848 | 35 | — | Golf course, hotel, buffet, LB's, Starbucks, lobby bar, pool/spa, Asian café, Lucky Dog. |
| Hard Rock Casino - Biloxi | 1,033 | 126 | 53,800 | 126,200 | 180,000 | 1,334 | 50 | 6 | Restaurants, gift shops, boutique, entertainment showroom, lounges. |
| Hollywood Casino - BSL | 715 | 57 | 40,000 | 146,000 | 186,000 | 1,116 | 21 | 6 | Restaurants, golf course, RV park, convention center, and hotel. |
| Imperial Palace - Biloxi | 2,286 | 290 | 67,580 | 126,564 | 194,144 | 2,038 | 61 | 16 | Restaurants, hotel, showroom, banquet facilities, retail shop, pool/spa. |
| Island View Casino - Gulfport | 1,192 | 162 | 82,935 | 98,197 | 181,132 | 2,064 | 47 | — | Restaurants, buffet, room service, and gift shop. |
| Isle of Capri - Biloxi | 681 | 98 | 57,252 | 618,700 | 675,952 | 1,329 | 31 | 9 | Lava Bar, buffet, Tradewinds Market Place, and restaurant. |
| New Palace Casino - Bilox | 550 | 83 | 26,260 | 9,500 | 35,760 | 814 | 14 | — | Restaurants, hotel, swimming pool, and bars. |
| Silver Slipper - Lakeshore | 647 | — | 36,826 | 63,174 | 100,000 | 996 | 27 | 5 | Live entertainment, restaurants, Bon Marche, gen. store, and fishing. |
| Treasure Bay - Biloxi | 896 | 18 | 24,557 | 715 | 25,272 | 807 | 22 | — | |
| **Region totals** | **12,456** | **1,649** | **544,070** | **3,808,005** | **4,352,075** | **14,613** | **423** | **65** | |
| **North River region** | | | | | | | | | |
| Bally's - Robinsonville | 599 | 46 | 46,535 | 153,543 | 200,078 | 1,268 | 22 | — | Restaurants, entertainment. |
| Fitzgerald's - Robinsonville | 933 | 161 | 38,088 | 522,912 | 561,000 | 1,303 | 36 | — | Hotel and restaurants. |
| Gold Strike - Robinsonville | 1,608 | 249 | 50,486 | 1,347,597 | 1,398,083 | 1,397 | 58 | 16 | Restaurants, Millenium Theater, arcade, and hotel. |
| Grand Casino - Tunica | 2,088 | 506 | 136,000 | 204,000 | 340,000 | 1,602 | 66 | 14 | Restaurants, RV park, arcade, golf course, Kid's Quest, events center, and clay shooting. |
| Hollywood - Robinsonville | 794 | 71 | 54,000 | 337,613 | 391,613 | 1,289 | 31 | 6 | Live entertainment, restaurants, RV park, indoor pool, and golf. |
| Horseshoe - Robinsonville | 1,978 | 99 | 63,000 | 222,500 | 285,500 | 1,741 | 74 | 16 | Restaurants, blues museum, entertainment facility, and health club. |
| Isle of Capri - Lula | 561 | 47 | 63,500 | 65,000 | 128,500 | 1,304 | 15 | — | Live entertainment, restaurants, health club, and blues museum. |
| Resorts - Robinsonville | 651 | 65 | 35,000 | 151,924 | 186,924 | 1,116 | 18 | — | Hotel and dining. |
| Sam's Town - Tunica | 936 | 115 | 66,000 | 30,000 | 96,000 | 1,338 | 38 | 21 | Hotel, gift shop, and restaurants. |
| Sheraton - Robinsonville | 737 | 55 | 32,800 | 121,000 | 153,800 | 1,050 | 29 | — | Restaurants and hotel. |
| **Region totals** | **10,885** | **1,414** | **585,409** | **3,156,089** | **3,741,498** | **13,408** | **387** | **73** | |
| **South River region** | | | | | | | | | |
| Ameristar - Vicksburg | 817 | 68 | 44,530 | 211,151 | 255,681 | 1,381 | 36 | — | F&B, entertainment, gift shop, convenience store, RV park, and Subway. |
| Diamond Jacks Casino Vkb | 492 | 32 | 32,000 | 30,900 | 62,900 | 814 | 20 | — | Restaurants, retail and lodging. |
| Harlow's Casino Resort | 432 | 77 | 33,000 | 50,000 | 83,000 | 837 | 15 | 7 | Hotel, two restaurants, entertainment arena. |
| Horizon Casino - Vicksburg | 236 | 117 | 20,909 | 15,091 | 36,000 | 695 | 11 | 8 | Live entertainment, restaurants, and hotel. |
| Jubilee - Greenville | 286 | 27 | 17,634 | 6,413 | 24,047 | 626 | 11 | — | Live entertainment & restaurants. |
| Isle of Capri - Natchez | 222 | 9 | 28,500 | 36,937 | 65,437 | 633 | 12 | — | Live entertainment, hotel, & restaurants. |
| Lighthouse - Greenville | 224 | — | 22,000 | — | 22,000 | 648 | 9 | — | Restaurants & live entertainment. |
| Rainbow - Vicksburg | 338 | 18 | 25,000 | 5,000 | 30,000 | 830 | 10 | — | Restaurants, gift shop, and hotel. |
| **Region totals** | **3,047** | **348** | **223,573** | **355,492** | **579,065** | **6,464** | **124** | **15** | |
| **State totals** | **26,388** | **3,411** | **1,353,052** | **7,319,586** | **8,672,638** | **34,485** | **934** | **153** | |

SOURCE: "Mississippi Gaming Commission—Public Information: Quarterly Survey Information: January 1, 2008–March 31, 2008," in *Quarterly Reports—1st Quarter 2008: Property Data,* Mississippi Gaming Commission, 2008, http://www.mgc.state.ms.us/ (accessed July 18, 2008)

1999 but threatened bankruptcy again in 2001, blaming the state's $100 million minimum tax. The legislature cut the tax to $50 million for 2001 and $60 million for subsequent years to help keep the casino in business.

On April 1, 2001, the legislature ended the so-called phantom cruises of the riverboat casinos, ruling that it would actually be illegal for them to leave the docks. All riverboats were allowed to begin dockside gambling. However, their tax rate was increased from 18.5% to 21.5%.

According to the Louisiana Gaming Control Board, in *Report to the Louisiana State Legislature, 2007–2008* (2008, https://web01.dps.louisiana.gov/lgcb.nsf/8d7ba772b 324df7186256eb4006fc77e/9e7b358f689ff3218625742f006

FIGURE 4.3

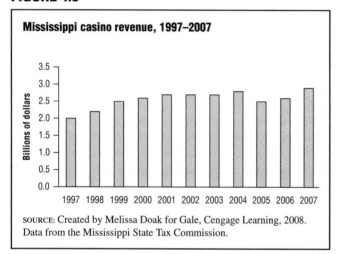

Mississippi casino revenue, 1997–2007

SOURCE: Created by Melissa Doak for Gale, Cengage Learning, 2008. Data from the Mississippi State Tax Commission.

44768/$FILE/2007-2008%20Annual%20Report.pdf), the state's riverboat casinos admitted nearly 25.5 million people during the fiscal year that ran from July 1, 2006, to June 30, 2007. (See Table 4.6.) The attendance figure, down from twenty-eight million in FY 2005, was likely lower because Hurricanes Katrina and Rita severely damaged two riverboat casinos on Lake Charles (*Harrah's Pride* and *Harrah's Star*) and one on Lake Pontchartrain (*Bally's*). The total adjusted gross revenue for the riverboats in FY 2007 was nearly $1.8 billion.

Harrah's, Louisiana's one land-based casino in New Orleans, reopened in February 2006 after having been closed by Hurricane Katrina nearly six months previously. The Louisiana Gaming Control Board notes that in FY 2005, 6.8 million people gambled at the casino; in FY 2006 only 2.7 million people gambled at the casino. Revenues were just $198 million in FY 2006, but were up to $399 million in FY 2007. The state's three racinos (racetracks at which slot machines are available), which were not damaged by the hurricanes, grossed nearly $366 million in slot machine revenue during FY 2007, up from $350 million the year before.

The Louisiana Gaming Control Board explains that the total gross casino revenue in Louisiana for FY 2007 was $2.4 billion, holding steady with FY 2005. Revenues in 2007 were double that from FY 1998, when casinos started operating in Louisiana. (See Figure 4.4.) The state took in approximately $443,710 in taxes from the casinos and racinos during FY 2007, down from $507.5 million a year earlier.

TABLE 4.6

Louisiana riverboat gaming activity, fiscal year 2006–07

| Licensee | D/B/A and location | Date of commencement | Admissions | Total AGR | Fee remittance |
|---|---|---|---|---|---|
| Catfish Queen Partnership in Commendam | Belle of B.R.-Baton Rouge | 09/30/94 | 1,202,882 | 103,250,792 | 22,198,920 |
| Belle of Orleans, L.L.C.[a] | Amelia Belle-Amelia | 07/07/95 | 109,866 | 7,501,022 | 1,612,720 |
| Grand Palais Riverboat, Inc. | Isle of Capri-Westlake | 07/12/96 | 2,036,489 | 138,900,790 | 29,863,670 |
| PNK (SCB) Partnership[b] | Sugar Cane Bay-Lake Charles | 12/08/93 | 0 | 0 | 0 |
| PNK (Baton Rouge) Partnership[c] | Riviére-Baton Rouge | 10/24/93 | 0 | 0 | 0 |
| Eldorado Casino Shreveport Joint Venture | Eldorado Casino Resort-Shreveport | 12/20/00 | 3,287,248 | 144,265,216 | 31,017,021 |
| Horseshoe Entertainment, L.L.P. | Horseshoe-Bossier City | 07/09/94 | 2,669,843 | 282,847,987 | 60,812,317 |
| Louisiana Casino Cruises, Inc. | Hollywood-Baton Rouge | 12/28/94 | 1,433,492 | 139,861,593 | 30,070,242 |
| Louisiana Riverboat Gaming Partnership | Diamond Jacks-Bossier City | 05/20/94 | 1,953,168 | 98,889,256 | 21,261,190 |
| PNK (Bossier City), Inc. | Boomtown-Bossier City | 10/04/96 | 1,732,563 | 97,455,537 | 20,952,940 |
| PNK (Harvey), L.P. | Boomtown Casino-Harvey | 08/06/94 | 2,370,420 | 178,032,344 | 38,276,954 |
| PNK (Lake Charles), L.L.C. | L'Auberge Du Lac-Lake Charles | 05/23/05 | 4,736,290 | 308,847,220 | 66,402,152 |
| Red River Entertainment of Shreveport Partnership in Commendam | Sam's Town-Shreveport | 05/20/04 | 2,014,043 | 128,995,042 | 27,733,934 |
| St. Charles Gaming Company, Inc. | Isle of Capri-Westlake | 07/29/95 | 774,204 | 32,397,904 | 6,965,549 |
| Treasure Chest Casino, L.L.C. | Treasure Chest-Kenner | 09/05/94 | 1,164,737 | 120,720,241 | 25,954,852 |
| **Totals** | | | **25,485,245** | **$1,781,964,944** | **$383,122,463** |

[a]Relocated to St. Mary Parish from its original berth site on Lake Pontchartrain in Orleans Parish.
[b]Formerly Harrah's Lake Charles, L.L.C. acquired by Pinnacle Entertainment, Inc.; currently in construction stage with anticipated opening in Fall, 2009.
[c]Formerly Harrah's Star Partnership acquired by Pinnacle Entertainment, Inc.; currently in development stage with anticipated opening in Summer, 2010.

SOURCE: "Louisiana State Police Riverboat Gaming Activity Summary, Fiscal Year 2006–2007," in *Report to the Louisiana State Legislature, 2007–2008,* Louisiana Gaming Control Board, 2008, https://web01.dps.louisiana.gov/lgcb.nsf/8d7ba772b324df7186256eb4006fc77e/9e7b358f689ff3218625742f006447 68/$FILE/2007–2008%20Annual%20Report.pdf (accessed July 21, 2008)

**FIGURE 4.4**

## Louisiana casino revenue, 1997–2007

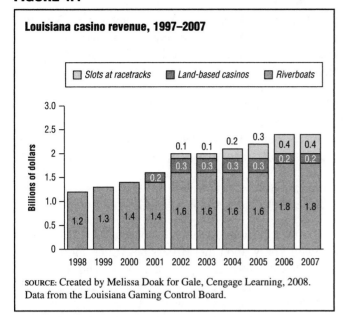

SOURCE: Created by Melissa Doak for Gale, Cengage Learning, 2008. Data from the Louisiana Gaming Control Board.

**TABLE 4.7**

## Indiana gaming taxes, selected statistics, fiscal year 2007

| Fiscal year 2007 | Win | Wagering tax | Admission tax | Total tax |
|---|---|---|---|---|
| Argosy | $ 480,655,921 | $153,171,412 | $ 11,711,655 | $164,883,067 |
| Belterra | $ 171,928,620 | $ 45,158,983 | $ 5,899,989 | $ 51,058,972 |
| Blue Chip | $ 267,254,458 | $ 85,188,799 | $ 9,853,938 | $ 95,042,737 |
| Caesars | $ 341,020,147 | $104,849,844 | $ 9,959,031 | $114,808,875 |
| Casino Aztar | $ 123,451,731 | $ 29,479,589 | $ 4,492,467 | $ 33,972,056 |
| French Lick | $ 110,920,428 | $ 13,493,576 | $ 4,020,488 | $ 17,514,064 |
| Grand Victoria | $ 149,924,858 | $ 37,446,789 | $ 5,393,811 | $ 42,840,600 |
| Horseshoe | $ 444,320,933 | $140,596,714 | $ 12,354,255 | $152,950,969 |
| Majestic Star I | $ 138,112,435 | $ 33,944,598 | $ 4,749,774 | $ 38,694,372 |
| Majestic Star II | $ 115,111,365 | $ 27,178,788 | $ 4,749,774 | $ 31,928,562 |
| Resorts | $ 321,254,597 | $ 97,354,462 | $ 10,431,951 | $107,786,413 |
| **Totals** | **$2,663,955,493** | **$767,863,554** | **$83,617,133** | **$851,480,687** |

SOURCE: "FY 2007 Tax Overview," in *2007 Annual Report to Governor Mitch Daniels*, Indiana Gaming Commission, 2007, http://www.in.gov/legislative/igareports/agency/reports/IGC04.pdf (accessed July 18, 2008)

The state has four major casino markets: Shreveport–Bossier City, New Orleans, Lake Charles, and Baton Rouge. The Shreveport market was the eleventh-largest casino market in the United States in 2007. (See Table 4.3.) A wide variety of games are allowed at Louisiana casinos, including blackjack, poker, craps, roulette, baccarat, keno, bingo, and slot machines. In "Louisiana State Police Video Gaming Division Revenue Report" (August 2008, https://web01.dps.louisiana.gov/lgcb.nsf/d8805955b3ee279586256e9b0049dc26/dbdfe1ea6d07e2f6862574ce0052a38e/$FILE/AUGUST%202008%20REVENUES.Video%20Poker.pdf), the Louisiana Gaming Control Board indicates that the state also had 14,377 slot machines in truck stops, bars, restaurants, and other noncasino locations as of August 2008. The machines generated $53.4 million in revenue that month.

## INDIANA

In 1993 the state of Indiana legalized gambling on up to eleven riverboats in specific areas of the state—in the northwestern corner along Lake Michigan; at the southern border along the Ohio River; and around Patoka Lake in the southern part of the state. The Patoka Lake site initially received a riverboat license, but it was later vetoed by the U.S. Army Corps of Engineers.

The first riverboat began operation in December 1995 in Evansville. By December 1996 six riverboats were operating. In 2002 new legislation permitted dockside operation of the riverboats in counties that would accept it. Permanent mooring allows patrons to access the casinos anytime during operating hours rather than just during cruise boarding times. The measure was intended to make Indiana casinos more competitive with those in Illinois.

The new law also changed the wagering tax structure from a 22.5% flat tax on adjusted gross receipts to a graduated tax rate of 15% to 35%. A portion of the increased tax revenue is distributed to counties that do not have casinos. The admissions tax, which remained at $3 per person, is split among the state, county, and city: each gets $1 per person.

The Indiana Gaming Commission notes in *2007 Annual Report to Governor Mitch Daniels* (2007, http://www.in.gov/legislative/igareports/agency/reports/IGC04.pdf) that in 2007 there were eleven riverboats operating in Indiana. Five of the casinos were along Lake Michigan in the far northern part of the state and six along the Ohio River in the far southern part. Together, the eleven riverboats had 18,600 slot machines and 681 table games. Games allowed included blackjack, craps, roulette, baccarat, and poker. Eight of the riverboats were docked at locations with associated land-based hotels, restaurants, and entertainment venues. The other three were docked at pavilions offering only dining and shopping. The casinos employed 15,672 people.

According to the Indiana Gaming Commission, the total riverboat admission in Indiana was 27.5 million people during FY 2007. The total win during FY 2007 was nearly $2.7 billion. (See Table 4.7.) In 2007 the combined northwestern Indiana/northeastern Illinois market was the third-largest casino market in the United States in terms of gross revenue, and the southeastern Indiana market was the twelfth largest. (See Table 4.3.) Admission and wagering taxes paid in FY 2007 totaled $851.5 million.

## ILLINOIS

Illinois legalized riverboat gambling in 1990, the second state to do so. The Illinois Gaming Board was authorized to grant up to ten casino licenses, each of which would allow up to two vessels to be operated at a single specific dock site. Each dock site could have no more than twelve hundred gaming positions, and all wagering was to be cashless. Originally, riverboats were required to cruise during gambling, but they were later allowed to operate dockside.

Nine Illinois riverboat casinos generated $2 billion in adjusted gross revenue in 2007, up from $1.9 billion in 2006. (See Figure 4.5.) According to the Illinois Gaming Board, in *2007 Annual Report* (2008, http://www.igb.state .il.us/annualreport/2007igb.pdf), the vast majority ($1.7 billion, or 88.2%) of the 2007 revenue was from electronic gambling devices; the remainder was from table games. Admissions totaled 16.5 million in 2007, up from 16.2 million the year before.

Illinois levies an admissions tax and a wagering tax. In 2005 the admissions tax stood at $2 per person at Casino Rock Island and $3 per person for all other casinos. Wagering taxes start at 15% for casinos with adjusted gross revenue of less than or equal to $25 million and increase as revenue increases. Casino taxes are shared by the state and communities in which the casinos are located. The Illinois Gaming Board states that the casino industry paid $115.7 million in local taxes in FY 2007 (see Table 4.8) and $718.2 million in state taxes. The state received 86% of admissions and wagering taxes, and the cities and counties received 14%.

**FIGURE 4.5**

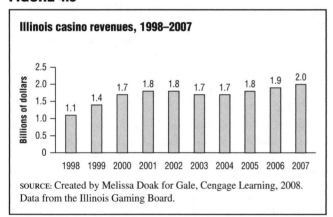

**Illinois casino revenues, 1998–2007**

SOURCE: Created by Melissa Doak for Gale, Cengage Learning, 2008. Data from the Illinois Gaming Board.

## MISSOURI

The legalization of riverboat gambling in Missouri started in 1992 with a referendum approved by 64% of the voters. That was followed by a court case, a constitutional amendment (that was defeated by voters), and wrangling over the definition of "games of skill." Eventually, in 1994 the general assembly passed a bill that defined games of skill and authorized riverboats to be located in artificial basins. The first two licenses for riverboat casinos were issued later that year. However, because the casinos could not offer games of chance, such as slot machines, competition from riverboats in Illinois kept customers away, and the casinos were not profitable.

After a petition drive, voters passed an initiative that allowed "only upon the Mississippi River and the Missouri River, lotteries, gift enterprises, and games of chance to be conducted on excursion gambling boats and floating facilities." The result was significant: revenues from casino riverboats during the first quarter of FY 1996 were more than twice what they had been during the first quarter of the previous year. Initially, the casinos were only allowed to hold two-hour gambling excursions. In 2000 the law was changed to allow continuous boarding. However, the original $500 loss limit per excursion that had been approved in 1992 still applies. Patrons are allowed to purchase only $500 worth of chips or tokens in any two-hour period, preventing them from losing more than that amount within the "excursion" period.

The Missouri Gaming Commission notes that in 2007 eleven riverboat casinos operated in six markets: St. Louis, Kansas City, Caruthersville, St. Joseph, LaGrange, and Boonville. All the riverboats remain dockside. Games allowed include blackjack, poker, and other card games, slot machines, craps, roulette, and several wheel games. Gaming revenue topped $1 billion for the first time during FY 2001 and reached $1.6 billion in FY 2007 (July 1, 2006, through June 30, 2007). (See Figure 4.6.)

**TABLE 4.8**

**Local distribution of Illinois gaming taxes, 2003–07**

|  | 2003 | 2004 | 2005 | 2006 | 2007 | % change '07 to '06 |
|---|---|---|---|---|---|---|
| Alton | $6,915,011 | $6,774,624 | $7,097,896 | $7,554,349 | $7,724,803 | 2.26% |
| East Peoria | 8,707,604 | 8,253,947 | 8,117,498 | 7,901,581 | 8,011,938 | 1.40% |
| Rock Island | 2,755,559 | 2,670,644 | 2,714,536 | 2,649,411 | 2,411,087 | −9.00% |
| Joliet | 29,494,538 | 28,775,387 | 31,721,572 | 34,864,387 | 36,168,333 | 3.74% |
| Jo Daviess | 0 | 0 | 0 | 0 | 0 | N/A |
| Metropolis | 8,163,312 | 8,469,446 | 8,413,434 | 9,330,506 | 9,921,866 | 6.34% |
| Aurora | 14,253,797 | 12,923,396 | 13,606,013 | 15,105,581 | 15,449,378 | 2.28% |
| East St. Louis | 9,926,617 | 10,483,145 | 10,545,446 | 10,820,363 | 11,738,204 | 8.48% |
| Elgin | 21,844,186 | 22,880,350 | 23,066,119 | 24,132,235 | 24,301,668 | 0.70% |
| **Total** | **$102,060,624** | **$101,230,939** | **$105,282,514** | **$112,358,413** | **$115,727,277** | **3.00%** |

SOURCE: "Distribution of Gaming Taxes: Distributions to Local Governments," in *2007 Annual Report*, Illinois Gaming Board, 2008, http://www.igb.state.il.us/annualreport/2007igb.pdf (accessed July 18, 2008)

FIGURE 4.6

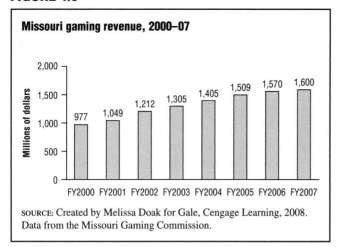

**Missouri gaming revenue, 2000–07**

SOURCE: Created by Melissa Doak for Gale, Cengage Learning, 2008. Data from the Missouri Gaming Commission.

FIGURE 4.7

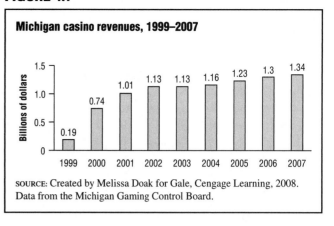

**Michigan casino revenues, 1999–2007**

SOURCE: Created by Melissa Doak for Gale, Cengage Learning, 2008. Data from the Michigan Gaming Control Board.

## MICHIGAN

Pari-mutuel horse racing (betting in which those who bet on the top competitors share the total amount bet and the house gets a percentage) was legalized in Michigan in 1933. During the 1970s the state lottery was legalized and a concerted effort began to allow casino gambling in Detroit. The casino efforts were unsuccessful until 1994, when the Windsor Casino opened just across the river in Windsor, Ontario. By that time, more than a dozen tribal casinos were operating around the state of Michigan, and Detroit was in an economic downturn. Attitudes toward casino gambling changed, and in November 1996 Michigan voters narrowly approved ballot Proposal E, which authorized the operation of up to three casinos in any city that had a population of 800,000 people or more and was located within 100 miles (161 km) of any other state or country in which gaming was permitted. Casino gaming also had to be approved by a majority of voters in the city. Proposal E was subsequently modified and signed into law in 1997. Out of eleven casino proposals submitted, three were accepted: Atwater/Circus Circus Casino (later called MotorCity Casino), owned by Detroit Entertainment; Greektown Casino, owned by the Sault Ste. Marie Tribe of Chippewa Indians; and the MGM Grand, owned by MGM Grand Detroit Casino. The casinos were granted permission to open at temporary locations, with permanent facilities planned for a proposed waterfront casino district.

The first casino, MGM Grand, opened in July 1999 in a former Internal Revenue Service building. Later that year the MotorCity Casino started operations in a former bread factory. The Greektown Casino opened in November 2000 in the heart of the city. It was the first tribally owned casino to open off a reservation. Detroit became the largest city in the country to allow casino gambling.

The plan for a downtown casino district was eventually abandoned because of rising real estate prices and local opposition, and the number of hotel rooms initially proposed was cut back after marketing studies showed that many casino customers were regional and did not need overnight lodging. The permanent casinos were also delayed by several lawsuits. However, work began on the permanent MGM Grand Detroit Casino and MotorCity Casino in the summer of 2006. The MGM Grand Detroit opened in October 2007. The MotorCity Casino opened in stages throughout 2007, with a grand opening in June. Greektown Casino filed for bankruptcy protection in May 2008. However, it opened an expanded casino in August 2008 and was expected to open its hotel in 2009.

In *Annual Report to the Governor: Calendar Year 2007* (April 15, 2008, http://www.michigan.gov/docu ments/mgcb/annrerp07_231975_7.pdf), the Michigan Gaming and Control Board states that the Detroit casinos together grossed more than $1.3 billion in 2007. (See Figure 4.7.) Each casino paid 8.1% of adjusted gross receipts as a state wagering tax to be deposited in Michigan's School Aid Fund. MotorCity and Greektown paid an additional 4%; 3.5% went into the state's general fund and 0.5% went to the Michigan Agriculture Equine Industry Development Fund. MGM was no longer required to pay the additional 4% because it had opened in its permanent location. The combined 8.1% State Wagering Taxes deposited in the School Aid Fund totaled $108.1 million in 2007. An additional $41.5 million was deposited in the General Fund and $5.9 million was deposited in the Agricultural Equine Industry Development Fund.

Unlike casinos in some other states, Detroit's casinos are not permitted under the Michigan Liquor Control Code to provide free alcoholic drinks. Games offered at Detroit casinos include baccarat, blackjack, casino war, craps, keno, poker, roulette, slot machines, and video poker.

## IOWA

Gambling was outlawed in the state of Iowa from the time of its statehood in 1846 until 1972, when a provision in the state constitution that prohibited lotteries was repealed. In 1973 the general assembly authorized bingo

FIGURE 4.8

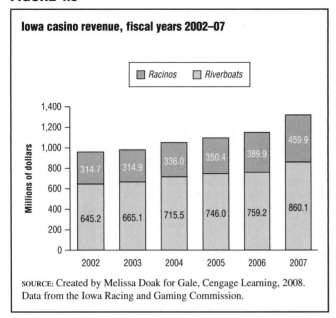

**Iowa casino revenue, fiscal years 2002–07**

SOURCE: Created by Melissa Doak for Gale, Cengage Learning, 2008. Data from the Iowa Racing and Gaming Commission.

and raffles by specific parties. A decade later pari-mutuel wagering at dog and horse tracks was legalized, followed by a state lottery in 1985. In 1989 gambling aboard excursion boats was authorized for counties in which voters approved gambling referenda. Between 1989 and 1995 referenda authorizing riverboat gambling were approved in more than a dozen counties. The Iowa Racing and Gaming Commission granted licenses for riverboat gambling in ten counties: Clarke, Clayton, Clinton, Des Moines, Dubuque, Lee, Polk, Pottawattamie, Scott, and Woodbury. By law, the residents of these counties vote every eight years on a referendum to allow riverboat gambling to continue. In 1994 pari-mutuel racetracks gained approval to operate slot machines.

In FY 2007 ten riverboat casinos and three racetrack casinos operated in Iowa. Games included bingo, blackjack, craps, keno, minibaccarat, poker, roulette, slots, and video poker. In *2007 Annual Report* (March 1, 2008, http://www.iowa.gov/irgc/Annual%20Report%202007 .pdf), the Iowa Racing and Gaming Commission indicates that in 2007 admissions to riverboats totaled 16.4 million and to racinos totaled 6.9 million. The riverboats are required by law to meet space requirements for non-gamblers and to provide shopping and tourism options. Slots are allowed at racetracks only if a specific number of live races are held during each racing season.

During FY 2007 Iowa casino revenues totaled $860.1 million, and racino revenues totaled $459.9 million. (See Figure 4.8.) In other words, nearly two-thirds (65%) of gambling revenue in Iowa was collected on riverboat casinos. The Iowa Racing and Gaming Commission notes in *Iowa Racing and Gaming Commission: Gaming Revenue by FY* (2007, http://www.state.ia.us/irgc/FYTD07 .pdf) that $278.2 million in gaming taxes were collected by cities, counties, and the state in 2007. Iowa's gaming

tax rate ranges from 5% to 24%, depending on revenue and the type of venue. In 2007 racinos paid $2.3 million in city taxes, $2.3 million in county taxes, and $98.4 million in state taxes, as well as contributions to the gamblers' treatment and endowment funds and regulatory and daily licensing fees. Riverboat casinos paid $4.3 million in city taxes, $4.3 million in county taxes, and $166.6 million in state taxes, as well as contributions to the gamblers' treatment and endowment funds and regulatory and daily licensing fees.

## COLORADO

During the 1800s gambling halls and saloons with card games were prevalent throughout the mining towns of Colorado. However, gambling was outlawed in the state around the turn of the twentieth century.

In November 1990 Colorado voters approved a constitutional amendment permitting limited-stakes gaming in the towns of Black Hawk and Central City, near Denver, and Cripple Creek, near Colorado Springs. The first Colorado casinos opened in October 1991 and had gross revenues of nearly $8.4 million during their first month of operation.

According to the Colorado Gaming Commission, in *2007 Annual Report* (2008, http://www.revenue.state .co.us/Gaming/Documents/2007annual.pdf), only blackjack, poker, and slot machines are permitted in Colorado's casinos. The maximum single bet is $5. Any increase in betting limits, additional types of games, or new gambling locations require a statewide vote authorizing a change in the constitutional amendment. Since 1992 there have been seven votes on whether to expand casino gaming to additional locations; each time expansion has been defeated by at least a two-to-one margin.

The Colorado Gaming Commission states that forty-one casinos operated in the state in December 2007. They had gross revenues of $816 million during FY 2007. (See Figure 4.9.) Annual revenue grew steadily from 1997

**FIGURE 4.9**

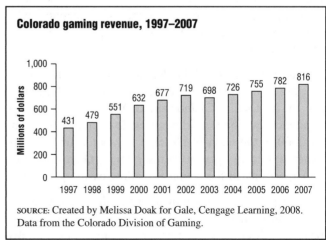

**Colorado gaming revenue, 1997–2007**

SOURCE: Created by Melissa Doak for Gale, Cengage Learning, 2008. Data from the Colorado Division of Gaming.

through 2007, leveling off for a brief period between 2002 and 2004. In *Gaming in Colorado: Fact Book and 2007 Abstract* (2008, http://www.revenue.state.co.us/Gaming/Documents/Fact07.pdf), the Colorado Gaming Commission notes that the Black Hawk casinos have historically been the most successful in the state, accounting for 70% to 75% of casino gaming revenue each year, followed by the Cripple Creek market (20% to 25% of the total) and Central City (5% to 10%). In 2007 Black Hawk casinos took in 71% of casino revenues, and Cripple Creek took in 19%.

From 2002 through 2007 Colorado's casinos had an adjusted gross revenue of $4.5 billion and paid $618.2 million in gaming taxes. The tax money was used to fund historical restoration projects and to offset the costs of casino gaming to state and local governments (including regulatory costs associated with the casino industry).

The gaming tax rate, which is set by the gaming commission annually, is based on each casino's adjusted gross proceeds (the amount of money wagered minus the amount paid out in prizes). In 2007 the tax ranged from 0.25% for casinos with less than $2 million in adjusted gross proceeds to 20% for establishments with adjusted gross proceeds of more than $15 million.

In addition, the casinos pay annual device fees: $75 per slot machine and game table to the state and $750 to $1,265 to local jurisdictions. In *Gaming Update* (October 2008, http://www.revenue.state.co.us/Gaming/Documents/GU1008.pdf), the Colorado Gaming Commission reports that in August 2008 there were 17,029 slot machines and 229 table games operating in the state.

## SOUTH DAKOTA

Commercial casino gambling in South Dakota is restricted to the town of Deadwood in Lawrence County. A rustic mountain town about 60 miles (97 km) from Mount Rushmore, Deadwood was designated a National Historic Landmark and is listed on both the National and South Dakota Registers of Historic Places. It had 139 casinos in June 2007, more than 80 of them historic. The games allowed are blackjack, poker, and slot machines.

The rocky history of gambling in Deadwood is described by Katherine Jensen and Audie Blevins in *The Last Gamble: Betting on the Future in Four Rocky Mountain Mining Towns* (1998). The gold rush of 1876 brought large numbers of people into the town, and it soon became packed with saloons and gambling halls. The town became associated with notorious characters such as Wild Bill Hickok (1837–1876), Poker Alice (1851–1930), and Calamity Jane (1852–1903).

Even though gambling was outlawed in the Dakota Territory in 1881, it continued quite openly in Deadwood with the apparent complicity of the local sheriff. Accord-

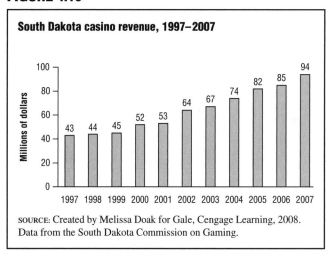

**FIGURE 4.10**

**South Dakota casino revenue, 1997–2007**

SOURCE: Created by Melissa Doak for Gale, Cengage Learning, 2008. Data from the South Dakota Commission on Gaming.

ing to Jensen and Blevins, gambling opponents complained in 1907 that the town's gambling halls "operated as openly as grocery stores, running twenty-four hours a day." On a busy Saturday night in 1947, South Dakota's attorney general sent sixteen raiders into the bars of Deadwood to show the town that the state meant business. The blatant days of gambling were over in Deadwood, although locals say the establishments continued to operate quietly for the next four decades.

In 1984 a group of Deadwood businessmen and community leaders began working to bring legalized gambling back to Deadwood, primarily to raise money to preserve the town's historic buildings. The group developed the slogan "Deadwood You Bet" and had it printed on hundreds of buttons. Despite widespread local support, the idea failed at the ballot box in 1984 and was voted down by the legislature in 1988. The measure made it onto the ballot in November 1988 following a massive petition effort. In 1989 South Dakota voters approved limited-stakes casino gambling for Deadwood. Originally, the casinos could only offer a $5 maximum bet. This limit was raised to $100 in 2000.

In *Annual Report, Fiscal Year 2007* (2007, http://www.state.sd.us/drr2/reg/gaming/annual_report/fy07_annual_report.pdf), the South Dakota Commission on Gaming indicates that Deadwood's casinos had a total combined gross revenue of $94.4 million in FY 2007, an 11% increase from the previous fiscal year. (See Figure 4.10.) From FY 1990 through June 2007 gross revenue totaled $966 million. The casinos pay an 8% gaming tax on their adjusted gross revenue and an annual fee of $2,000 per card game or slot machine. In FY 2007, $7.4 million in taxes on gross revenues were collected, raising the total taxes on gross revenues collected between FY 1990 and FY 2007 to $74.7 million. Besides these taxes, device taxes, city taxes, and application, license, and device testing fees were also collected.

# CHAPTER 5
# NATIVE AMERICAN TRIBAL CASINOS

Casinos operated by Native American tribes made $26 billion in 2007. (See Figure 5.1.) The American Gaming Association (AGA) reports in *2008 State of the States: The AGA Survey of Casino Entertainment* (2008, http://www.americangaming.org/assets/files/aga_2008_sos.pdf) that commercial casinos made $34.1 billion during the same year. Therefore, in 2007 Native American casinos took in 43% of total casino revenues, the same percentage as in 2005.

According to the U.S. Census Bureau (April 30, 2008, http://www.census.gov/popest/national/asrh/NC-EST2007-asrh.html), 4.5 million people in the United States (approximately 1.5% of the total population) identified themselves as Native American or Alaskan Native in 2007. In "Indian Gaming Facts" (2008, http://www.indiangaming.org/library/indian-gaming-facts/index.shtml), the National Indian Gaming Association (NIGA) indicates that in 2007 there were 562 federally recognized tribes in the United States. Furthermore, 225 tribes ran 423 gaming enterprises in 2007. The NIGA reports in *An Analysis of the Economic Impact of Indian Gaming in 2005* (2005, http://www.indiangaming.org/NIGA_econ_impact_2005.pdf) that more than twenty-two million Americans visited tribal gaming facilities in 2005, generating $22.6 billion in gross revenue from gaming and an additional $2.7 billion in gross revenue from hospitality and entertainment services related to gaming. In 2006 tribal gaming facilities generated $25.7 billion in revenues. (See Figure 5.2.)

## HISTORY

The growth of tribal casinos can be traced to the late 1970s, when Native American tribes began operating bingo halls to raise funds for tribal purposes. Tribes in Florida and Wisconsin tried opening high-stakes bingo games on their reservations. Bingo games were legal in those states but subject to restrictions on the size of the

jackpot and how often games could be held. The Oneida Tribe of Wisconsin and the Seminole Tribe of Florida took their respective states to court, arguing that the tribes were sovereign nations and not subject to state limitations on gambling.

In 1981 the U.S. Fifth Circuit Court of Appeals ruled in *Seminole Tribe of Florida v. Butterworth* (658 F.2d 310) that the tribe could operate a high-stakes bingo parlor because the state of Florida did not have regulatory power over the tribe, a sovereign governing entity. A similar ruling was issued in *Oneida Tribe of Indians v. State of Wisconsin* (518 F.Supp. 712 [1981]). Both cases concluded that the states' gambling laws were regulatory, or civil, in nature rather than criminal, because the states already allowed bingo games to take place.

Other tribes also sued, and the issue eventually reached the U.S. Supreme Court. In *California v. Cabazon Band of Mission Indians* (480 U.S. 202 [1987]), the Court ruled that California could not prohibit a tribe from conducting activities (in this case, high-stakes bingo and poker games) that were legal elsewhere in the state. In 1989 the Bay Mills Indian Community opened the King's Club in Brimley, Michigan, the first Native American gambling hall to offer slot machines and blackjack.

## GAMBLING CLASSES

In 1988 Congress passed the Indian Gaming Regulatory Act, in response to the court decisions. The act allows federally recognized tribes to open gambling establishments on their reservations if the state in which they are located already permits legalized gambling. It set up a regulatory system and three classes of gambling activities:

- Class I—social gaming for minimal prizes and traditional gaming (e.g., in tribal ceremonies or celebrations)

- Class II—bingo and bingolike games, lotto, pull tabs (paper tickets that have tabs concealing symbols or

FIGURE 5.1

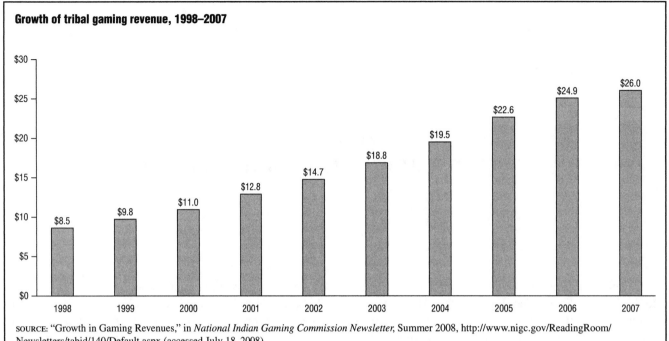

**Growth of tribal gaming revenue, 1998–2007**

SOURCE: "Growth in Gaming Revenues," in *National Indian Gaming Commission Newsletter*, Summer 2008, http://www.nigc.gov/ReadingRoom/ Newsletters/tabid/140/Default.aspx (accessed July 18, 2008)

**FIGURE 5.2**

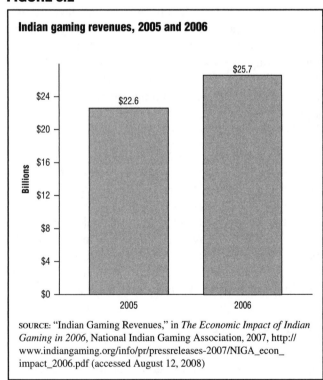

**Indian gaming revenues, 2005 and 2006**

SOURCE: "Indian Gaming Revenues," in *The Economic Impact of Indian Gaming in 2006*, National Indian Gaming Association, 2007, http:// www.indiangaming.org/info/pr/pressreleases-2007/NIGA_econ_ impact_2006.pdf (accessed August 12, 2008)

numbers), tip jars (lotterylike games played with preprinted tickets), punch boards (thick cardboard with symbols or numbers concealed behind foil), and nonbanking card games (such as the type of poker that is played against other players instead of the house)

• Class III—banking card games (card games in which the player bets against the house), casino games, slot machines, pari-mutuel betting (in which those who bet on the top competitors share the total amount bet and the house gets a percentage) on horse and dog racing and jai alai, electronic facsimiles of any game of chance, and any other forms of gaming not included in Class I or II

Class I gaming is regulated exclusively by the tribes and requires no financial reporting to other authorities. Class II and III games are allowed only if such games are already permitted in the state where the tribe is located. According to the U.S. Government Accountability Office (GAO), the investigatory branch of Congress, court rulings have maintained that tribes can operate casinos where state-run lotteries exist and charitable casino nights are permitted.

Class II and III operations require that the tribe adopt a gaming ordinance that is approved by the National Indian Gaming Commission (NIGC), a government body set up to regulate gaming on tribal lands. In addition, Class III gaming requires that the tribe and state have an agreement, called a tribal-state compact (or treaty), that is approved by the U.S. secretary of the interior. A compact is supposed to balance the interests of the state and the tribe in regard to standards for operation and maintenance, the applicability of state and tribal laws and regulations, and the amount needed by the state to defray its regulatory costs. Tribes may have compacts with more than one state and may have different compacts for different types of gambling operations.

## REGULATION

Native American casinos are regulated at three levels of government: federal, state, and tribal. Federal regulation is performed by the NIGC, which oversees the licensing of gaming employees and management and reviews tribal gaming ordinances. The NIGC also has enforcement powers. For example, in June 2004 the commission temporarily closed a casino operated by the Coyote Valley Band of Pomo Indians in Redwood Valley, California, for allegedly operating Class III gambling devices without a compact with the state. However, most violations do not result in closure, but in notification followed by fines. In 2006, for instance, the Santa Rosa Rancheria Tachi-Yokut Tribe was found in violation for failing to conduct proper background checks on casino employees. The tribe had ninety days to check the background of the employees in question or face fines of up to $25,000 per day. Most violations concern tribes' failure to submit annual audits by required deadlines.

The federal government also has criminal jurisdiction over cases involving embezzlement, cheating, and fraud at tribal gaming operations, because such crimes are federal offenses.

State regulation is spelled out in the tribal-state compacts. They cover matters such as the number of slot machines that may be operated; limits on types and quantities of card games that can be offered; minimum gambling ages in the casinos; authorization for casino workers to unionize; public health and safety issues; compulsive gambling issues; the effects of tribal gaming on other state enterprises; and how much revenue should be paid to the state and how often.

The tribes themselves are the primary regulators of tribal gaming. The NIGA, a trade organization for Native American casinos, reports in *An Analysis of the Economic Impact of Indian Gaming in 2005* that $245 million was spent by the tribes on regulation of their industry in 2005.

## FEDERAL RECOGNITION

Native American casinos must be a tribal endeavor, not an individual endeavor—that is, a random group of Native Americans cannot start a tribal casino. Only a tribe's status as a sovereign entity, granted by the federal government, allows it to conduct gaming.

The list of federally recognized tribes is maintained by the Bureau of Indian Affairs (BIA), an agency of the U.S. Department of the Interior. The most current list, which includes 561 tribes, was published in "Indian Entities Recognized and Eligible to Receive Services from the United States Bureau of Indian Affairs" (*Federal Register*, vol. 72, no. 55, March 22, 2007).

Throughout U.S. history, tribes have received federal recognition through treaties with the U.S. government, via congressional actions, or through BIA decisions. Most tribes were officially recognized during the eighteenth and nineteenth centuries. In the twenty-first century recognition can be achieved either through an act of Congress or through a series of actions, known as the "federal acknowledgment process," that can take many years. Under the Code of Federal Regulations, Title 25, Part 83 (April 1, 2001, http://edocket.access.gpo.gov/cfr_2001/aprqtr/25cfr83.7.htm), a group of Native Americans must meet seven criteria to be federally recognized as a tribe:

- They must have been identified as an Native American entity on a substantially continuous basis since 1900.

- A predominant portion of the group must comprise a distinct community and have existed as a community from historical times to the present.

- They must have maintained political influence or authority over their members as an autonomous entity from historical times until the present.

- They must submit a copy of the group's current governing documents, including membership criteria.

- The group's membership must consist of individuals who descended from a historical Native American tribe or from historical Native American tribes that combined and functioned as a single autonomous political entity.

- The membership of the group must be composed primarily of people who are not members of an existing acknowledged Native American tribe.

- The tribe must not be the subject of congressional legislation that has terminated or forbidden a federal relationship.

Federal recognition is important to Native American tribes if they are to be eligible for billions of dollars in federal assistance. According to the BIA (July 25, 2008, http://www.doi.gov/bia/), in 2008 the federal government held about 66 million acres (27 million ha) of land in trust for federally recognized Native Amerian tribes and their members. If a tribe does not have a land base, the federal government can take land in trust for the tribe once it receives recognition. That land is no longer subject to local jurisdiction, including property taxes and zoning ordinances.

Most tribes require that a person have a particular degree of Native American heritage (usually 25%) to be an enrolled member. Some tribes require proof of lineage. The BIA states that in 2008 federally recognized tribes had approximately 1.7 million members.

One of the most contentious issues related to tribal casinos is the authenticity of the tribes themselves. Critics charge that some Native American groups want federal recognition only as a means to enter the lucrative gambling business. The GAO examines this issue in *Indian Issues: Improvements Needed in Tribal Recognition Process* (November 2001, http://www.gao.gov/new.items/d0249.pdf). There were 193 tribes with gambling facilities in 2001. According to the GAO, 170 (88%) of the tribes could trace their federal recognition at least back to the time of the Indian Reorganization Act of 1934 or similar legislation from the 1930s. About 59% of those tribes were engaged in gambling operations in 2001. By contrast, 45% of the tribes recognized since 1960 were engaged in gambling operations.

The GAO indicates that the procedures established by the BIA in 1978 to ensure that the recognition of tribes be uniform and objective had become too long and inconsistent. Backlogs became constant because the number of petitions for recognition began to climb during the 1990s. However, the GAO explains in *Indian Issues: Timeliness of the Tribal Recognition Process Has Improved, but It Will Take Years to Clear the Existing Backlog of Petitions* (February 10, 2005, http://www.gao.gov/new.items/d05347t.pdf) that by 2005 the backlog of cases had been steadily reduced and was expected to be completed by 2008. Regardless, other sources, such as the press release "Sen. Webb, Reps. Moran & Scott, Virginia Indian Tribes Call for Federal Recognition, Legislative Action, Reform of BIA System" (November 8, 2007, http://moran.house.gov/list/press/va08_moran/TribesPress Webb.shtml) and *Process of Federal Recognition of Indian Tribes* (September 19, 2007, http://frwebgate.access.gpo.gov/cgi-bin/getdoc.cgi?dbname=110_senate_hearings&docid=f:38917.pdf), report waits of as long as fifteen, twenty, or even thirty years.

## REVENUES

Because tribes are sovereign governments, they are not required by law to make public statements of their revenues, so financial information on individual tribal casinos is not publicly released. Each year the NIGC announces total gaming revenue from the previous year for all tribal gaming facilities combined. It also breaks down the revenue by U.S. region and revenue class. The NIGC indicates in the press release "NIGC Announces 2007 Indian Gaming Revenues" (June 18, 2008, http://www.nigc.gov/ReadingRoom/PressReleases/PressReleasesMain/PR93062008/tabid/841/Default.aspx) that in fiscal year 2007 tribal casinos made $26 billion, up from $24.9 billion in fiscal year 2006. This revenue is broken down by region in Table 5.1.

Tribal casinos in Region II (California and northern Nevada) were the most profitable in 2007, earning $7.8 billion. (See Table 5.1.) Because there are no tribal casinos in northern Nevada, all of this revenue was actually from California tribal casinos. California tribes with gaming facilities earned 30% of all tribal casino revenue nationwide. Their market share was $1 billion more than that reported for commercial casinos on the Las Vegas Strip during 2007, according to the Nevada State Gaming Control Board, in *State of Nevada Gaming Revenue Report: Year Ended December 31, 2007* (2008, http://gaming.nv.gov/documents/pdf/1g_07dec.pdf).

The second-most profitable region for tribes with gaming operations during 2007 was Region VI, which encompasses the states of Alabama, Connecticut, Florida, Louisiana, Mississippi, New York, and North Carolina. The region took in $6.4 billion in casino revenues, or 25% of total tribal revenue. (See Table 5.1.) Casinos

**TABLE 5.1**

**Tribal gaming revenues by region, fiscal years 2007 and 2006**

[$ in thousands]

| | Fiscal year 2007 | | Fiscal year 2006 | | Increase (decrease) | | |
|---|---|---|---|---|---|---|---|
| | Number of operations | Gaming revenues | Number of operations | Gaming revenues | Number of operations | Gaming revenues | Revenue percentage |
| Region I | 43 | 2,208,190 | 46 | 2,080,369 | (3) | 127,821 | 6.1% |
| Region II | 58 | 7,796,488 | 56 | 7,674,794 | 2 | 121,693 | 1.6% |
| Region III | 44 | 2,840,585 | 45 | 2,718,914 | (1) | 121,672 | 4.5% |
| Region IV | 109 | 4,217,960 | 122 | 4,069,940 | (13) | 148,021 | 3.6% |
| Region V | 100 | 2,553,034 | 98 | 2,125,906 | 2 | 427,127 | 20.1% |
| Region VI | 28 | 6,399,841 | 27 | 6,219,100 | 1 | 180,742 | 2.9% |
| **Totals** | 382 | 26,016,098 | 394 | 24,889,022 | (12) | 1,127,075 | 4.53% |

Region I   Alaska, Idaho, Oregon, and Washington.
Region II   California, and Northern Nevada.
Region III   Arizona, Colorado, New Mexico, and Southern Nevada.
Region IV   Iowa, Michigan, Minnesota, Montana, North Dakota, Nebraska, South Dakota, Wisconsin and Wyoming.
Region V   Kansas, Oklahoma, and Texas.
Region VI   Alabama, Connecticut, Florida, Louisiana, Mississippi, North Carolina, and New York.

SOURCE: "National Indian Gaming Commission Tribal Gaming Revenues (in Thousands) by Region, Fiscal Year 2007 and 2006," in *NIGC Announces 2007 Indian Gaming Revenues*, National Indian Gaming Commission, June 18, 2008, http://www.nigc.gov/ReadingRoom/PressReleases/PressReleasesMain/PR93062008/tabid/841/Default.aspx (accessed July 18, 2008)

FIGURE 5.3

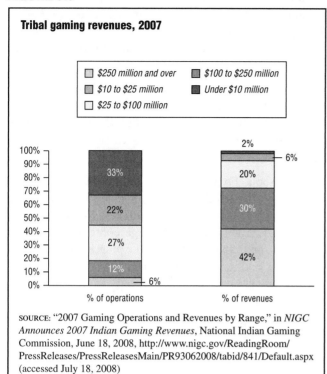

**Tribal gaming revenues, 2007**

Legend:
- $250 million and over
- $10 to $25 million
- $25 to $100 million
- $100 to $250 million
- Under $10 million

SOURCE: "2007 Gaming Operations and Revenues by Range," in *NIGC Announces 2007 Indian Gaming Revenues*, National Indian Gaming Commission, June 18, 2008, http://www.nigc.gov/ReadingRoom/PressReleases/PressReleasesMain/PR93062008/tabid/841/Default.aspx (accessed July 18, 2008)

operating in Connecticut, especially Foxwoods, are thought to be the largest source of that region's revenue.

The GAO reports in *Indian Issues: Improvements Needed in Tribal Recognition Process* that in 1988, the year the Indian Gaming Regulatory Act was passed, tribal gambling revenues were $171 million. That amount grew to $9.8 billion by 1999. Revenues reported by the NIGC for 1998 through 2007 are shown in Figure 5.1. Over this period, tribal casino revenues grew from $8.5 billion to $26 billion, an increase of more than 206%. By contrast, the AGA indicates in *2008 State of the States* that revenues at commercial casinos grew from $19.7 billion in 1998 to $34.1 billion in 2007, an increase of 73%.

Tribal gaming revenues reported by the NIGC for 2007 are broken down by revenue class in Figure 5.3. About 33% of tribal gambling operations reported revenues of less than $10 million each. In "NIGC Announces 2007 Indian Gaming Revenues," the NIGC states that sixty-nine operations (18% of the total number) earned $100 million or more. Those sixty-nine facilities took in 72% of all tribal casino revenue.

The Indian Gaming Regulatory Act requires that net revenues from tribal gaming be used:

- To fund tribal government operations or programs
- To provide for the general welfare of the tribe and its members
- To promote tribal economic development
- To donate to charitable organizations
- To help fund operations of local government agencies

Tribes with gaming operations may distribute gaming revenues to individual tribe members through per capita payments but are not required to do so. Such payments must be approved by the U.S. secretary of the interior as part of the tribe's Revenue Allocation Plan and are subject to federal income tax.

## TRIBAL-COMMERCIAL CASINO VENTURES

Building casinos can be expensive. Tribes that have built them have had to borrow large sums of money and/or obtain investors to do so. In general, the law requires that tribes partner with companies for no more than five years at a time and limits the companies' take to 30% of the total revenue. Under some circumstances, the partnership can last seven years and the companies' portion can be as much as 40% of total revenue. These five- to seven-year contracts can also be renewed if both parties and the state government agree to the renewal.

The NIGC (2008, http://www.nigc.gov/ReadingRoom/ManagementContracts/ApprovedManagementContracts/tabid/491/Default.aspx) reports that in 2008 fifty-three tribes had management contracts in place with commercial companies. Nearly one-third of the contracts were with gaming companies based in Las Vegas and Reno, Nevada. Harrah's Entertainment was a partner in six of these contracts.

Native American casinos have often faced fierce opposition from commercial casino operators hoping to thwart competition. For example, tribal casinos in California could cut deeply into the Nevada casino business because California residents, who have long provided a large share of Nevada's gambling revenue, could gamble closer to home. However, some commercial casino operators have seen expanded opportunities for revenue through partnerships with Native American tribes, and some tribes—especially small tribes—have welcomed the investment capital and management experience offered by commercial partners.

For example, Thunder Valley Casino is a $215 million venture about 30 miles (48 km) northeast of Sacramento, California. The casino, which opened in June 2004, is owned by the United Auburn Indian Community, which has around 250 adult members. The casino was financially backed and managed by Station Casinos of Las Vegas. The tribe selected the company because it was willing to put up $200 million to build the casino and agreed to manage the casino for the tribe; in return Station receives 24% of the casino's net revenues. Before the casino opened, tribe members lived in poverty on a 3-acre (1.2-ha) reservation. However, with the casino came full health, dental, and vision insurance for each tribe member. Gaming revenues also funded the United Auburn Indian Community Tribal School, which has a teacher-student ratio of 1 to 7. The casino is building on its success. Babette Hermann reports in "From Termination to Triumph" (*Indian Country Today*, February 6, 2008) that in 2007 the tribe announced plans to build a new 650-room resort hotel at Thunder Valley Casino.

Casino ventures between companies and small tribes are particularly controversial. According to Timothy Egan, in "Lawsuit in California Asks, Whose Tribe Is It, Anyway?" (*New York Times*, April 10, 2002), critics suggest that small tribes are being manipulated by outside investors who only want to cash in on tribal casinos. The California Nations Indian Gaming Association insists that small tribes should not be denied the tremendous economic opportunities offered by casinos. Egan notes that Susan Jensen, a spokesperson for the group, said, "The reason some of these tribes have only one or two people left is because Indians were exterminated."

### Tribal Casinos off the Reservation

Another hot topic is the construction of tribal casinos on land outside reservations. Brad Knickerbocker reports in "Tribal Casinos Push beyond the Reservations" (*Christian Science Monitor*, October 14, 2005) that by 2005 three dozen tribes had applied to the BIA to build casinos outside their reservations. Many of these tribes had casinos on their reservations and were looking to expand into different markets, many closer to major cities. To build a new casino on nonreservation land, tribes must convince the BIA that they have claim to a parcel of land where they would like to build the new casino. The BIA can then put the land into a trust for the tribe.

In 2008 the U.S. House of Representatives considered two bills, H.R. 2176: To Provide for and Approve the Settlement of Certain Land Claims of the Bay Mills Indian Community, (http://www.govtrack.us/congress/bil .xpd?bill=h110-2176) and H.R. 4115: To Provide for and Approve the Settlement of Certain Land Claims of the Sault Ste. Marie Tribe of Chippewa Indians (http://www .govtrack.us/congress/bill.xpd?bill=h110-4115), that would have authorized the construction of casinos in Michigan hundreds of miles from the reservation lands of the Bay Mills Indian Community and the Sault Ste. Marie Tribe of Chippewa Indians. On June 25, 2008, the House failed to pass the bills, preventing the expansion of off-reservation gambling.

### THE STORY OF NATIVE AMERICAN CASINOS IN TWO STATES

#### Connecticut

Tribal casinos are not required by law to make their financial records public. Even though exact figures are not known, various reports indicate that the tribal casinos operating in Connecticut are extremely profitable. For example, in *2006–07 Indian Gaming Industry Report* (2006), the economist Alan Meister estimates the annual revenue of Connecticut's tribal casinos to be $2.3 billion.

As of June 2008, only two tribal casinos were operating in Connecticut. Foxwoods Casino and Resort is operated by the Mashantucket Pequot in Ledyard, and the Mohegan Sun is operated by the Mohegan in nearby Uncasville. Both are located in a rural area of eastern Connecticut.

In "About Foxwoods" (2007, http://www.foxwoods .com/AboutFoxwoods/), Foxwoods describes itself as being the world's largest casino complex. In 2007 it had 6 casinos, 1,416 hotel rooms, 25 large conference rooms, a spa, a golf and country club, a shopping mall, dozens of restaurants, and a 1,400-seat theater. Foxwoods had over seven thousand slot machines, four hundred gaming tables, and the world's largest bingo hall. It also offers keno and sports gambling. The resort receives about forty thousand visitors every day.

The Mohegan Sun (2008, http://www.mohegansun .com/gateway/index.html) had twelve hundred hotel rooms, thirty-six restaurants, and three casinos in 2008. The complex also included a ten-thousand-seat arena, a showroom, an extensive retail complex, and its own gas station.

Foxwoods in particular has an interesting history. According to Kim Isaac Eisler, in *Revenge of the Pequots: How a Small Native American Tribe Created the World's Most Profitable Casino* (2001), a law passed in Connecticut in the 1980s allowed the wagering of "play money" on casino games such as blackjack, roulette, craps, and poker. The law was championed by the Mothers against Drunk Driving organization to encourage high schools to hold casino-type events following proms to reduce drunk driving by teenagers. Under this law, the Mashantucket Pequot Tribe was able to get a license for a "charity" gambling casino. It also procured $60 million from the resort developer Sol Kerzner (1935–) to begin construction.

Foxwoods opened in 1992. At that time, slot machines were not permitted. In 1994 the tribe negotiated a deal with Lowell P. Weicker Jr. (1931–), the governor of Connecticut, that provided the tribe with exclusive rights to operate slot machines within the state. In return, the tribe agreed to make yearly payments to the state of $100 million or 25% of the revenue from their slot machines, whichever was greater. By 1997 Foxwoods was considered the largest and most profitable casino in the United States.

The Mohegan tribe also signed in 1994 its own compact with Weicker to operate a casino. The Mashantucket Pequots granted the Mohegan tribe permission to include slot machines in its new casino. In return, the state set the annual payment required from each tribe at $80 million or 25% of their slot revenue, whichever was greater. The Mohegan Sun opened in 1996 after receiving financing from Kerzner.

The Mashantucket Pequot's standing as a tribe is not without controversy. In *Without Reservation: How a Controversial Indian Tribe Rose to Power and Built the World's Largest Casino* (2001), Jeff Benedict claims that the Pequots never should have been legally recognized as a tribe by the federal government because some members were not actually descendants of the historic Pequot tribe. The tribe achieved its recognition by an act of Congress. Benedict made his allegations a major part of his unsuccessful run for Congress during the summer of 2002. He later helped found the Connecticut Alliance against Casino Expansion (CAACE), a nonprofit coalition that lobbies against additional casinos in Connecticut and successfully led the drive to repeal the state's "Las Vegas Night" law that provided the legal opening for the original casinos. CAACE also seeks federal legislation to reform the tribal recognition process.

In Connecticut, legalized gambling is regulated by the Division of Special Revenue, which conducts licensing, permitting, monitoring, and education. It also ensures that the correct revenues are transferred to the state's general fund and to each municipality that hosts a gaming facility or charitable game. Table 5.2 shows the annual and cumulative revenues paid into the general fund by Foxwoods and Mohegan Sun. The Division of Special Revenue indicates in "Gaming Revenue and Statistics" (July 16, 2008, http://www.ct.gov/dosr/lib/dosr/stmt2008.pdf) that Connecticut collected nearly $2.7 billion from Foxwoods between 1993 and June 2008 and nearly $2 billion from Mohegan Sun between 1997 and June 2008. These casino revenues represented 39.5% of all gaming payments to the state general fund between 1972 and 2008. (See Figure 5.4.)

### California

In *Gaming Tribe Report* (June 6, 2008, http://www.nigc.gov/Portals/0/NIGC%20Uploads/readingroom/listandlocationoftribalgamingops/tribe%20&%20operation%20report%202008a-state.pdf), the NIGC indicates that in 2008 fifty-five tribes in California had gaming operations, by far the most of any state. According to the NIGC, in "NIGC Announces 2007 Indian Gaming Revenues," the state's tribal casinos earned nearly $7.8 billion in fiscal year 2007, approximately one-third of the nationwide tribal total and more than the casinos on the Las Vegas Strip. Industry analysts predict that this percentage will continue to grow as the California market matures. According to the National Conference of State Legislatures, in "Federal and State Recognized Tribes" (December 2007, http://www.ncsl.org/programs/statetribe/tribes

**TABLE 5.2**

Connecticut tribal gaming payments to state general fund, 1993–2008

|  | Casino | | |
| --- | --- | --- | --- |
| FYE | Foxwoods | Mohegan Sun | Subtotal |
| 1993 | $30,000,000 | | 30,000,000 |
| 1994 | 113,000,000 | | 113,000,000 |
| 1995 | 135,724,017 | | 135,724,017 |
| 1996 | 148,702,765 | | 148,702,765 |
| 1997 | 145,957,933 | $57,643,836 | 203,601,769 |
| 1998 | 165,067,994 | 91,007,858 | 256,075,852 |
| 1999 | 173,581,104 | 113,450,294 | 287,031,398 |
| 2000 | 189,235,039 | 129,750,030 | 318,985,069 |
| 2001 | 190,683,773 | 141,734,541 | 332,418,314 |
| 2002 | 199,038,210 | 169,915,956 | 368,954,166 |
| 2003 | 196,300,528 | 190,953,944 | 387,254,472 |
| 2004 | 196,883,096 | 205,850,884 | 402,733,980 |
| 2005 | 204,953,050 | 212,884,444 | 417,837,494 |
| 2006 | 204,505,785 | 223,020,826 | 427,526,611 |
| 2007 | 201,380,257 | 229,095,455 | 430,475,712 |
| 2008 | 190,037,675 | 221,373,298 | 411,410,973 |
|  | $2,685,051,226 | $1,986,681,366 | 4,671,732,592 |

Notes:
Revenue transferred on cash basis per fiscal year. FYE = Fiscal Year End.
The above transfers represent:
a) Actual lottery transfers through fiscal year 2008 as reported by the Connecticut Lottery Corporation.
b) Collection of parimutuel taxes, net of payments to municipalities and other entities, for the former jai alai and greyhound facilities.
c) Collection of parimutuel taxes, net of payments to municipalities and other entities, for races conducted through fiscal year 2008 for off-track betting (OTB).
d) Estimated sealed ticket and bingo revenue through fiscal year 2008.
e) Actual casino contributions through July 15, 2008, based on reported video facsimile/slot machine revenue through fiscal year 2008.
From its inception in 1976 through June 30, 1993, the OTB system was state operated. For that period, transfers represented the fund balance in excess of division needs. The OTB system was sold to a private operator effective July 1, 1993 and since then transfers are based on a statutory parimutuel tax rate.

SOURCE: Adapted from "Transfers to General Fund," in *Gaming Revenue and Statistics*, State of Connecticut, Division of Special Revenue, July 16, 2008, http://www.ct.gov/dosr/lib/dosr/stmt2008.pdf (accessed August 8, 2008)

**FIGURE 5.4**

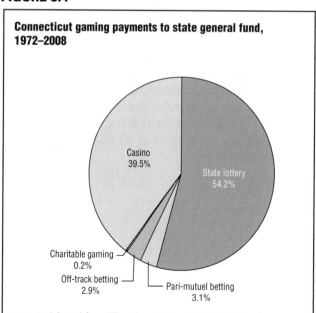

Connecticut gaming payments to state general fund, 1972–2008

SOURCE: Adapted from "Transfers to General Fund," in *Gaming Revenue and Statistics*, State of Connecticut, Division of Special Revenue, July 16, 2008, http://www.ct.gov/dosr/lib/dosr/stmt2008.pdf (accessed August 8, 2008)

.htm#state), the state had 115 federally recognized tribes in 2007, 20% of the national total. Most are described as small extended family groups living on a few acres of federal trust property called *rancherias*. Some tribes have only a handful of members.

Before 2000 California tribes were largely limited to bingo halls because state law prohibited the operation of slot machines and other gambling devices, certain card games, banked games, and games where the house collects a share of the amount wagered. In 2000 California voters passed Proposition 1A, which amended the state constitution to permit Native American tribes to operate lottery games, slot machines, and banking and percentage card games on tribal lands. The constitutionality of the measure was immediately challenged in court.

In January 2002 the California governor Gray Davis (1942–) signed sixty-two gambling compacts with California tribes. The compacts allowed each tribe to have a maximum of two thousand slot machines. The governor also announced plans to cap the number of slot machines in the state at forty-five thousand. At the time, there were already forty thousand slot machines in operation and dozens of tribal casinos in the planning stages. The governor put a moratorium on new compacts while Proposition 1A made its way through the courts. In August 2002 a U.S. district court ruled that tribal casinos were entitled to operate under the provisions of the state gaming compacts and Proposition 1A.

In 2003 the state of California suffered a severe budget crisis. Davis was ultimately forced out of office through a special recall election in which Arnold Schwarzenegger (1947–) became the governor. In the press release "Schwarzenegger Far off the Mark on Tribal Governments" (September 23, 2003, http://www.cniga.com/media/pressrelease _detail.php?id=40), the California Nations Indian Gaming Association (CNIGA) states that in televised campaign ads Schwarzenegger promised voters to make tribal casinos "pay their fair share," arguing that "their casinos make billions, yet pay no taxes and virtually nothing to the state." The CNIGA was outraged, calling the remarks "hurtful" and accusing Schwarzenegger of having "a complete and almost frightening lack of understanding of the legal status of Indians and tribal governments." The CNIGA also reminded voters that the gaming tribes paid more than $100 million per year into a special fund designated to pay for the effects of tribal gaming on local communities.

In June 2004 Schwarzenegger signed new compacts that preserved the exclusive gaming rights of five California tribes: the Pala Band of Mission Indians, the Pauma Band of Mission Indians, the Rumsey Band of Wintun Indians, the United Auburn Indian Community, and the Viejas Band of Kumeyaay Indians. The slot machine cap was also raised above two thousand machines per tribe. In exchange, the tribes agreed to pay the state $1 billion up front and a licensing fee for each new slot machine added above the current limit. Payments were expected to total between $150 million and $275 million per year through the compacts' expiration date in 2030.

Schwarzenegger also announced plans to negotiate similar deals with other tribes in the state. However, several tribes decided to fight the new compacts. The Rincon Indian Tribe sued the state, arguing that the new compacts showed favoritism to some tribes and put others at an economic disadvantage. A federal judge, however, ruled against the Rincon. The judge reasoned that all tribes are sovereign entities, so different gambling deals can be structured by different tribes.

The state continued to form tribal compacts that permitted casino expansion in exchange for higher taxes. One of the more notable deals was made with the Agua Caliente Band of Cahuilla Indians. The tribe owned two casinos in Palm Springs. In August 2006 the state agreed to let the tribe open a third casino with five thousand slot machines if the tribe paid an estimated $1.9 billion in taxes over the following twenty-three years. Many Californians were concerned that if such deal-making were allowed to continue, casinos could be as prevalent as shopping malls and lead to higher instances of gambling addiction.

# CHAPTER 6
# THE ECONOMIC AND SOCIAL EFFECTS OF CASINOS

Assessing the effects of casinos on society is complicated because many factors have to be considered. Most relate to economics, but some address quality of life and moral issues. Proponents of casino gambling consider it part of the leisure and entertainment sector—like amusement parks or movie theaters. In a casino, participants exchange their money for a good time. Those who support casino gambling generally do not see it as a moral issue.

Opponents are less unified in their opinions. Some disapprove of gambling on religious grounds, because it contradicts moral principles of thrift, hard work, and sober living. Others are wary of an industry that was associated with mobsters, swindlers, and corrupt politicians throughout much of its history in this country. Still others point out that casinos provide a place for those who are prone to problem gambling to act on those urges. Easy accessibility to casinos, they suggest, encourages some people to gamble who otherwise would not and should not. Outlawing casinos is one way to protect people from their own bad judgment.

There is also the so-called NIMBY factor: "not in my backyard." Some people support casinos in theory and may even visit them on vacation, but they do not want them in their hometown, for whatever reason. According to the American Gaming Association (AGA), in *2004 State of the States: The AGA Survey of Casino Entertainment* (2004, http://www.americangaming.org/assets/files/2004_Survey_for_Web.pdf), four out of ten Americans did not want a casino in their own neighborhoods in 2003. Local residents and politicians are often opposed to casinos because they fear increased traffic and crime and may want to protect their community's image. Also, many state governments are running lotteries and do not want competition from casinos for their residents' gambling dollars.

## NATIONAL PUBLIC OPINION

According to Paul Taylor, Cary Funk, and Peyton Craighill of the Pew Research Center, in *Gambling: As the Take Rises, So Does Public Concern* (May 23, 2006, http://pewresearch.org/assets/social/pdf/Gambling.pdf), 42% of the people surveyed in 2006 said casinos are detrimental to their communities, whereas 34% said casinos have a positive impact. However, a smaller percentage of people who lived near a casino (38%) had negative views of casinos' influence on their communities than those who did not live near a casino (42%). (See Table 6.1.) The AGA finds in *2008 State of the States: The AGA Survey of Casino Entertainment* (2008, http://www.americangaming.org/assets/files/aga_2008_sos.pdf) that more than two-thirds (69%) of those surveyed in 2007 believed casinos brought widespread economic benefits to other industries and businesses in their region. Furthermore, in *2007 State of the States: The AGA Survey of Casino Entertainment* (2007, http://www.americangaming.org/assets/files/aga_2007_sos.pdf), the AGA indicates that in 2006, 67% of those surveyed agreed that legalized casino gambling was a good way for cities and states to generate revenue without having to raise taxes.

Elected officials and civic leaders had an even more positive view of casinos in their communities. The AGA reports in *2005 State of the States: The AGA Survey of Casino Entertainment* (2005, http://www.americangaming.org/assets/files/uploads/2005_State_of_the_States.pdf) that a 2004 poll asked 201 elected officials and civic leaders about the effects of casinos in their communities: 79% said casinos had had a positive impact, whereas only 13% saw a negative impact. Some 63% praised casinos as helping other businesses, and 79% touted casinos as being responsible corporate citizens.

## THE EFFECTS OF NATIVE AMERICAN CASINOS

Native American tribes that encounter opposition to their casino plans attribute opposition to the same issues faced by corporate casinos, although some also see racism as a factor.

TABLE 6.1

**Public opinion on the impact of casinos on local communities, 2006**

OVERALL, WOULD YOU SAY CASINOS HAVE A POSITIVE OR NEGATIVE IMPACT ON THE LOCAL COMMUNITY?

| | All adults | Casino nearby | Casino not nearby | Been to casino? | |
| --- | --- | --- | --- | --- | --- |
| | | | | Yes | No |
| | % | % | % | % | % |
| Positive | 34 | 40 | 30 | 52 | 26 |
| Negative | 42 | 38 | 45 | 27 | 49 |
| Both/neither (volunteered) | 10 | 12 | 8 | 10 | 9 |
| Don't know | 14 | 10 | 17 | 11 | 16 |
| | 100 | 100 | 100 | 100 | 100 |

SOURCE: Paul Taylor, Cary Funk, and Peyton Craighill, "Are Casinos Good for the Local Community," in *Gambling: As the Take Rises, So Does Public Concern*, Pew Research Center, May 23, 2006, http://pewresearch.org/assets/social/pdf/Gambling.pdf (accessed August 8, 2008)

## The Pros

The National Indian Gaming Association (NIGA) notes in *An Analysis of the Economic Impact of Indian Gaming in 2005* (2005, http://www.indiangaming.org/NIGA_econ_impact_2005.pdf) that tribal gaming and associated businesses had:

- Generated revenues of $22.6 billion in 2005 from Native American gaming

- Generated another $2.7 billion in gross revenue from related hospitality and entertainment services

- Created six hundred thousand jobs

- Paid $6.9 billion in wages

- Paid $7.6 billion in federal taxes and revenue savings

- Paid $2.2 billion in state taxes, revenue sharing, and regulatory payments

- Paid more than $100 million to local governments

- Funded essential tribal programs, such as schools, hospitals, water and sewer systems, roads, police and firefighting programs, and cultural and social projects

Jonathan B. Taylor and Joseph P. Kalt find in *The American Indians on Reservations: A Databook of Socioeconomic Change between the 1990 and 2000 Censuses* (2005) that income increased by 35% between 1990 and 2000 on non-Navajo gaming reservations, whereas income only grew by 14% on nongaming, non-Navajo reservations. (Navajo do not have casinos, and the Navajo reservation has more than ten times the membership of any other Native American tribe.)

Most tribal lands are located in areas of the country that have limited natural resources and industry, so tribal casinos often bring much needed wealth to the tribes and their neighbors. The NIGA (August 2004, http://www.in

diangaming.org/info/Final_Impact_Analysis.pdf) points to specific instances in which gaming helped revitalize impoverished communities in and around Native American lands. For example, in 1995 Del Norte was one of the more indigent counties in California: the biggest economic development in the works was a new maximum-security prison in Crescent City. Then the Tolowan Tribe opened Elk Valley Rancheria and Casino, also in Crescent City. It quickly became the county's largest employer, providing over five thousand new jobs for tribal and nontribal members of the community by 2004. Using money from the casino, the tribe helped finance a $35 million wastewater-treatment plant in the county. Another example is the Tunica-Biloxi Tribe in central Louisiana, which was one of the poorest parishes (counties) in the state until the tribe built the Paragon Casino and Resort in 1994. NIGA reports that the casino contributes greatly to the local economy by providing jobs and scholarships.

## The Cons

Critics contend that tribal casinos:

- Unfairly compete against local hotels, restaurants, and pari-mutuel operators

- Hurt state lottery sales

- Place an increased burden on states to address problems resulting from pathological gambling

- Introduce opportunities for money laundering (the act of engaging in transactions designed to hide or obscure the origin of illegally obtained money) and organized crime

Some critics suggest that casinos encourage and perpetuate a cycle of dependence: tribe members who were formerly dependent on the federal government are now dependent on their tribal governments. They believe that, ultimately, casinos will hurt the culture and political stability of the tribes.

In *Gambling in the Golden State: 1998 Forward* (May 2006, http://www.library.ca.gov/crb/06/04/06-004.pdf), Charlene W. Simmons of the California State Library catalogs all the known positive and negative effects that Native American casinos had had on California communities. According to Simmons, Native American casinos led to slightly higher incidences of bankruptcy and crime, particularly violent crimes such as aggravated assault. The casinos also strained the local infrastructure. Most of the casinos brought many people into rural areas with narrow two-lane roads and limited sewage systems. Even though casinos helped the economies of their immediate communities, they often siphoned money away from adjacent communities: people spent their money at casinos rather than at stores and eating establishments in their own neighborhoods.

## THE LACK OF BALANCED DATA

In 1996 Congress created the National Gambling Impact Study Commission (NGISC) to examine the economic and social impacts of legalized gambling. After conducting hearings in Las Vegas, Nevada; Atlantic City, New Jersey; Chicago, Illinois; San Diego, California; and Biloxi, Mississippi, the commission published *Final Report* (June 1999, http://govinfo.library.unt.edu/ngisc/reports/fullrpt.html), which included the following assessments:

- Casinos are associated with increased per capita income in the construction, hotel, lodging, recreation, and amusement industries but decreased per capita income for those working in local restaurants and bars.

- The financial benefits of casinos are particularly impressive in economically depressed communities.

- Casinos create full-time entry-level jobs that are badly needed in areas suffering from chronic unemployment and underemployment.

- Unemployment rates, welfare payments, and unemployment insurance declined by approximately one-seventh in communities close to newly opened casinos.

- In terms of income, health insurance, and pensions, casino jobs in the destination resorts of Las Vegas and Atlantic City are better than comparable jobs in the service industries.

- Small business owners located near casinos often suffer from the loss of business.

- Tribal casino workers have complained about the lack of job security, an absence of federal and state anti-discrimination laws, and the lack of workers' compensation benefits.

- Elected officials from casino towns expressed support for casinos because they improved the quality of life in their towns and funded community improvements.

- Problems with pathological gambling increased in seven out of nine communities surveyed.

- The AGA is the largest source of funding for research on pathological gambling.

- Many casinos train management and staff to identify problem gamblers among customers or employees.

- Many tribal casinos contribute money to nonprofit groups dealing with problem gambling.

The commission concluded that a lack of objective research data on gambling issues is a major hurdle in determining the extent of its effects on society. The U.S. General Accounting Office (GAO; now the U.S. Government Accountability Office) followed up the commission's report with *Impact of Gambling: Economic Effects More Measurable than Social Effects* (April 2000, http://www.gao.gov/new.items/gg00078.pdf). The GAO finds some evidence that pathological gambling in areas with casinos results in increased crime and family problems, such as intimate partner violence and child abuse, divorce, and homelessness. However, the GAO suggests that some of these effects might actually be primarily due to other problems that usually accompany pathological gambling, such as alcohol or drug abuse.

## PURE ECONOMICS

The AGA notes in *2008 State of the States* that in 2007 commercial casinos took in over $34.1 billion. In *National Indian Gaming Commission Newsletter* (Summer 2008, http://www.nigc.gov/LinkClick.aspx?link=NIGC+Uploads%2fNewsletters%2fSummer.2008.pdf&tabid=140&mid=760), the National Indian Gaming Commission indicates that tribal casinos took in $26 billion that same year. As such, American casinos—commercial and tribal—took in $60.1 billion during 2007, making the casino industry an extremely big business. Most casinos have been huge successes for their investors, who range from middle-class stockholders in major corporations to billionaires such as Donald Trump (1946–) and Stephen A. Wynn (1942–). Most tribal casinos have been economically successful as well, bringing unimagined wealth to Native Americans, many of whom were at the very bottom of the U.S. economic ladder only a decade ago. Casinos are also labor-intensive businesses that employ hundreds of thousands of people, who support their families, pay taxes, and buy goods and services—factors that contribute to the economic health of their communities.

The economic effects of casinos on local and state governments are also significant. Commercial casinos pay billions of dollars every year to government agencies in the form of application fees, regulatory fees, wagering taxes, and admission taxes. Even though governments incur increased costs for more police, roads, and sewers, casino taxes and fees help fund programs that improve the quality of life in the immediate vicinity or state. Tribal casinos, though exempt from state and local taxation, pay billions of dollars each year to compensate states and municipalities for regulatory and public-service expenses.

## DIRECT GOVERNMENT REVENUE
### From Commercial Casinos

In *2008 State of the States*, the AGA reports that commercial casinos generated tax revenues of $5.8 billion in 2007, up from $5.2 billion in 2006. (See Figure 6.1.) Nevada generated the most gambling tax revenue in 2007 ($1 billion), followed by Indiana ($842 million) and Illinois ($834 million). (See Figure 6.2.) According to the AGA, racetrack casinos paid taxes of $2.2 billion to local and state governments in 2007, up 54.6% from the previous year. The biggest increases were in Pennsylvania, which paid $461.1 million in taxes in 2007, a 2555% increase from

FIGURE 6.1

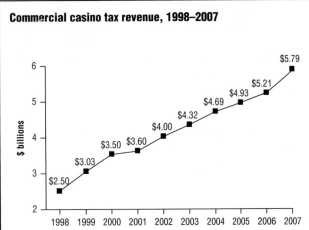

**Commercial casino tax revenue, 1998–2007**

2006, and in Florida, which paid $101.2 million in taxes in 2007, a 1862% increase from the previous year. These increases were due to the opening of three new racetrack casinos in Pennsylvania and one in Florida.

Gaming taxes can be a substantial portion of a state's revenue. For example, Amanda Fehd reports in "Nevada Senate Approves State Education Budget" (Associated Press, June 1, 2007) that Nevada's budget in 2007 was $18 billion. Fees and taxes paid by casinos made up about 28% of the state budget. Total taxes collected in Mississippi in 2007 amounted to $6.4 billion, as reported by the U.S. Census Bureau, in "State Government Tax Collections: 2007" (February 29, 2008, http://www.cen sus.gov/govs/statetax/0725msstax.html). According to the Mississippi Gaming Commission, in "Tax Revenues from Gaming" (September 8, 2008, http://www.mstc.state .ms.us/taxareas/misc/gaming/stats/gamtax.pdf), gaming taxes amounted to approximately 5% of those taxes, with $332 million collected during the fiscal year (FY) ending June 30, 2007.

The AGA notes in *2005 State of the States* that in 2004, 67% of elected officials and civic leaders with

**FIGURE 6.2**

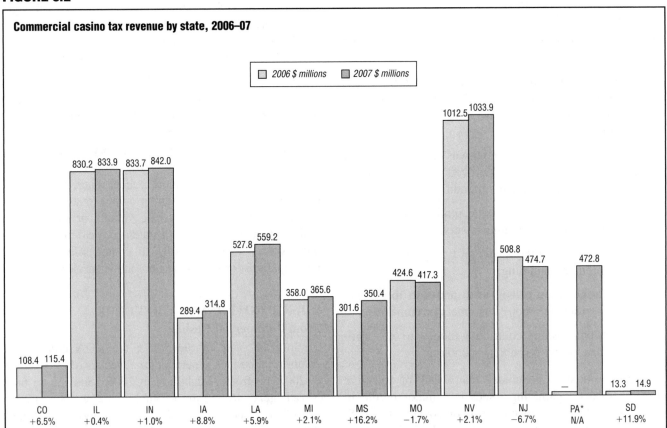

**Commercial casino tax revenue by state, 2006–07**

*There are no 2006 statistics for Pennsylvania because stand-alone casinos there only became operational in 2007.

casinos in their communities said that the casinos had increased the tax revenue in their communities. More important, 73% of those community leaders agreed that such tax revenue and casino-development agreements allowed their communities to complete projects that would not have been feasible without the additional revenue.

## From Native American Casinos

The Indian Gaming Regulatory Act requires that net revenues from tribal gaming be used to fund tribal government operations and programs, to promote tribal economic development, to donate to charitable organizations, and to help fund operations of local government agencies.

The revenues earned by tribal casinos are not taxable because the casinos are operated by tribal governments: just as the U.S. government does not tax the states for revenue earned from lottery tickets, it does not tax tribal governments for revenue earned from casinos. Therefore, tribal casinos generate less tax revenue than commercial casinos. Tribe members who live on reservations and are employed at tribal enterprises, such as casinos, are not subject to state income taxes. However, tribe members do pay federal income tax, Federal Insurance Contributions Act tax, and Social Security tax on their wages, even if those wages are earned at tribal enterprises. Wages paid to tribe members living off reservations and to nontribe employees are subject to state income taxes.

In *Analysis of the Economic Impact of Indian Gaming in 2005*, the NIGA reports that tribal casinos and associated business generated $6.1 billion in federal taxes during 2005. That amount included employer and employee Social Security taxes, personal and corporate income taxes, and excise taxes. In addition, Native American gaming produced $1.5 billion in federal revenue savings through reduced welfare and unemployment payments.

According to the NIGA, tribal governments spent $323 million on regulatory costs in 2005, including $245 million on tribal regulatory entities, $66 million paid to state agencies, and $12 million paid to the National Indian Gaming Commission for oversight expenses.

## EMPLOYMENT AND CAREERS

In 2007, 360,818 people were employed in commercial casinos. (See Table 6.2.) Tribal casinos employed 248,000 people in 2006. (See Figure 6.3.) Employment was slightly down from the previous year, but up significantly from 1998. (See Figure 6.4.) Because they are employed in an entertainment and hospitality industry, gaming workers need excellent communication and customer-service skills, but the financial aspect of casino activities also requires personal integrity and the ability

**TABLE 6.2**

**Commercial casino jobs by state, 2006–07**

| State | 2006 | 2007 | Change |
|---|---|---|---|
| Nevada | 215,041 | 201,953[a] | −6.1% |
| New Jersey | 45,043 | 41,672 | −7.5% |
| Mississippi | 29,529[b] | 30,572 | +3.3% |
| Louisiana | 17,859 | 18,009 | +0.8% |
| Indiana | 15,600 | 15,671 | +0.5% |
| Missouri | 10,900 | 12,160 | +11.6% |
| Iowa | 9,732 | 10,434 | +7.2% |
| Illinois | 8,819 | 8,337 | −5.5% |
| Colorado | 7,829 | 7,925 | +1.2% |
| Michigan | 6,961 | 7,650 | +9.9% |
| Pennsylvania | —[c] | 4,877 | N/A |
| South Dakota | 2,003 | 1,558[d] | −22.2% |
| **Total** | **369,316** | **360,818** | **22.3%** |

[a]Figure for locations with gross gaming revenue in excess of $1 million for fiscal year2007.
[b]Mississippi employment figures for 2006 have increased compared to last year's reported figures due to a calculation error in the *2007 State of the States*.
[c]There are no 2006 statistics for Pennsylvania because stand-alone casinos there only became operational in 2007.
[d]The significant decrease in the number of employees in South Dakota comes mainly from a change in data collection. 2007 data came from the South Dakota Department of Labor, while 2006 data was collected by the South Dakota Gaming Commission.

SOURCE: "Commercial Casino Jobs by State, 2006 vs. 2007," in *2008 State of the States: The AGA Survey of Casino Entertainment*, American Gaming Association, 2008, http://www.americangaming.org/assets/files/aga_2008_sos.pdf (accessed August 1, 2008)

**FIGURE 6.3**

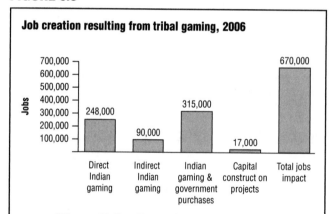

SOURCE: "Direct and Indirect Increase in Employment, 2006 Gains Due to Class II and Class III Indian Gaming," in *The Economic Impact of Indian Gaming in 2006*, National Indian Gaming Association, 2007, http://www.indiangaming.org/info/pr/press-releases-2007/NIGA_econ_impact_2006.pdf (accessed August 12, 2008)

to maintain composure when dealing with angry or emotional patrons. A high school diploma or the equivalent is usually preferred for all entry-level jobs. Table 6.3 describes the duties, qualifications, training requirements, and earnings of several categories of casino workers.

All casino employees—from managers to dealers to slot repair technicians—must be at least twenty-one years old and have licenses from the appropriate regulatory agency. Obtaining a license requires a background investigation—applicants can be disqualified from casino employment for a variety of reasons, including links to organized crime, a felony record, and gambling-related offenses. Requirements for education, training, and experience are up to individual casinos. The Bureau of Labor Statistics (April 14, 2007, http://www.bls.gov/oco/ocos275.htm) considers the overall employment outlook for the industry to be good, as increasing competition should result in more jobs for gaming workers. Occupations in gaming are predicted to be among the fastest growing U.S. occupations between 2006 and 2016, which are projected to grow by 23% during this period.

The growth of the casino employment market has spurred a related increase in vocational and professional training for casino workers. The University of Nevada, Las Vegas, only 1.5 miles (2.4 km) from the Strip, offers a major in gaming management that includes instruction in gaming operations, marketing, hospitality, security, and regulations. At Tulane University's School of Continuing Studies in New Orleans, students can choose from several programs lasting between one and four years, including a bachelor's degree in casino resort management. Students pursuing a degree in hospitality and tourism management at the University of Massachusetts can specialize in casino management. Central Michigan University, which is located near the Soaring Eagle Casino and Resort operated by the Saginaw Chippewa Tribe, offers a business degree in gaming and entertainment management, including coursework in the protection of casino table games, gaming regulations and control, the mathematics of casino games, and the sociology of gambling. The Casino Career Institute, which includes a large mock casino, is a division of Atlantic Cape Community College in downtown Atlantic City. When it opened in 1978, it was the first gaming school in the country affiliated with a community college.

**FIGURE 6.4**

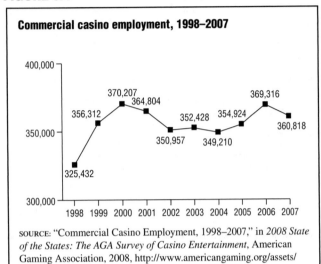

Commercial casino employment, 1998–2007

**TABLE 6.3**

Casino occupations, 2008

| Title | Responsibilities | Education training | Median salary |
|---|---|---|---|
| Gaming managers | Plan, organize, direct, control, or coordinate gaming operations in a casino. Formulate gaming policies. Interview, hire, train, and evaluate new workers and create work schedules and station assignments. | Associates or Bachelor's degree. Hands-on experience may be substituted for formal education. Most managers gain experience in other casino jobs, typically as dealers, and have a broad knowledge of casino rules, regulations, procedures, and games. | $62,820 |
| Gaming supervisors | Oversee gaming operations and personnel in an assigned area. Circulate among the tables to ensure that all stations and games are attended to each shift. Interpret the casino's operating rules for patrons. Plan and organize activities for guests staying at a casino hotels. Address service complaints. | Associates or Bachelor's degree. Hands-on experience may be substituted for formal education. Most supervisors gain experience in other gaming jobs before moving into supervisory positions. | 41,160 |
| Slot key persons (also called slot attendants or slot technicians) | Coordinate and supervise the slot department and its workers. Verify and handle payoff winnings to patrons, reset slot machines after payoffs, refill slot machines with money, make minor repairs and adjustments to the machines, enforce safety rules and report hazards. | No formal eduation requirements, but completion of technical training helpful. Most positions are entry-level and provide on-the-job training. | 22,720 |
| Gaming and sports book writers and runners | Assist in the operation of games such as bingo. Scan tickets presented by patrons and calculate and distribute winnings. May operate equipment that randomly selects the numbers, announce numbers selected, pick up tickets from patrons, collect bets, or receive, verify, and record patrons' cash wagers. | High school diploma or GED. Usually trained on the job. | 18,800 |
| Gaming dealers | Operate casino table games such as craps, baccarat, blackjack, or roulette. Determine winners of game, calculate and pay winning bets, and collect losing bets. May be required to monitor patrons to determine if they are following the rules of the game. | Completion of a training program at a vocational or technical school. An in-depth knowledge of casino games may be substituted for formal education. Most casinos require employees to audition for such jobs. | 14,730 |

SOURCE: Adapted from "Gaming Services Occupations," in *Occupational Outlook Handbook, 2008–09 Edition*, U.S. Department of Labor, Bureau of Labor Statistics, 2008, http://www.bls.gov/oco/ocos275.htm (accessed August 12, 2008)

## Employment at Commercial Casinos

According to the AGA, in *2008 State of the States*, commercial casinos employed 360,818 people in 2007. Nevada accounted for 56% of the total. (See Table 6.2.) In addition, racetrack casinos in Delaware, Florida, Iowa, Louisiana, Maine, New Mexico, New York, Oklahoma, Pennsylvania, Rhode Island, and West Virginia employed 27,258 people during 2007, up 22.2% from 2006. A large proportion of this increase was due to the opening of new racetrack casinos in Florida and Pennsylvania.

Employment at commercial casinos grew rapidly during the 1990s, then stagnated overall between 2000 and 2005, before rising in 2006 and then falling again in 2007. Despite the 2007 drop, overall employment figures in the casino industry rose from 325,432 in 1998 to 360,818 in 2007, an increase of 11%. (See Figure 6.4.) Casino employment rose dramatically in Missouri (11.6%) and Michigan (9.9%) between 2006 and 2007, but fell in Nevada (6.1%) and New Jersey (7.5%). (See Table 6.2.)

Even though employment numbers fell and then rose again between 2000 and 2005, commercial casino wages rose steadily. According to the AGA, in 2007 commercial casinos paid $13.8 billion in wages, up from $13.3 billion in 2006.

## Employment at Native American Casinos

In *The Economic Impact of Indian Gaming in 2006* (2007, http://www.indiangaming.org/info/pr/press-releases-2007/NIGA_econ_impact_2006.pdf), the NIGA reports that tribal gambling directly employed 248,000 people in 2006. (See Figure 6.3.) About 178,000 of those jobs were at tribal casinos; the other jobs were at ancillary facilities such as restaurants and hotels. Another ninety thousand jobs were attributed to the indirect effects of tribal casinos—for example, businesses at which casino workers spent their wages. The NIGA estimates that tribal casinos were indirectly responsible for 315,000 other jobs by purchasing goods and services from businesses around the country. Capital construction projects (e.g., casino building) were associated with the creation of seventeen thousand other jobs. In total, the NIGA credits tribal gaming for the employment of 670,000 people during 2006.

The NIGA estimates that in 2006 roughly 25% of tribal casino employees were Native Americans and 75% were non–Native Americans. In some cases the percentages reflected the fact that several tribes had fewer members than employees.

Historically, employees at tribal casinos have not been covered by the federal labor laws that protect workers at commercial casinos. As sovereign entities, tribes were considered excluded from Title VII of the Civil Rights Act of 1964 and Title I of the Americans with Disabilities Act of 1990, which prohibit discrimination in employment on the basis of race, sex, physical impairment, and other criteria. In addition, the National Labor Relations Act exempts government entities from the requirement that they allow employees to form unions. Tribes, having been ruled to be sovereign governments by both the National Labor Relations Board (NLRB) and a federal court, operated under their own laws and blocked unions if they chose to do so.

However, some court cases have held that Occupational Safety and Health Administration requirements, the Fair Labor Standards Act, and the Employee Retirement Income Security Act do apply to tribal businesses conducted on reservations. Furthermore, the NLRB, after a 2004 challenge by UNITE HERE, a union that represents hotel and restaurant employees, overturned thirty years of precedent and ruled in *San Manuel Indian Bingo & Casino* (341 NLRB 1055 [2004] aff'd. 475 F.3d 1306 [D.C. Cir. 2007]) that the San Manuel Indian Bingo and Casino in Southern California could not stop the formation of a union.

The NLRB (http://www.nlrb.gov/shared_files/Regional%20Decisions/2008/34-RC-02261-05-02-08Attachment.pdf) explains that in 2007 *San Manuel Indian Bingo & Casino* was used as a precedent to rule against the Mashantucket Pequot Tribe's contention that employment at Foxwoods could not be regulated by federal law because of the tribe's status as a sovereign nation. On October 24, 2007, a Decision and Direction of Election was issued to allow the United Auto Workers and the American Federation of Labor and Congress of Industrial Organizations to organize dealers at Foxwoods. The election was held on November 24, 2007, and most employees voted in favor of the union. Employer appeals were overruled by the NLRB (2008, http://www.nlrb.gov/shared_files/ALJ%20Decisions/2008/JD-NY-09-08.htm). The union was officially certified on June 30, 2008 (http://www.nlrb.gov/shared_files/Board%20Decisions/352/v35292.pdf).

## TOURISM

According to the AGA, in *2006 State of the States: The AGA Survey of Casino Entertainment* (2006, http://www.americangaming.org/assets/files/2006_Survey_for_Web.pdf), 72% of those polled in 2005 said casinos can play an important role in a community's entertainment and tourism options.

### Las Vegas

No destination better represents the marriage between gambling and tourism than Las Vegas. It has had its ups and downs, however. In the early 1990s the city experienced a steep decline in revenues because of competition from legal gambling on riverboats and tribal casinos in other states. To counteract this development, the city began a drive to shift its focus from an adult playground to a family destination. As part of the campaign, $12 billion was spent to refurbish almost every hotel on the Strip and to add entertainment facilities. Theme hotels became the big draw. Adult entertainment along the Strip, such as topless shows, gave way to magic shows, circus events, and carnival rides. The Las Vegas Convention and Visitors Authority focused advertising on families. The result was a huge increase in visitors.

However, children distracted their parents from gambling. Casino owners noticed that the changes did not bring in more gambling revenue, so during the late 1990s the city began to change its image again. Adult entertainment made a comeback along the Strip: casino-hotels began offering more topless and nude shows, although managers insisted that the nudity presented at their casinos would always be tasteful and artistic. They were anxious not to offend shareholders of their parent corporations or to alienate women, potential gamblers who make up nearly 60% of Las Vegas visitors. MGM Grand shut down its family theme park in 2001.

Theresa Howard reports in "Vegas Goes for Edgier Ads" (*USA Today*, August 3, 2003) that in early 2003 the Las Vegas Convention and Visitors Authority launched a somewhat risqué ad campaign with the slogan "What Happens Here, Stays Here." It may have been part of the reason that Las Vegas tourism and casino revenue increased substantially in 2005 and 2006. (See Figure 4.2 in Chapter 4.) The resurgence of travel (it slowed for two years after the September 11, 2001, terrorist attacks) may have been another factor.

Las Vegas tourism faces one particular future challenge: It relies heavily on visitors from California, so the advent of tribal gaming in California could create stiff competition.

### Atlantic City

Tourism in Atlantic City increased following the introduction of casino gambling, but not as fast or as much as many had hoped. From the 1880s to the 1940s Atlantic City was a major tourist destination, particularly for people living in the Northeast. Visitors went for the beaches and to walk along the town's boardwalk and piers, which featured carnival-like entertainment. During the 1950s and 1960s the town fell into economic depression as tourists ventured farther south to beaches in Florida and the Caribbean.

Casino gambling was legalized in 1976 in the hopes that the city would recapture its former glory and rival Las Vegas as a tourist destination. Progress was slow through the 1980s and early 1990s. Even though visitors began to go to Atlantic City, they mostly arrived by bus or car and stayed only for a day or two. In 1984 the state established the Casino Reinvestment Development Authority (CRDA) to revitalize the city using the funds from a 1.25% tax on casino revenues.

The economic troubles that had ravaged the town's businesses before gambling was legalized were not easily overcome. Vacant lots, buildings in disrepair, and housing projects surrounded the casinos. The overall atmosphere was not particularly appealing to vacationers or convention-goers. Mike Kelly notes in "Gambling with Our Future: City Poised to Hit Jackpot, or Lose Everything" (*The Record* [West Paterson, New Jersey], July 1, 1993) that in 1993 the city was "trapped in a web of poverty and blight." At that time, the typical visitor was a retiree who arrived by bus and stayed only for the day. According to Kelly, Atlantic City's thirty million annual visitors actually represented about five million people making multiple trips.

In the late 1990s initiatives by the CRDA and other groups began to pay off. Hundreds of new homes were built, and commercial businesses were established. One of the largest convention centers in the country (it has 31 acres [12.5 ha] of space) opened in May 1997. The city's image began to improve, and tourism showed a moderate surge. Regardless, city and casino officials still see three factors that limit tourism growth in Atlantic City: lack of a major airport, lack of usable land, and cold winters. Restrictions on smoking on the casino floor, which went into effect in 2008, also worry officials.

## CRIME

*Officials must realize that legal gambling will attract an unsavory element that can jeopardize the safety and well-being of the city's residents and the many visitors who come to gamble.*

—Federal Bureau of Investigation, *FBI Law Enforcement Bulletin* (January 2001)

When gambling was legalized in Nevada in 1931, the law kept corporations out of the casino business by requiring that every shareholder obtain a gaming license. This law, which was designed to safeguard the integrity of the casinos, unintentionally gave organized crime a huge advantage. The nation was in the midst of the Great Depression (1929–1939), and building a flashy casino-hotel was expensive. Few legitimate businessmen had the cash to finance a casino, and banks were reluctant to loan money for what they saw as a poor investment. Organized crime groups had made fortunes selling bootleg liquor during Prohibition (1920–1933), so they were able to make the capital investments needed to build and operate lavish casino-hotels that attracted visitors.

The marriage between casinos and organized crime in Nevada lasted for decades but was eventually ended by gaming officials and law enforcement. In the twenty-first century, there is no strong evidence of organized crime activity in the casino industry. Regulatory agencies keep a watchful eye on casinos to make sure mobsters and their associates do not gain a new foothold.

Casinos keep an equally watchful eye on their patrons and employees. The casino floor is constantly monitored by a host of security guards and cameras. Observers watch dealers and patrons at the gaming tables and all money-counting areas. Some casinos use high-tech facial recognition programs to scan incoming patrons and quickly identify any known felons or other undesirables. Even though the industry does not release data on crimes committed by casino employees, analysts believe employee theft and embezzlement account for millions of dollars in losses each year.

Vice crimes, particularly prostitution, as well as weapons crimes also occur. Details of the type of crimes found around casinos are illustrated by the Missouri Gaming Commission, in *Annual Report to the General Assembly: Fiscal Year 2006* (2006, http://www.mgc.dps.mo.gov/annual%20reports/2006_ar/annual2006.pdf). Commission agents filed 1,767 charges between July 2005 and June 2006. (See Table 6.4.) This total included charges for acts committed at the casinos as well as arrests made for criminal activities that did not occur on casino property. More than eight hundred (46%) cases involved people who obstructed the judicial process in cases involving gambling. Over three hundred people were charged with violating gambling laws, and 189 people were charged with stealing.

**TABLE 6.4**

**Arrests made by Missouri Gaming Division troopers, by charges filed, July 2005–June 2006**

| Type of charge | Number |
|---|---|
| Assault | 50 |
| Burglary | 3 |
| Damaged property | 7 |
| Dangerous drugs | 63 |
| Family offense | 8 |
| Flight/escape | 21 |
| Forgery | 45 |
| Fraud | 56 |
| Gambling laws | 304 |
| Health & safety | 2 |
| Liquor laws | 8 |
| Miscellaneous federal charges | 14 |
| Motor vehicle | 142 |
| Obstruction of judicial process | 812 |
| Obstructing police | 21 |
| Peace disturbance | 1 |
| Prostitution | 1 |
| Robbery | 2 |
| Sex offenses | 6 |
| Sexual assault | 2 |
| Stealing | 189 |
| Stolen property | 6 |
| Weapons | 4 |
| **Total charges** | ***1,767** |

*These totals reflect the number of charges filed by agents of the commission. The number of individuals arrested will be lower as some individuals may have multiple charges filed as a result of an individual incident. These totals also include arrests made attendant to outstanding warrants for criminal activity that did not occur on property of excursion gambling boats.

SOURCE: "Charges Filed," in *Annual Report to the General Assembly, Fiscal Year 2006*, Missouri Gaming Commission, 2006, http://www.mgc.dps.mo.gov/annual%20reports/2006_ar/annual2006.pdf (accessed August 2, 2008)

The amount of crime in a community with a casino has a direct relationship to the maturity of the casino, according to Earl L. Grinols and David B. Mustard, in "Casinos, Crime, and Community Costs" (*Review of Economics and Statistics*, vol. 88, no. 1, April 2006). The researchers collected crime data from all 3,165 counties in the United States with and without casinos between 1977 and 1996. Their analysis shows that when a casino first opened in a county, crime changed very little, but slowly rose and then grew steadily in subsequent years. Even though increased employment and expanded law enforcement might reduce crime initially, over time these effects were overtaken by factors related to casinos. Grinols and Mustard note, "Specifically, problem and pathological gamblers commit crime as they deplete their resources, nonresidents who visit casinos may both commit and be victims of crime, and casino-induced changes in the population start small but grow." Overall, 8.6% of property crimes and 12.6% of violent crimes (which include robberies) in counties with casinos were due to the presence of the casinos. They find "mixed evidence" about whether casino openings increase crime rates in neighboring counties.

## SUICIDE

The possible link between casino gambling and suicide rates has been the subject of much investigation. For example, in December 1997 David P. Phillips, Ward R. Welty, and Marisa M. Smith concluded in "Elevated Suicide Levels Associated with Legalized Gambling" (*Suicide and Life-Threatening Behavior*, vol. 27, no. 4) that "visitors to and residents of major gaming communities experience significantly elevated suicide levels." The researchers found that in Atlantic City "abnormally high suicide levels" for visitors and residents appeared only after casinos opened. However, five years later Richard McCleary et al., in "Does Legalized Gambling Elevate the Risk of Suicide?" (*Suicide and Life-Threatening Behavior*, vol. 32, no. 2, July 2002), found little to no correlation between suicide rates and the presence of casino gambling in U.S. communities. After comparing the 1990 suicide rates of 148 metropolitan areas in different regions of the country, the researchers found that the presence of casinos could account for only 1% of the regional differences in suicide rates. They also compared "before and after" suicide rates for cities in which gambling had been legalized. Even though increased suicide rates were noted in Atlantic County, New Jersey, and Harrison County, Mississippi, after the advent of gambling, the increases were not considered statistically significant. McCleary et al. noted that suicide rates dropped significantly in Lawrence County, South Dakota, after casino gambling was introduced in the town of Deadwood.

In "Risk Factors for Suicide Ideation and Attempts among Pathological Gamblers" (*American Journal on Addictions*, vol. 15, no. 4, 2006), David C. Hodgins,

TABLE 6.5

**Twenty states with highest suicide rates, by number and rate per 100,000 population, 2005**

| State | Deaths | Rate |
|---|---|---|
| Montana | 206 | 22.0 |
| Nevada | 480 | 19.9 |
| Alaska | 131 | 19.8 |
| New Mexico | 342 | 17.8 |
| Wyoming | 90 | 17.7 |
| Colorado | 800 | 17.2 |
| Idaho | 228 | 16.0 |
| Arizona | 945 | 15.9 |
| South Dakota | 121 | 15.6 |
| Oregon | 560 | 15.4 |
| Oklahoma | 522 | 14.7 |
| North Dakota | 92 | 14.5 |
| Arkansas | 400 | 14.4 |
| Tennessee | 856 | 14.4 |
| West Virginia | 255 | 14.1 |
| Utah | 348 | 14.0 |
| Kentucky | 566 | 13.6 |
| Maine | 175 | 13.3 |
| Florida | 2,347 | 13.2 |

SOURCE: Adapted from "2005, United States Suicide Injury Deaths and Rates per 100,000," in *WISQARS Injury Mortality Reports, 1999–2005*, Centers for Disease Control and Prevention, National Center for Injury Prevention and Control, 2008, http://webappa.cdc.gov/sasweb/ncipc/mortrate10_sy.html (accessed August 2, 2008)

Chrystal Mansley, and Kylie Thygesen find that suicidal ideation and suicide attempts are more likely among pathological gamblers. However, the history of suicidal thoughts generally preceded problem gambling behavior by an average of more than ten years. The researchers conclude that previous mental health disorders, such as clinical depression, put individuals more at risk for both suicide and gambling problems. In other words, gambling itself does not cause suicide attempts.

Nevada, a state in which gambling is widely practiced, had the third-highest suicide rate in the nation in 2005. (See Table 6.5.) The Centers for Disease Control and Prevention indicates in *WISQARS Injury Mortality Reports, 1999–2005* (2008, http://webappa.cdc.gov/sasweb/ncipc/mortrate10_sy.html) that the suicide rate in Nevada was 19.9 suicides per 100,000 population in 2005. This was nearly twice the national average of 11.1 per 100,000 population. Many mental health experts attribute Nevada's high suicide rate to the huge inflow of new residents who lack a support system of family and friends. Loneliness and despair are more likely to overwhelm such people than those who have an emotional safety net in place. In general, suicide rates are higher in the western states than in any other region. Even Utah, which allows no legal gambling, had the seventeenth-highest suicide rate in 2005, with a rate of fourteen suicides per one hundred thousand population.

## BANKRUPTCY

Establishing a definitive link between gambling habits and bankruptcy is difficult. The Council on Compul-

sive Gambling of New Jersey notes in the press release "Correlation between Gambling and Bankruptcy Holding Strong" (August 22, 2001, http://www.800gambler.org/ArticleDetails.aspx?ContentID=90) that a 2001 study by SMR Research Corporation of Hackettstown, New Jersey, attributes 14.2% of U.S. bankruptcy filings to gambling problems. The researchers compare bankruptcy-filing rates during 2000 for 3,109 counties. They find that the 244 counties in which casinos operated had a bankruptcy rate that was 13.6% higher than counties without a casino. The AGA disputes the researchers' findings by pointing out that other factors were not considered, such as liberal bankruptcy laws and the ease with which credit cards can be obtained.

Ernest Goss and Edward A. Morse of Creighton University examine in *The Impact of Casino Gambling on Individual Bankruptcy Rates from 1990 to 2002* (August 25, 2005, http://papers.ssrn.com/sol3/papers.cfm?abstract_id=801185) the bankruptcy rates between 1990 and 2002 in 253 counties with casinos. According to their analysis, those counties actually saw a drop in bankruptcies when the casinos first opened. The researchers reason that the insurgence of revenue and jobs brought in by the casino likely helped the residents' financial situation. However, after a casino was open for nine years bankruptcies trended the other way. Eventually, the bankruptcy rate in a county with a casino was 2.3% higher on average than a county without a casino.

## COMPULSIVE GAMBLING

The AGA indicates in *2003 State of the States: The AGA Survey of Casino Entertainment* (2003, http://www.americangaming.org/assets/files/AGA_survey_2003.pdf) that participants were asked in 2002 to indicate who they thought bore the most responsibility for addressing compulsive gambling in the United States. Most respondents (63%) said gamblers themselves should be held most responsible, whereas 15% thought the society at large should take the most responsibility, and 10% put the burden on the owners of gambling facilities. In *2008 State of the States*, the AGA explains that in 2007 a majority (84%) of casino gamblers set a budget before they began gambling, and that half of gamblers allowed themselves to lose no more than $100 per day.

### Self-Exclusion Programs

Many casinos operate self-exclusion programs in which people can voluntarily ban themselves from casinos. A number of states also offer self-exclusion programs for all casinos within their borders. For example, Missouri's Voluntary Exclusion Program (http://www.mgc.dps.mo.gov/nav_prob_gamb_main.htm) was created in 1996 after a citizen requested that he be banned from the riverboats because he was unable to control his gambling. The Missouri Gaming Commission requires that the casinos remove self-excluded people from their direct marketing lists, deny them check-cashing privileges and membership in players' clubs, and cross-check for their names on the list before paying out any jackpots of $1,200 or more. The casinos are not responsible for barring listed people from the casinos, but anyone listed is to be arrested for trespassing if he or she violates the ban and is discovered in a casino. However, self-excluded people can enter the casino for employment purposes.

Programs in other states are similar. If a self-excluded person is discovered in an Illinois casino, his or her chips and tokens are taken away and their value is donated to charity. The Illinois self-exclusion program runs for a minimum of five years. After that time, people can be removed from the program if they provide written documentation from a licensed mental health professional that they are no longer problem gamblers. Self-exclusion in Michigan is permanent; a person who chooses to be on the Disassociated Persons List is banned for life from Detroit casinos. In New Jersey the Casino Control Commission allows people to voluntarily suspend their credit privileges at all Atlantic City casinos. The commission maintains a list of those who have joined the program and shares the list with the casinos.

Besides casinos and states, companies that provide the ATMs and cash-advance services for casinos have put self-exclusion programs into place. For example, Global Payments provides self-exclusion and even self-limit services for people with gambling problems. Those who put their names on the self-exclusion list are denied money or cash advances, whereas the self-limit program puts a limit on how much money patrons can withdraw in a specified period.

**Hotlines and Treatment**

All the states operate gambling hotlines that either refer callers to other groups for help or provide counseling over the phone. According to the Mississippi Council on Problem and Compulsive Gambling (2008, http://www.msgambler.org/), 55% of the callers to its hotline in 2007 obtained the number through a casino. Nora K. Bock of the Division of Alcohol and Drug Abuse explains in *A Report of the Compulsive Gambling Program* (December 2006, http://www.dmh.mo.gov/ada/progs/CG%20Annual%20Report%20FY06%20for%20web%202-07.pdf) that Missouri operates a gambling hotline that received 2,827 calls in FY 2005, down substantially from FY 2004, when the hotline received 3,686 calls. Between its inception and the end of 2005 the hotline had received nearly twenty thousand calls.

Missouri also offers free treatment to residents suffering from problem gambling and to their families. The program is administered by the Department of Mental Health through a network of private mental health providers who have been certified as compulsive-gambling counselors. Casinos are required to pay $2 to the state for each person who enters the casinos. Up to $0.01 of this fee can be deposited in the state's compulsive gamblers fund, which funds the treatment. Bock notes that in 2006, 407 people received free treatment for gambling addiction through this program.

Iowa's Department of Public Health tracks statistics on clients admitted to its gambling treatment program. In "Profile of Gamblers Admitted to Treatment for State Fiscal Year 2007" (2007, http://www.1800betsoff.org/common/pdf/profile_of_gamblers.pdf), the department indicates that in comparison to other Iowa residents, gamblers admitted to the treatment program tended to be older, less educated, single, and unemployed. Howard J. Shaffer et al. of Harvard Medical School explain in *The Iowa Department of Public Health Gambling Treatment Services: Four Years of Evidence* (October 25, 2002, http://www.1800betsoff.org/common/pdf/Iowa_harvard_report.pdf) that gamblers held an average of $14,000 in gambling debt and lost about $522 weekly. Over half (58%) of clients said their primary wagering in the past six months had been done on slot machines. Another 14% said their primary wagering had been at table games in casinos. In 2006, 29% of clients were aged twenty-five to thirty-nine, 41% were aged forty to fifty-four, and 22% were aged fifty-five and over. (See Table 6.6.) Clients were overwhelmingly white (93%). Nearly six out of ten (58%) were employed full time, 11% were employed part time, and 11% were looking for work. Two-thirds (64%) had a monthly individual income of over $1,000, and nearly one-third (31%) had declared bankruptcy.

**AGA Educational Efforts**

In *Code of Conduct for Responsible Gaming* (September 15, 2003, http://www.americangaming.org/assets/files/Code_with_bookmarks.pdf), the AGA describes the actions that AGA members pledge to take to ensure that responsible gambling is conducted and encouraged at casinos. These actions include the proper training of employees and the promotion of responsible gambling on company Web sites and through brochures and signs posted at the casinos. AGA members also agree to provide opportunities for patrons to self-exclude themselves from casino play.

**UNDERAGE GAMBLING**

The legal gambling age in all commercial casinos in the United States is twenty-one; in tribal casinos it varies from eighteen to twenty-one.

The AGA indicates in *2003 State of the States* that participants were asked in 2002 who they thought bore the most responsibility for addressing the problem of underage gambling in the United States. Respondents

**TABLE 6.6**

**Clients admitted to the Iowa Gambling Treatment Program, by selected characteristics, 2006**

| Age | Total | Percent |
|---|---|---|
| <25 | 58 | 8% |
| 25–39 | 207 | 29% |
| 40–54 | 289 | 41% |
| ≥55 | 154 | 22% |
| **Gender** | | |
| Male | 352 | 49% |
| Female | 356 | 51% |
| **Race** | | |
| No response | 14 | 2% |
| African Am/black | 27 | 4% |
| American Indian | 4 | 0.5% |
| Asian | 4 | 0.5% |
| Caucasian/white | 660 | 93% |
| **Employment status** | | |
| Employed full time (35 or more hours per week) | 411 | 58% |
| Employed part time (less than 34 hours per week) | 80 | 11% |
| Not in labor force | 140 | 20% |
| Unemployed (looking for work in past 30 days) | 78 | 11% |
| **Individual monthly income** | | |
| $0 | 146 | 21% |
| $1–$499 | 23 | 3% |
| $500–$1,000 | 84 | 12% |
| >$1,000 | 456 | 64% |
| **Bankruptcy** | | |
| Yes | 221 | 31% |
| No | 488 | 69% |
| **Total debt** | | |
| $0 | 56 | 8% |
| $1–$4,999 | 96 | 13% |
| $5000–$9,999 | 69 | 10% |
| $10,000–$19,999 | 90 | 13% |
| $20,000–$49,999 | 142 | 20% |
| $50,000–$99,999 | 103 | 14% |
| $100,000–$299,999 | 139 | 20% |
| ≥$300,000 | 14 | 2% |

SOURCE: Adapted from "Profile of Clients Admitted to IGTP Agencies in FY2006," in *Iowa Gambling Treatment Program Historical Summary*, Iowa Department of Public Health, June 2007, http://www.legis.state.ia.us/lsadocs/SC_MaterialsDist/2007/SDDPW000.PDF (accessed August 1, 2008)

**TABLE 6.7**

**Contacts with minors in casinos in Detroit, MI, by selected statistics, 2007**

| | MGM Grand 1/1/07– 12/31/07 | Motor City 1/1/07– 12/31/07 | Greektown 1/1/07– 12/31/07 | Totals |
|---|---|---|---|---|
| 1. The number of minors who were denied entry into the casino. | 685 | 4,861 | 792 | 6,338 |
| 2. The number of minors who were physically escorted from the casino premises. | 13 | 1 | 10 | 24 |
| 3. The number of minors who were detected participating in gambling games other than slot machines. | 1 | 1 | 2 | 4 |
| 4. The number of minors who were detected using slot machines. | 4 | 0 | 2 | 6 |
| 5. The number of minors who were taken into custody by a law enforcement agency on the casino premises. | 13 | 1 | 9 | 23 |
| 6. The number of minors who were detected illegally consuming alcohol on the casino premises. | 0 | 0 | 2 | 2 |

SOURCE: Adapted from "Casino Licensees' Reported Contacts with Minors on Licensed Casino Premises during Calendar Year 2007," in *Annual Report to the Governor, Calendar Year 2007*, Michigan Gaming Control Board, April 2008, http://www.michigan.gov/documents/mgcb/annrerp07_231975_7.pdf (accessed July 18, 2008)

said owners of gambling facilities should be held most responsible (39%), followed by gamblers themselves (24%) and the society at large (22%). When asked to rate the job that the casino gaming industry was doing in preventing underage gambling, a majority (65%) rated the casino industry as doing a fairly good or very good job. The reputation of the casino industry for doing a good job in preventing "underage use of their product" was considered superior to that of the gun (42%), alcohol (38%), and tobacco (30%) industries.

The Nevada Gaming Commission reports in *Nevada Gaming Control Act and Ancillary Statutes* (August 2008, http://www.gaming.nv.gov/stats_regs.htm) that as of January 2000, Regulation 14 banned slot machines with themes that were "derived from or based on a product that is currently and primarily intended or marketed for use by persons under 21 years of age."

The so-called slots-for-tots regulation is supposed to prevent the introduction of slot machines displaying cartoon characters that might appeal to children. The issue receives particular attention in Nevada because the state's casinos allow escorted children to walk through the casino. Most states prohibit the passage of minors through the gambling area.

The AGA lists in *Code of Conduct for Responsible Gaming* a number of rules that member casinos should follow to ensure that minors do not gamble in casinos. For example, they should not display cartoon figures, pictures of underage people, or pictures of collegiate sports athletes on the casino floor. They are also supposed to stop any minor from loitering on the casino floor, and casino employees are to be trained to deal with minors who attempt to buy alcohol or gamble.

Casinos seem to be successful in following the guidelines. For example, data compiled by the Michigan Gaming Control Board are shown in Table 6.7. A total of 6,338 minors tried to enter the three Detroit casinos in 2007, but were denied entry. Twenty-four minors were caught on casino premises and escorted out by casino personnel, and twenty-three other minors were taken into custody by law enforcement agencies.

## POLITICS

Gambling and politics have always been linked, largely because casinos and other gaming establishments are so heavily regulated, the number of licenses available is often limited, and so much money can be made by people who get those licenses. Lobbying (a common factor in the political system) can easily turn into influence peddling and bribery at all levels of government.

Some jurisdictions have become so concerned about the confluence of political pressure and money that they prohibit casino license applicants from making contributions to political candidates. Mississippi decided to prevent this temptation by setting no limit on the number of casinos that can be built. State officials claimed their policy would prevent the bribery, extortion, and favoritism that had plagued neighboring Louisiana, where the number of licenses available for riverboat casinos was set at fifteen. Those licenses were so highly prized that Governor Edwin Edwards (1927–) extorted $3 million from people who wanted them. In May 2000 he was convicted of racketeering, extortion, and fraud and sentenced to ten years in prison.

On the federal level, politics and gambling intersect on issues that affect more than one state or Native American tribe. At that intersection, some people see opportunities to make a lot of money. One such operator was Jack Abramoff (1958–), a prominent lobbyist in Washington, D.C., who pleaded guilty to fraud, tax evasion, and conspiracy to bribe public officials in January 2006. He was sentenced to five years and ten months in prison and ordered to pay $21 million in restitution.

Many credit Abramoff and his colleagues with securing the defeat of the Internet Gambling Prohibition Act of 1999. The bill was one of the first anti–Internet gambling bills proposed in Congress. It was passed in the U.S. Senate in 1999 and was put forth in the U.S. House of Representatives the following year. At the time, Abramoff was working for eLottery, an Internet site that wanted to sell state lottery tickets online. Their business was threatened by the legislation, so Abramoff sent money to conservative special interest groups to get them to pressure conservative House members to drop the bill because it contained exceptions for horse racing and jai alai. Through procedural maneuvering, a two-thirds majority was needed to pass the bill; it failed. When the bill's original supporters demanded that it be revived, Abramoff targeted ten Republican House members in vulnerable districts with media and direct-mail campaigns that accused them of being "soft on gambling" if they voted for the bill. The representatives received so much pressure from their constituents that the House Republican leadership, fearing the party might lose four seats in the 2000 election, decided not to bring the bill up for another vote.

Later in his career, Abramoff and his team defrauded Native American tribes out of millions of dollars. Typically, he promised that, as their lobbyist, he could secure funding from the government for special projects, such as wider roads or new schools, and that he could keep the government from interfering in their operations, including casinos. In return, the tribes paid his lobbying firm and a public relations company over $85 million.

In some instances, Abramoff worked against a tribe behind the scenes and then offered to help it out for huge sums of money. For example, in 2002 he and his colleagues were instrumental in shutting down the Speaking Rock Casino in El Paso, Texas. He then went to the Tigua Tribe, which operated the casino, and claimed that he and his colleagues could get Congress to reopen the casino. The tribe paid $4.2 million in lobbying fees, but the casino never reopened.

# CHAPTER 7
# LOTTERIES

A lottery is a game of chance in which people pay for the opportunity to win prizes. Part of the money taken in by a lottery is used to award the winners and to pay the costs of administering the lottery. The money left over is profit. Lotteries are extremely popular and legal in more than a hundred countries.

In the United States all lotteries are operated by state governments, which have granted themselves the sole right to do so. In other words, they are monopolies that do not allow any commercial lotteries to compete against them. The profits from U.S. lotteries are used solely to fund government programs. As of August 2008, lotteries operated in forty-two states and the District of Columbia. In addition, lottery tickets could be legally purchased by any adult physically present in a lottery state, even if that adult did not reside in the state.

According to the North American Association of State and Provincial Lotteries (NASPL), Americans wagered $57.4 billion in lotteries in fiscal year (FY) 2006. U.S. lottery sales were up from $52.6 billion in FY 2005, an increase of 9%.

## LOTTERY HISTORY
### Early History

The drawing of lots to determine ownership or other rights is recorded in many ancient documents. The practice became common in Europe in the late fifteenth and early sixteenth centuries. Lotteries were first tied directly to the United States in 1612, when King James I (1566–1625) of England created a lottery to provide funds to Jamestown, Virginia, the first permanent British settlement in North America. Lotteries were used by public and private organizations after that time to raise money for towns, wars, colleges, and public works projects.

An early American lottery, conducted by George Washington (1732–1799) in the 1760s, was designed to finance construction of the Mountain Road in Virginia. Benjamin Franklin (1706–1790) supported lotteries to pay for cannons during the American Revolution (1775–1783). John Hancock (1737–1793) ran a lottery to finance the rebuilding of Faneuil Hall in Boston. Lotteries fell into disfavor in the 1820s because of concerns that they were harmful to the public. New York was the first state to pass a constitutional prohibition against them.

### The Rise and Fall of Lotteries

The southern states relied on lotteries after the Civil War (1861–1865) to finance Reconstruction (1865–1877). The Louisiana lottery, in particular, became widely popular. According to the Louisiana Lottery Corporation, in "History of Lottery" (September 2008, http://www.louisianalottery.com/assets/docs/fact%20sheets/HistoryofLotteries.pdf), in 1868 the Louisiana Lottery Company was granted permission by the state legislature to operate as the state's only lottery provider. In exchange, the company agreed to pay $40,000 per year for twenty-five years to the Charity Hospital of New Orleans. The company was allowed to keep all other lottery revenues and to pay no taxes on those revenues. The Louisiana lottery was popular nationwide—93% of its revenue came from out of state. It was also extremely profitable, returning a 48% profit to its operators.

In 1890 Congress banned the mailing of lottery materials. The Louisiana lottery was abolished in 1894 after Congress passed a law against the transport of lottery tickets across state lines. Following its closure, the public learned that the lottery had been operated by a northern crime syndicate that regularly bribed legislators and committed widespread deception and fraud. The resulting scandal was huge and widely publicized. Public opinion turned against lotteries, and by the end of the nineteenth century they were outlawed across the country.

Negative attitudes about gambling began to soften during the early twentieth century, particularly after the failure of Prohibition (1920–1933). The state of Nevada legalized casino gambling in the 1930s, and gambling for charitable purposes became more commonplace across the country. Still, lingering fears about fraud kept public sentiment against lotteries for two more decades.

### Rebirth in the 1960s

In "History of the New Hampshire Lottery" (2008, http://www.nhlottery.org/AboutUs/History.aspx), the New Hampshire Lottery Commission notes that in 1963 the New Hampshire legislature authorized a sweepstakes to raise revenue. The state had no sales or state income tax at that time, and it desperately needed money for education programs. Patterned after the popular Irish Sweepstakes, the game was much different from the lotteries of the twenty-first century. Tickets were sold for $3, and drawings were held infrequently. The biggest prizes were tied to the outcomes of particular horse races at the Rockingham Park racetrack in Salem, New Hampshire. Nearly $5.7 million was wagered during the lottery's first year.

The New York Lottery states in "New York Lottery's Mission" (October 2, 2008, http://www.nylottery.org/ny/nyStore/cgi-bin/ProdSubEV_Cat_333652_NavRoot_305.htm) that New York introduced a lottery in 1967. It was particularly successful, grossing $53.6 million during its first year. It also enticed residents from neighboring states to cross state lines and buy tickets. Twelve other states established lotteries during the 1970s (Connecticut, Delaware, Illinois, Maine, Maryland, Massachusetts, Michigan, New Jersey, Ohio, Pennsylvania, Rhode Island, and Vermont). Analysts suggest that lotteries became so firmly entrenched throughout the Northeast for three reasons: each state needed to raise money for public projects without increasing taxes, each state had a large Catholic population that was generally tolerant of gambling, and history shows that states are most likely to start a lottery if one is already offered in a nearby state. For example, Ron Stodghill and Ron Nixon report in "For Schools, Lottery Payoffs Fall Short of Promises" (*New York Times*, October 7, 2007) that Michael F. Easley (1950–), the governor of North Carolina, said before his state established a lottery, "Our people are playing the lottery. We just need to decide which schools we should fund, other states' or ours."

During the 1980s lottery fever spread south and west. Seventeen states (Arizona, California, Colorado, Florida, Idaho, Indiana, Iowa, Kansas, Kentucky, Missouri, Montana, Oregon, South Dakota, Virginia, Washington, West Virginia, and Wisconsin) plus the District of Columbia started lotteries. Six more states (Georgia, Louisiana, Minnesota, Nebraska, New Mexico, and Texas) started lotteries during the 1990s. They were joined after 2000 by North Carolina, North Dakota, Oklahoma, South Car-

olina, and Tennessee. Most people approve of lotteries. More people approve of lotteries than actually buy tickets and participate, although the gap between approval and participation rates seems to be narrowing.

## LOTTERY GAMES

Early lottery games were simple raffles in which a person purchased a ticket preprinted with a number. The player might have had to wait for weeks for a drawing to determine if the ticket was a winner. These types of games, called passive drawing games, were the dominant lottery games in 1973. By 1997 they had ceased to exist, as consumers demanded more exciting games that provided quicker payoffs and more betting options.

Nearly all states that operate lotteries offer cash lotto and instant games. Players of lotto games select a group of numbers from a large set and are then awarded prizes based on how many picked numbers offer a second set of numbers chosen in a random drawing. Most lotto tickets sell for $1, and drawings are held once or twice per week to determine the winning numbers. Scratch-off instant games are paper tickets on which certain spaces have been coated with a scratch-off substance that when removed reveals numbers or text underneath that must match posted sequences to win.

Most states offer other numbers games, such as three- and four-digit games. Pull tabs, spiel, keno, and video lottery games are much less common. Pull tabs are two-ply paper tickets that must be separated to reveal symbols or numbers underneath that must match posted sequences to win. Spiel is an add-on feature to a lotto game that provides an extra set of numbers for a fee that must be matched to numbers selected in the random drawing to win. Keno is a lotto game in which a set of numbers is selected from a large field of numbers; players select a smaller set of numbers and are awarded prizes based on how many of their numbers match those in the drawn set. Video lottery terminals are electronic games of chance played on video screens that simulate popular casino games such as poker and blackjack. Keno and video lottery games are considered by many to be casino-type games, especially because they can be played every few minutes (in the case of fast keno) or at will (in the case of video lottery terminals), which makes them more controversial and generally less acceptable than more traditional lottery games.

As of 2008, many lottery games were conducted using computer networks. Retail outlets have computer terminals that are linked by phone lines to a central computer at the lottery commission, which records wagers as they are made. The computer network is a private, dedicated network that can be accessed only by lottery officials and retailers. Players can either choose their numbers themselves or allow the computer to select numbers randomly, an option known as Quick Pick. The computer link allows retailers to validate winning tickets.

Most lotto drawings are televised live. Some states also air lottery game shows in which contestants compete for money and prizes. For instance, *The Big Spin*, the California State Lottery's thirty-minute game show, has been broadcast since 1985. Contestants, who are chosen through lottery drawings or special promotions, spin a big wheel to win cash prizes in front of a cheering audience.

Lottery winners generally have six months to one year to collect their prizes, depending on state rules. If the top prize, usually called the jackpot, is not won, the amount of the jackpot usually rolls over to the next drawing, increasing the jackpot. Lotteries are often most popular when the jackpot has rolled over several times and grown to an unusually large amount.

Most states allow players to choose in advance how a jackpot will be paid to them—either all at once (the cash lump-sum prize) or in installments (an annuity, usually paid out over twenty or twenty-five years). Either way, in most states taxes are subtracted from the prize.

## Scratch Games

In 1974 Massachusetts became the first state to offer an instant lottery game using scratch-off tickets. By 2008 games involving scratch tickets (or "scratchers," as they are called in some states) were extremely popular. Lottery organizations offer many different scratch games with various themes.

Scratch games run for a specified period, usually for several months to a year. Many scratch tickets allow a player to win multiple times on each ticket. The top prize amounts are often hundreds of thousands of dollars. However, some of the games offer prizes besides money, including merchandise, trips, vehicles, and tickets to sporting events and concerts. For example, in 2006 a Missouri scratch game gave away a seat at a table at the World Poker Tour tournament. The total winnings for such prizes often include payment by the lottery commission of federal and state income taxes on the value of the prizes.

Many lotteries have teamed with sports franchises and other companies to provide popular products as prizes. For example, in June 2008 the New Jersey Lottery Commission announced a scratch game in which a Harley-Davidson motorcycle was the top prize. Many brand-name promotions feature famous celebrities, sports figures and teams, or cartoon characters. These merchandising deals benefit the companies through product exposure and advertising; the lotteries benefit because the companies share advertising costs.

In 2008 most states offered "high-profit point tickets"—scratch tickets priced as high as $30, which are often part of a holiday or themed promotion. (Traditional scratch tickets sell for $1 to $5.) The higher-priced tickets appeal to many scratch players because they offer more valuable prizes and payouts than regular-priced tickets. However, in "'Zero' Chance Lottery Tickets Stun Some Players" (CNN.com, July 7, 2008), Jason Carroll and Susan Chun report that in 2008 state lotteries came under fire for continuing to sell the high-priced scratch-off tickets even after the top prize had been won. In fact, Scott Hoover of Washington and Lee University sued the state of Virginia for a breach of contract after he bought a scratch-off ticket called "Beginner's Luck" and later learned the top prizes had already been won.

Most lotteries operate toll-free numbers or Web sites that provide information on scratch-game prizes. Patrons can find out which prizes have been awarded and which remain to be claimed.

## Second-Chance Games

Sometimes even nonwinning lottery tickets have value. Most state lotteries run occasional second-chance drawings—and even third-chance drawings—in which holders of nonwinning tickets for particular games can still win cash or prizes. For example, the New York Lottery held a second-chance drawing during the summer of 2006 in which holders of nonwinning Subway Series scratch tickets could win Mets and New York Yankees tickets and merchandise. The grand prize winner in Florida's $100,000 Hold 'Em Poker second-chance drawing in December 2007 won a seat at a World Poker Tour tournament with a buy-in of $10,000, a week's accommodation at the tournament site, additional spending money, and tickets to the tournament finals. Winners of quarterly second-chance drawings in Nevada may be awarded either $2,500 in cash or thirty $10 scratch-off tickets.

## Video Lottery Games

Video lottery games are highly profitable computer games that are played on video lottery terminals (VLTs). They are monitored and controlled by a central computer system overseen by a state's lottery agency. VLTs were operated in nine states in 2008: Delaware, Louisiana, Montana, New Mexico, New York, Oregon, Rhode Island, South Dakota, and West Virginia. Three of these states, Rhode Island, Delaware, and West Virginia, launched the first multistate, progressive video lottery game in 2006 (a progressive jackpot is one that increases with each game played). Known as Ca$hola, the game begins with a $250,000 jackpot.

VLTs in Louisiana, Montana, and South Dakota are owned by private entities. Those in Rhode Island are leased by the state to private operators. VLTs in the other states are owned by state lottery commissions. In Delaware, New York, and Rhode Island, VLTs are only allowed at racetracks. Except in New York, profits from the VLTs are split between the racetracks and the state lotteries. The VLTs in New York were challenged in court because the state's constitution requires that lottery proceeds benefit education programs. Some VLT revenue was going to racetracks, so the courts declared the diversion of lottery revenue unconstitutional. In 2005 the state legislature amended the law. Under the new legislation the money for the racetrack owners comes out of the state's general fund and all the money gathered from the VLTs goes to education.

In Iowa, VLTs were introduced in 2003, and eventually nearly six thousand VLTs were bringing in over $1.1 billion in revenue. However, according to the Cedar Rapids *Gazette Online* (July 15, 2006), calls to the state's hotline for gambling problems rose 17% in 2005, largely because of VLTs, and the state legislature shut down the VLT program in May 2006.

Video lottery games have become controversial because many people consider them hard-core gambling. They allow continuous gambling for large sums of money, as opposed to lotto play, which features drawings only once or twice a week. Opponents of video lottery games contend that they are much more addictive than traditional lottery games because of their availability and instant payoffs. They also contend that the games have a special appeal to young people, who are accustomed to playing video games.

### Multistate Games

POWERBALL. During the 1980s lottery officials realized that multistate lotteries could offer higher payoffs than single-state lotteries because the costs of running one game could be shared. The Multi-State Lottery Association (MUSL) was formed in 1987 as a nonprofit association of states offering lotteries. It administers a variety of games, the best known of which is Powerball. In this lotto game each ticket has six numbers: five numbers are selected out of fifty-five numbers, and then a separate number, the Powerball, is selected out of forty-two numbers. The odds of winning the jackpot are about 146 million to 1. Drawings have been held twice weekly since the first drawing on April 22, 1992. The largest jackpot ever paid out, in February 2006, was $365 million. It was split evenly among eight coworkers in Lincoln, Nebraska.

As of August 2008, MUSL (http://www.musl.com/musl_members.html) had thirty-one members. Each member state offered at least one MUSL game, and twenty-nine member states, the District of Columbia, and the U.S. Virgin Islands offered the Powerball. Each member keeps 50% of its own Powerball ticket sales; the rest is paid out in prizes.

MEGA MILLIONS. Mega Millions is a popular multistate game that is offered in twelve states. Players choose six numbers from two separate number pools: five numbers from 1 to 56, and one number from 1 to 46. All six numbers must be chosen in the drawing to win the jackpot. The odds of winning the jackpot are about 175 million to 1. Drawings are held twice weekly.

Mega Millions was originally known as the Big Game. The first Big Game drawing took place on September 6, 1996. It became popular and soon offered jackpots of more than $50 million. Its largest jackpot was won in May 2000—two winners, one in Michigan and one in Illinois, split $363 million.

However, Big Game sales lagged during FY 2001, so game operators renamed it Mega Millions and increased the initial jackpot to $10 million, twice what it had been for the Big Game. Ticket sales increased dramatically. In 2005 the minimum jackpot was raised to $12 million when California joined the lottery. The biggest Mega Millions jackpot was in March 2007—$390 million was split between a couple in Woodbine, New Jersey, and another person in Dalton, Georgia.

## HOW LOTTERIES OPERATE

In 2008 most lotteries were administered directly by state lottery boards or commissions. The lotteries in Connecticut, Georgia, Kentucky, Louisiana, and Tennessee were operated by quasi-governmental or privatized lottery corporations. In most states enforcement authority regarding fraud and abuse rested with the attorney general's office, state police, or the lottery commission. The amount of oversight and control that each legislature has over its lottery agency differs from state to state.

Even though lotteries are a multimillion-dollar business, lottery commissions employ only a few thousand people nationwide. Lottery commissions set up, monitor, and run the games offered in their states, but the vast majority of lottery sales are by retail outlets that contract to sell the games.

### Retailers

According to the NASPL (2008, http://www.naspl .org/index.cfm?fuseaction=content&PageID=9&Page Category=31), over 191,000 retailers sold lottery tickets in the country in 2008. California had the most retailers (19,000), followed by Texas (16,281) and New York (15,900). Half of all lottery retailers were convenience stores. Other outlets included various kinds of stores, nonprofit organizations (churches and fraternal organizations), service stations, restaurants and bars, bowling alleys, and newsstands.

Retailers get commissions on lottery sales and bonuses when they sell winning tickets. They also get increased store traffic and media attention, especially if they become known as "lucky" places to purchase lottery tickets. Some state lottery Web sites list the stores where winners purchased their tickets. For example, in "Lucky Retailers" (April 6, 2006, http://www.calottery.com/SecondaryNav/RetailLocations/LuckyRetailers/), the California State Lottery notes that one retailer in Port Hueneme, California, sold six winning million-dollar-plus tickets between 1987 and 1994.

Lottery tickets are often impulse purchases, so retailers sell them near the checkout. This also allows store operators to keep an eye on ticket vending machines to prevent play by underage customers. Because convenience stores increasingly offer pay-at-the-pump gasoline sales—transactions that are likely to decrease in-store traffic—lottery officials in Minnesota and several other states are contemplating ways to sell and print tickets at the gas pumps. In fact, a patent (U.S. Patent 6364206, http://www.patentstorm.us/patents/6364206.html) was issued in 2002 that would enable lottery ticket transactions at gas pumps. In 2008 the New Jersey Lottery Commission was considering selling lottery tickets in mass-merchandise stores, such as Target and Home Depot.

## LOTTERY PLAYER DEMOGRAPHICS

Jeffrey M. Jones of the Gallup Organization states in *One in Six Americans Gamble on Sports* (February 1, 2008, http://www.gallup.com/poll/104086/One-Six-Americans-Gamble-Sports.aspx) that in 2008, 46% of adults had purchased a lottery ticket within the previous year. Many state lottery commissions conduct demographic studies to get a better picture of lottery players, largely because they want to better target them in marketing campaigns. The findings in two states provide some insight into lottery players.

### Texas

In *Demographic Survey of Texas Lottery Players 2007* (December 5, 2007, http://www.uh.edu/cpp/txlottery.pdf), the University of Houston's Center for Public Policy states that only 38% of Texans played the lottery in 2007, which was the lowest level since the lottery began in 1992. (See Figure 7.1.) People with an income of $75,000 to $100,000 were the most likely to play (50%), whereas people with an income of less than $12,000 were the least likely to play (28.6%). (See Table 7.1.) Men were more likely than women to play the lottery (41.5% and 36.1%, respectively). Older people were more likely than younger people to play the lottery, and people who were employed at least part time (45.2%) were more likely than retired people (33.2%) or unemployed people (17.1%) to play the lottery. These figures suggest that a worsening economy may be partially responsible for the drop in lottery players in 2007.

The amount of money various demographic groups spent on the lottery differed greatly, however. Young people, Native Americans, males, and individuals with

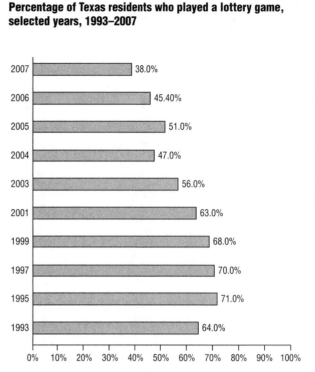

**FIGURE 7.1**

**Percentage of Texas residents who played a lottery game, selected years, 1993–2007**

| Year | Percentage |
|------|-----------|
| 2007 | 38.0% |
| 2006 | 45.40% |
| 2005 | 51.0% |
| 2004 | 47.0% |
| 2003 | 56.0% |
| 2001 | 63.0% |
| 1999 | 68.0% |
| 1997 | 70.0% |
| 1995 | 71.0% |
| 1993 | 64.0% |

SOURCE: "Figure 1. Percentage of Respondents Playing Any Lottery Game," in *Demographic Survey of Texas Lottery Players 2007*, University of Houston, Center for Public Policy, December 2007, http://www.uh.edu/cpp/txlottery.pdf (accessed July 18, 2008). Data from 2007 University of Houston Center for Public Policy (CPP) survey data, 2006 University of North Texas survey reports and survey reports from 1993–2005.

less education were likely to spend the most on the lottery. (See Table 7.1.) The most popular game was Lotto Texas; about 85% of people who played lottery games played Lotto Texas, and over one-third (34.6%) of those purchased tickets at least once a week. Individuals spent the most money on scratch games, with the average player spending $33.27 per month on such games.

### South Carolina

According to the South Carolina Education Lottery, in *Player Profile Study 2006* (September 2006, http://www.statelibrary.sc.gov/scedocs/L917/000391.ppt), 54% of those polled had played the South Carolina lottery in 2006. About 51% of females surveyed had played the lottery, as opposed to 49% of males. A higher percentage of African-Americans (62%) had played the lottery than whites (50%). Of all age groups, a higher percentage of people between thirty-five and fifty-four had played the lottery (58%) than any other age group.

Seventeen percent of players said they played the lottery more than once a week ("frequent players"), 13% said they played about once a week ("regular players"), and the rest said they played one to three times a month ("occasional players") or less ("infrequent players").

TABLE 7.1

**Percentage of Texas residents who played a lottery game in the past year by demographic characteristics and median dollars spent per month, 2007**

| Demographic factors | Percentage played | Median dollars spent |
|---|---|---|
| **Education** | | |
| Less than high school diploma | 27.3 | 61.00 |
| High school degree | 36.5 | 15.00 |
| Some college | 45.7 | 15.00 |
| College degree | 41.1 | 8.00 |
| Graduate degree | 32.1 | 5.00 |
| **Income** | | |
| Under $12,000 | 28.6 | 9.50 |
| $12,000 to $19,999 | 33.1 | 10.00 |
| $20,000 to $29,999 | 38.9 | 20.00 |
| $30,000 to $39,999 | 40.1 | 16.00 |
| $40,000 to $49,999 | 36.8 | 22.00 |
| $50,000 to $59,999 | 43.1 | 10.00 |
| $60,000 to $74,999 | 43.5 | 13.00 |
| $75,000 to $100,000 | 50.0 | 5.00 |
| Over $100,000 | 43.1 | 9.50 |
| **Race** | | |
| White | 37.9 | 10.00 |
| Black | 39.8 | 20.00 |
| Asian | 37.0 | 22.00 |
| Native American Indian | 41.2 | 49.00 |
| Other | 40.1 | 15.00 |
| **Hispanic origin** | | |
| Yes | 39.0 | 17.00 |
| No | 38.2 | 10.00 |
| **Gender** | | |
| Female | 36.1 | 10.00 |
| Male | 41.5 | 13.00 |
| **Age** | | |
| 18 to 24 | 17.0 | 12.00 |
| 25 to 34 | 35.7 | 27.00 |
| 35 to 44 | 41.7 | 10.00 |
| 45 to 54 | 46.2 | 12.00 |
| 55 to 64 | 46.4 | 9.00 |
| 65 or older | 32.2 | 12.00 |
| **Employment status** | | |
| Employed full/part time | 45.2 | 10.00 |
| Unemployed | 17.1 | 16.50 |
| Retired | 33.2 | 12.00 |

SOURCE: "Table 2. Any Game: Past-Year Lottery Play and Median Dollars Spent per Month by Demographics," in *Demographic Survey of Texas Lottery Players 2007*, University of Houston, Center for Public Policy, December 2007, http://www.uh.edu/cpp/txlottery.pdf (accessed July 18, 2008)

In South Carolina, high-school educated, middle-aged men in the middle of the economic spectrum were more likely to be "frequent players" than any other demographic group.

The South Carolina survey also reported where and when South Carolinians purchased their tickets. In 2006 people usually purchased tickets at a gas station or convenience store that sells gas (91%), as opposed to a grocery store (12%) and a convenience store without gas (8%). Most players purchased their tickets on the weekdays (44%), versus the weekend (32%), or both (18%). Sixty percent claimed to purchase their tickets after four in the afternoon. The most popular game was Powerball, which was played by 43% of those polled. Scratch tickets came in a close second (41%).

## GROUP PLAY

Groups of people frequently pool their money and buy lottery tickets, particularly for large jackpots. Group wins are beneficial to the lotteries because they generate more media coverage than solo wins and expose a wider group of friends, relatives, and coworkers to the idea that lotteries are winnable. However, pooling arrangements, even those between only two people, can lead to disagreements if a group actually wins a jackpot. Several such groups have ended up in court, but given the number of winners every year, such cases are relatively rare.

Some states have formalized group play. For example, the California State Lottery started the Jackpot Captain program in 2001 to help "group leaders" manage lotto pools. Lotto captains have access to a special Web site that gives them tips on organizing and running group play. They can download and print forms that help them track players, games, dates, and jackpots. As an incentive, lotto captains can participate in special drawings for cash and prizes. According to state lottery officials, far more people enrolled to be captains than was expected. The lottery described them as hard-core players who promote lottery games, recruit new players, and provide valuable feedback about lottery promotions. The most recent captains program was rolled out by Rhode Island in April 2008. The state began offering the PowerBall Group Play Program that allows group play captains access to a special group play page and a group play tool kit.

## WHY DO PEOPLE PLAY LOTTERIES?

A lottery is a unique gambling event because it costs only a small amount of money for a chance to win a large jackpot. Even though the odds are extremely long, the huge jackpot is the main selling feature. Rollover jackpots spur ticket sales. As more people buy tickets, the jackpot grows, whereas the odds of winning decrease. However, this does not deter people from buying tickets—sales actually increase under these circumstances.

Mark D. Griffiths and Richard T. A. Wood of Nottingham Trent University examine in *Lottery Gambling and Addiction: An Overview of European Research* (1999, https://www.european-lotteries.org/data/info_130/Wood.pdf) why people continue to play the lottery despite the long odds. Among the most common reasons are the lure of a large jackpot in exchange for a small investment; successful advertising; publicity about jackpot winners; ignorance of probability theory; televised drawings; overestimating the positive outcomes and underestimating the negative ones; the credibility of government backing; and players' belief in their own luck. However, perhaps the most important finding by Griffiths and Wood concerns the role of entrapment. According to the researchers, many people select the same numbers week after week. As time goes by and their numbers are not selected, they do not become discouraged. Instead, they think their chances of winning are getting better. Often, players experience near misses, in which two or more of their numbers come up in the jackpot drawing. This only convinces them that they are getting closer to the big win. They become increasingly entrapped in playing their numbers and fear skipping even one drawing. According to Wood and Griffiths, this mindset has its roots in a common myth that the probability of winning increases the longer a losing streak lasts.

Emily Haisley, Romel Mostafa, and George Loewenstein of Carnegie Mellon University find in "Subjective Relative Income and Lottery Ticket Purchases" (*Journal of Behavioral Decision Making*, vol. 21, no. 3, July 2008) that people who perceive themselves as poor are more likely to buy lottery tickets and are more likely to buy more lottery tickets than people who do not perceive themselves as poor. The researchers find that buying lottery tickets sets up a vicious cycle for poor people: it exploits individuals' desires to escape poverty, but it also contributes to their inability to improve their financial situation.

## THE EFFECTS OF LOTTERIES
### Economic Effects

Proponents of lotteries usually use economic arguments to justify their position. They point out that lotteries provide state governments with a relatively easy way to increase their revenues without imposing more taxes. The games are financially beneficial to the many small businesses that sell lottery tickets and to larger companies that participate in merchandising campaigns or provide advertising or computer services. In addition, lottery advocates surmise, the games provide cheap entertainment to people who want to play, while raising money for the betterment of all.

Lottery opponents also have economic arguments. They contend that lotteries contribute only a small percentage of total state revenues and, therefore, have a limited effect on state programs. Lotteries cost money to operate and lure people into parting with their money under false hopes. In addition, opponents contend that those targeted by lotteries come particularly from lower income brackets and may not be able to afford to gamble.

THE DIVISION OF LOTTERY MONEY. The sales amount is the total amount taken in by the lottery. This sales amount is then split between prizes, administrative costs, retailer commissions, and state profits. In general, 50% to 60% of U.S. lottery sales are paid out as prizes to winners. Administrative costs for advertising, employee salaries, and other operating expenses usually account for 1% to 10% of sales. On average, retailers collect 5% to 8% of sales in the form of commissions and approxi-

mately 2% as bonuses for selling winning tickets. The remaining 30% to 40% is profit turned over to the state.

According to the NASPL, U.S. state lotteries had approximately $57.4 billion in sales for FY 2006. National sales were up 9% over the previous fiscal year's sales of $52.6 billion. Every state reported sales were higher in 2006 than in 2005.

The NASPL's data show that during FY 2006 New York ($6.8 billion) had the highest lottery sales, followed by Massachusetts ($4.5 billion) and Florida ($4 billion). These three states accounted for 27% of national lottery sales. Seventeen states had lottery sales of more than $1 billion during FY 2006.

The states took in $17.1 billion in profits from the lottery in FY 2006. The states allocate their lottery profits in different ways. Table 7.2 shows each state's cumulative allocation of profits from each lottery's inception to June 2006. A total of $234.1 billion has been given to various beneficiaries since the beginning of lotteries in each state. New York topped the list with $30 billion in profits allocated to education since 1967. California followed with $18.5 billion to education, and New Jersey, $15.6 billion.

RETAILER PAYMENTS. According to the U.S. Census Bureau (March 17, 2008, http://www.census.gov/compendia/statab/cats/state_local_govt_finances_employment.html), $27.7 billion was given out as prizes in state lotteries in 2004. That was 61% of the total lottery revenue in that year. Administrative costs, including retailer compensation, made up approximately $2.7 billion (6%) of total revenue, whereas average state profit was $15 billion (33%).

The primary means of retailer compensation is a commission on each ticket sold. In other words, a lottery retailer keeps a certain percentage of the money taken in from lottery sales. Most states also have incentive-based programs for retailers that meet particular sales criteria. For example, the Wisconsin lottery pays retailers a bonus for increasing ticket sales by particular amounts. Lottery officials believe the incentive program, which encourages retailers to ask customers if they would like to buy lottery tickets, is more effective than an increase in commission. Retailers that sell a winning ticket of $600 or more in Wisconsin receive 2% of the value of the ticket (up to $100,000).

UNCLAIMED LOTTERY WINNINGS. Unclaimed lottery winnings add up to hundreds of millions of dollars each year, and each state handles them differently. Some states, such as New York, require that unclaimed winnings be returned to the prize pool. Other states allocate such funds to lottery administrative costs or to specific state programs. For example, in Texas unclaimed prizes go to funds that benefit hospital research and payment of indigent health

**TABLE 7.2**

## Cumulative lottery contributions to beneficiaries, by state, from start to June 30, 2006

[In millions]

**Arizona (1982)**

| | |
|---|---|
| Local transportation assistance fund | $558.00 |
| County assistance fund | $152.64 |
| Heritage fund | $298.53 |
| Economic development fund | $50.16 |
| Mass transit | $62.35 |
| Healthy Arizona | $40.65 |
| General fund (by category) | |
|     Education | $445.64 |
|     Health and welfare | $178.27 |
|     Protection and safety | $82.12 |
|     General government | $46.13 |
|     Inspection and regulation | $7.79 |
|     Natural resources | $6.82 |
| Department of Gaming (responsible gaming support) | $0.60 |
| Court appointed special advocate fund (unclaimed prizes) | $28.76 |
| Clean air fund (unclaimed prizes) | $0.50 |
| State general fund (unclaimed prizes) | $1.50 |
| | **$1,960.46** |

**California (1985)**

| | |
|---|---|
| Education | **$18,457.56** |

**Colorado (1983)**

| | |
|---|---|
| Capital Construction Fund | $439.80 |
| Division of Parks and Outdoor Recreation | $161.50 |
| Conservation Trust Fund | $646.30 |
| Great Outdoors Colorado Trust Fund | $461.60 |
| General Fund | $1.30 |
| School Fund | $28.90 |
| | **$1,739.40** |

**Connecticut (1972)**

| | |
|---|---|
| General Fund (to benefit education, roads, health and hospitals, public safety, etc.) | **$5,847.68** |

**D.C. (1982)**

| | |
|---|---|
| General Fund | **$1,340.00** |

**Delaware (1975)**

| | |
|---|---|
| General Fund | $2,321.50 |
| Health & Social Services—Problem Gambler Programs | $13.18 |
| | **$2,334.68** |

**Florida (1987)**

| | |
|---|---|
| Education Enhancement Trust Fund | **$15,203.00** |

**Georgia (1993)**

| | |
|---|---|
| HOPE scholarships | $3,580.43 |
| Pre-kindergarten program | $2,695.86 |
| Capital outlay and technology for primary and secondary schools | $1,800.00 |
| | **$8,076.29** |

**Idaho (1989)**

| | |
|---|---|
| Public schools (K–12) | $150.28 |
| Public buildings | $150.28 |
| | **$300.56** |

**Illinois (1974)**

| | |
|---|---|
| Illinois common school fund (K–12) | **$12,896.00** |

**Indiana (1989)**

| | |
|---|---|
| Build Indiana fund | $1,920.40 |
| Teachers' retirement fund | $462.60 |
| Police & fire pension relief fund | $276.30 |
| Help America Vote Act | $1.80 |
| | **$2,661.10** |

**TABLE 7.2**

## Cumulative lottery contributions to beneficiaries, by state, from start to June 30, 2006 [CONTINUED]

[In millions]

**Iowa (1985)**

| | |
|---|---|
| Iowa plan (economic development) | $170.32 |
| CLEAN fund (environment and agriculture) | $35.89 |
| Gambler's Treatment Program | $12.08 |
| Special appropriations | $13.77 |
| Sales tax | $135.98 |
| General fund | $647.23 |
| | **$1,015.27** |

**Kansas (1989)**

| | |
|---|---|
| Economic development initiatives fund | $6464.99 |
| Correctional instititions building fund | $76.28 |
| County reappraisal project (fiscal year 88–90) | $17.20 |
| Juvenile detention facilities fund | $25.19 |
| State general fund (fiscal year 1995–2004) | $121.19 |
| Problem gambling grant fund | $0.48 |
| | **$888.13** |

**Kentucky (1989)**

| | |
|---|---|
| Education | $214.00 |
| Vietnam Veterans | $32.00 |
| General fund | $1,387.60 |
| Post-secondary & college scholarships | $609.60 |
| Affordable housing & trust fund | $20.80 |
| Literacy programs & early childhood reading | $18.00 |
| | **$2,282.00** |

**Louisiana (1991)**

| | |
|---|---|
| Various state agencies | $147.30 |
| State general fund | $69.20 |
| Minimum foundation program—funding elementary & secondary education in public schools | $1,512.25 |
| Problem gambling | $5.50 |
| | **$1,734.25** |

**Maine (1974)**

| | |
|---|---|
| General fund | $732.00 |
| Outdoor heritage fund | $11.91 |
| | **$743.91** |

**Maryland (1973)**

| | |
|---|---|
| General fund | $9,270.87 |
| Subdivisions (for one year only fiscal year '84–85) | $31.25 |
| Stadium Authority | $442.63 |
| | **$9,744.75** |

**Massachusetts (1972)**

| | |
|---|---|
| Cities and towns | $12,028.14 |
| Arts Council | $189.90 |
| General fund | $2,991.44 |
| Compulsive gamblers | $10.46 |
| | **$15,219.94** |

**Michigan (1972)**

| | |
|---|---|
| Education (K–12) | **$12,916.63** |

**Minnesota (1989)**

| | |
|---|---|
| General fund | $866.49 |
| Environmental and natural resources trust fund | $381.40 |
| Game & fish fund | $61.47 |
| Natural resources fund | $61.47 |
| Other state programs | $36.70 |
| Compulsive gambling | $20.50 |
| | **$1,428.03** |

**Missouri (1986)**

| | |
|---|---|
| Public education | $1,915.34 |
| General revenue fund (1986–1993) | $542.54 |
| | **$2,457.88** |

**Montana (1987)**

| | |
|---|---|
| Property tax relief | $15.34 |
| Elementary and secondary schools | $34.09 |
| Juvenile detention | $2.53 |
| General fund | $78.20 |
| Study of socioeconomic impact on gambling | $0.10 |
| | **$130.26** |

**Nebraska (1993)**

| | |
|---|---|
| Compulsive gamblers assistance fund | $5.51 |
| Education innovation fund | $106.37 |
| Environmental trust fund | $103.81 |
| Solid waste landfill closure assistance fund | $18.46 |
| General fund | $5.00 |
| State fair support & improvement fund | $3.79 |
| Nebraska scholarship fund | $15.90 |
| | **$258.84** |

**New Hampshire (1964)**

| | |
|---|---|
| Education | **$1,080.10** |

**New Jersey (1970)**

| | |
|---|---|
| Education and institutions | **$15,571.20** |

**New Mexico (1996)**

| | |
|---|---|
| Public school capital outlay | $66.55 |
| Lottery tuition fund | $217.24 |
| | **$283.79** |

**New York (1967)**

| | |
|---|---|
| Education | **$30,000.00** |

**North Dakota (2004)**

| | |
|---|---|
| Compulsive gambling fund | $0.40 |
| State general fund | $7.27 |
| | **$7.67** |

**Ohio (1974)**

| | |
|---|---|
| Education | **$14,300.00** |

**Oklahoma(2005)**

| | |
|---|---|
| Education | **$68.95** |

**Oregon (1985)**

| | |
|---|---|
| Economic development | $1,570.00 |
| Public education | $2,715.00 |
| Natural resource programs | $367.00 |
| | **$4,652.00** |

**Pennsylvania (1972)**

| | |
|---|---|
| Older Pennsylvanians | **$15,500.00** |

**Rhode Island (1974)**

| | |
|---|---|
| General fund | **$2,600.00** |

**South Carolina (2002)**

| | |
|---|---|
| Education lottery fund | **$1,190.41** |

**South Dakota (1989)**

| | |
|---|---|
| General fund | $376.35 |
| Capital construction fund | $20.98 |
| Property tax reduction fund | $1,044.97 |
| Grant to human services | $1.92 |
| | **$1,444.22** |

**Tennessee (2004)**

| | |
|---|---|
| Lottery for education account | $620.56 |
| After school program | $16.32 |
| | **$636.88** |

**TABLE 7.2**

**Cumulative lottery contributions to beneficiaries, by state, from start to June 30, 2006** [CONTINUED]

[In millions]

**Texas (1992)**

| | |
|---|---|
| General revenue fund | $4,997.82 |
| Foundation school fund | $7,629.34 |
| Multicategorical teaching hospital | $100.00 |
| Tertiary care facility account | $131.07 |
| Health and Human Services Commission's Graduate Medical Program | $40.00 |
| | **$12,898.23** |

**Vermont (1978)**

| | |
|---|---|
| General fund | $212.46 |
| Education fund | $128.70 |
| | **$341.16** |

**Virginia (1988)**

| | |
|---|---|
| General fund (fiscal year 1989–1998) | $2,788.42 |
| Direct aid to public education K–12 (fiscal year 1999–present) | $3,003.89 |
| Literary fund (primarily for school construction additions and renovations) | $155.63 |
| Debt set-off collection | $13.10 |
| | **$5,961.04** |

**Washington (1982)**

| | |
|---|---|
| General fund | $1,836.13 |
| Education funds | $476.22 |
| Seattle Mariners Stadium (Safeco Field) | $42.43 |
| King County Stadium and Exhibition Center (Qwest Field) | $42.43 |
| Economic devel. strategic reserve | $2.53 |
| Problem gambling | $0.18 |
| | **$2,399.92** |

**West Virginia (1986)**

| | |
|---|---|
| Education | $903.12 |
| Senior citizens | $366.99 |
| Tourism | $346.08 |
| Bonds covering profit areas | $0.00 |
| General fund | $535.64 |
| Other | $1,079.37 |
| | **$3,231.20** |

**Wisconsin (1988)**

| | |
|---|---|
| Public benefit such as property tax relief | **$2,368.00** |
| **Total—US** | **$234,089.26** |

**Atlantic lottery (1976)**

| | |
|---|---|
| Lotteries Commission of New Brunswick | $1,468.82 |
| Provinces of Newfoundland and Labrador | $1,359.71 |
| Nova Scotia Gaming Corporation | $2,074.27 |
| Prince Edward Island Lotteries Commission | $234.36 |
| | **$5,137.16** |

**British Columbia (1974)**

| | |
|---|---|
| Government of British Columbia | **$8,287.50** |

**Loto-Québec (1970)**

| | |
|---|---|
| Consolidated fund | $20,387.00 |
| Government of Canada | $337.21 |
| Special commissions to non-profit organizations | $81.04 |
| Independent community action support fund | $167.41 |
| Agricultural Ministry | $41.80 |
| Ministry of Industry, Commerce, Science and Technology | $33.60 |
| Culture & Communication Ministry | $3.00 |
| Municipal affairs | $2.60 |
| Social Services Ministry | $249.00 |
| | **$21,302.66** |

**Ontario (1975)**

| | |
|---|---|
| Province of Ontario | **$24,900.00** |

**Western Canada (1974)**

| | |
|---|---|
| Member provinces and associate territories | **$5,318.00** |
| **Total—Canada** | **$64,945.32** |

## TABLE 7.2

**Cumulative lottery contributions to beneficiaries, by state, from start to June 30, 2006** [CONTINUED]

[In millions]

**Puerto Rico (1991)**

| | |
|---|---|
| Contingency fund to subsidize rent for elders economically disadvantaged | $36.00 |
| Municipality fund | $409.00 |
| Public health reform | $54.60 |
| General fund | $951.70 |
| | **$1,451.30** |

**Mexico (1991)**

| | |
|---|---|
| Education & health programs | $9.40 |

SOURCE: "Chart 21–06. Cumulative Lottery Contributions to Beneficiaries," North American Association of State and Provincial Lotteries, 2008, http://www.naspl.org/UploadedFiles/File/Cumulative_Lottery_Contributions06.pdf (accessed August 8, 2008)

---

care. The California State Lottery (November 22, 2005, http://www.calottery.com/Media/Education/Unclaimed/) turns the money over to educational programs—more than $580 million between 1985 and 2007.

**TAXES AND OTHER WITHHOLDING FROM LOTTERY WINNINGS.** Lottery winnings are usually taxable as personal income. All prizes greater than $600 are reported by the lotteries to the Internal Revenue Service. In general, the lottery agencies subtract taxes before awarding large prizes. For example, the New York Lottery in 2008 withheld federal, state, and local income taxes on prizes greater than $5,000. The lottery withheld 25% for federal taxes and 6.85% for state taxes. An additional 3.65% was withheld if the winner was a New York City resident. Non-U.S. residents faced even higher tax withholding rates. In addition, the New York Lottery is required by law to subtract past-due child support payments and collect repayment of public assistance from prizes of $600 or more.

### Education

Lottery proponents often advocate lotteries for their economic benefits to education. Some lotteries dedicate all or a portion of their profits toward K–12 or higher education. However, opponents often argue that these profits do not provide additional dollars for education but simply replace general fund dollars that would have been spent on education anyway.

Donald E. Miller of Saint Mary's College argues in "Schools Lose out in Lotteries" (*USA Today*, April 14, 2004) that educational spending per student gradually decreases once a state starts a lottery. He examined data for twelve states that had enacted lotteries for education between 1965 and 1990. According to Miller, before lotteries were set up average education spending in those states increased each year by approximately $12 per student. In the years immediately following the initiation of the lotteries, the states increased their education spend-

ing on average by nearly $50 per student. However, the increase fell sharply in following years and eventually lagged behind states without lottery-generated education funds. Miller suggests that legislators use lottery funds "to replace rather than add to existing sources of education funding."

Stodghill and Nixon note that in 2006 only 1% to 5% of public education money came from lotteries. Most of the money raised by lotteries is spent on marketing, prizes, and retail commissions. In addition, as more lotteries are created, they are competing for players, leading lotteries to increase the size of their prizes, which shrinks the percentage of money that goes to education. Miller finds that as money from the lottery simply replaces other funds, schools gain no additional funding.

**THE HOPE SCHOLARSHIP.** The Georgia Lottery Corporation (2008, http://www.galottery.com/stc/education/index.jsp) explains that it funds three educational programs: the Helping Outstanding Pupils Educationally (HOPE) scholarship program, a voluntary prekindergarten program, and grants for training teachers in advanced technologies and capital for educational facilities. The Georgia Lottery Corporation (2008, http://www.galottery.com/gen/education/hopeScholarship.jsp) notes that HOPE scholarships and grants are available to Georgia residents who enroll in certain programs at public and private institutions in the state. Students must have at least a 3.0 grade point average to qualify for HOPE money and have to maintain their eligibility in subsequent years. Most recipients are recent high school graduates who pursue college degrees.

In "Georgia's HOPE Program" (2008, http://www.gacollege411.org/finaid/scholarshipsandgrants/hopescholarship/default.asp), the Georgia Student Finance Commission explains that at public colleges the HOPE scholarship pays for tuition and fees and provides a $300 book allowance per academic year. Room and board expenses are not covered. In 2008 the HOPE scholarship provided $3,500 per academic year to full-time students (who can also qualify for the Georgia Tuition Equalization Grant of $900 per academic year). Part-time students attending private colleges were eligible for $1,750 per academic year. Georgia students who earned a General Education Diploma could receive a one-time $500 award that could be used toward tuition or books at a public or private college in Georgia. Between 1993 and 2008, $3.8 billion had been awarded to 1.1 million Georgia college students.

The HOPE scholarship program is one of the country's largest state-financed merit-based aid programs and is credited with significantly increasing the attendance of in-state residents at Georgia colleges. Similar programs include Kentucky's Educational Excellence Scholarship (http://www.kheaa.com/website/kheaa/kees?main=1)

and Florida's Bright Futures Scholarship (http://www
.floridastudentfinancialaid.org/ssfad/bf/).

## Social Effects

According to the NASPL, in "Lottery History" (2008,
http://www.naspl.org/index.cfm?fuseaction=content&PageID
=12&PageCategory=11), lotteries operate on every
continent except Antarctica. In the United States lotteries
enjoy unprecedented popularity. They are legal in forty-
two states and are generally considered a benign form of
entertainment with two enormous selling points: they
seem to offer a shortcut to the "American Dream" of
wealth and prosperity, and they are a voluntary activity
that raises money for the public good in lieu of increased
taxes. Opposition to lotteries is generally based on religious or moral reasons. Some people consider all forms
of gambling to be wrong, and state-sponsored lotteries
may be particularly abhorrent to them.

The National Gambling Impact Study Commission
(NGISC) complains in *Final Report* (June 1999, http://gov
info.library.unt.edu/ngisc/reports/fullrpt.html) about the
appropriateness of state governments pushing luck, instant
gratification, and entertainment as alternatives to hard
work, prudent investment, and savings. Such a message
might be particularly troubling if it is directed toward
lower-income people.

POVERTY, RACE, AND ETHNICITY. One of the most
common criticisms leveled against state lotteries is that
they unfairly burden the poor—that they are funded mostly
by low-income people who buy tickets, but benefit mostly
higher-income people. In economics terminology, a tax that
places a higher burden on lower-income groups than
higher-income groups (in terms of percentage of their
income) is called regressive. Even though the lottery is
not really a tax, many people consider it to be a form of
voluntary taxation because the proceeds fund government
programs. The economist Philip J. Cook, one of the co-
authors of the NGISC's *Final Report*, states "the tax that is
built into the lottery is the most regressive tax we know."

The NGISC expresses serious concern about the heavy
reliance of lotteries on less-educated, lower-income people. It also mentions that an unusually large number of
lottery outlets are concentrated in poor neighborhoods.

Joseph McCrary and Thomas J. Pavlak of the Vinson
Institute of Government Studies at the University of Geor-
gia review in *Who Plays the Georgia Lottery?: Results of a
Statewide Survey* (2002, http://www.ncalg.org/Library/
Studies%20and%20White%20Papers/Lotteries/Georgia%20
Lottery.pdf) a number of nationwide and state studies on
the relationship between income and lottery participation.
The researchers find that "the regressivity finding remains
largely consistent throughout the literature." McCrary and
Pavlak cite a common belief among lower-income people
that playing the lottery is their only chance to escape
poverty.

In "The Poor Play More" (*Chicago Reporter*, October
2002), Leah Samuel analyzes the lottery sales in Illinois
since 1997 by comparing lottery sales figures around the
state with income and demographic data from the 2000
census. The ten zip codes with the highest lottery sales for
the previous six fiscal years were all in Chicago. The
residents of all ten zip codes had average incomes of less
than $20,000 per year, compared to the city average of
$24,000 per year. Eight of the zip code areas had unem-
ployment rates more than the city average of 10%. Residents of half of the zip code areas were populated by at
least 70% African-Americans. Samuel finds that average
lottery sales per capita in the city's mostly African-American zip codes were 29% to 33% higher than in mostly
white or Hispanic zip code areas. The zip code with the
highest lottery sales in the state, 60619, coincided with
predominantly African-American and Latino low-income
communities on the city's south side. Residents of that zip
code spent nearly $23 million on lottery tickets during FY
2002. Samuel also finds that residents in poorer communities spent a larger portion of their income on lottery
tickets than did people in more affluent neighborhoods.
Lottery spending during FY 2002 was $224 per person in
zip codes that were at least 70% African-American and
$173 per person in zip codes that were at least 70% white.

Robert Gebeloff and Judy DeHaven report similar
findings in "Who Really Pays for the Lottery" (*Star-
Ledger* [Newark, New Jersey], December 6, 2005). Gebeloff and DeHaven gathered data on lottery sales in New
Jersey by zip code and compared that data to income and
population data for each zip code from 2000 to 2004. The
results clearly show that those who lived in poorer areas
bought far more lottery tickets than those living in wealthy
ones. People who resided in zip codes where the average
income was less than $52,151 spent an average of $250 per
year on the lottery, whereas those who lived in zip codes
with an average salary of $117,503 to $141,132 spent an
average of $115 on lottery tickets per year. Residents of
extremely wealthy neighborhoods—where the average salary was more than $141,132—spent $89 on lottery tickets
each year. In addition, less wealthy neighborhoods had
more lottery retailers per capita. The ratio of lottery
retailers per 5,000 people was 4 to 1 in low-income areas,
compared to roughly 1.5 to 1 in wealthy neighborhoods.

Haisley, Mostafa, and Loewenstein back up these
studies, finding that people who perceive themselves as
poor are more likely to buy lottery tickets than other
people. Poor people see the lottery as a way to improve
their financial situation. The researchers determine that
poor people spending money on the lottery is a factor in
their inability to improve their relative finances.

RACE AND ETHNICITY OF LOTTERY BENEFICIARIES.
McCrary and Pavlak report that African-Americans and
less-educated people are more likely to be active lottery

players than whites and more-educated people. Proceeds from the Georgia lottery fund only education programs. If these programs provide more benefits to the poor than to the wealthy, it could be argued that this compensates for the regressive nature of the state lottery.

However, Ross Rubenstein and Benjamin Scafidi, in "Who Pays and Who Benefits: Examining the Distributional Consequences of the Georgia Lottery for Education" (*National Tax Journal*, vol. 52, no. 2, June 2002), and Christopher Cornwell and David Mustard, in *The Distributional Impacts of Lottery Funded Merit-Based Aid* (1999), criticize Georgia's lottery for providing more benefits to white households than to minority households. Cornwell and Mustard claim that counties with the highest incomes and white populations receive significantly more HOPE scholarships.

In *HOPE Scholarship: Joint Study Commission Report* (2003, http://www.cviog.uga.edu/hope/report.pdf), the Vinson Institute of Government Studies argues that a county-by-county comparison of HOPE scholarship recipients is not appropriate because other factors affect these statistics—for example, whether a particular county contains a college or university. However, the institute does conclude that minorities in Georgia are "slightly less likely" than whites to get a HOPE scholarship.

The Vinson Institute reports that lottery play was inversely related to education level. In other words, people with fewer years of education played the lottery more often than those with more years of education. It also finds that lottery spending per person was highest in counties where African-Americans made up a larger percentage of the population.

Regarding the HOPE scholarship program, the Vinson Institute indicates that white students received a disproportionately high amount of the funds, compared to African-American students. In 1999 white students made up 66% of the freshman class in Georgia, but accounted for 74% of all HOPE scholars. By contrast, 26% of all freshmen were African-Americans, yet they accounted for only 21% of HOPE scholars. The Vinson Institute notes that this disproportionate relationship was true for every year examined, back to 1994. However, the institute states that the gap narrowed substantially over that time.

Analysis of Georgia's lottery-funded prekindergarten program provided completely different results. The Vinson Institute finds that the rate of enrollment in the prekindergarten program was higher in lower-income areas of the state than in affluent areas. It concludes that this particular lottery program is more beneficial to poorer people, African-Americans, and those who regularly play the lottery than to other groups in the state.

In "State Lotteries: Their Effect on Equal Access to Higher Education" (*Journal of Hispanic Higher Educa-*

*tion*, vol. 3, no. 1, 2004), Randall G. Bowden of Saint Leo University finds that minority and low-income students do not have proportionate access to higher education in lottery states.

**COMPULSIVE GAMBLING AND COGNITIVE DISTORTION.** The vast majority of states operate lotteries, and as a result, they are easily accessible to large numbers of people. Surveys show that lottery play is the most popular and widely practiced form of gambling in the United States. However, does the combination of easy and widespread access and general public acceptance mean that lottery players are more likely to develop serious gambling problems?

Dean Gerstein et al. conclude in *Gambling Impact and Behavior Study: Report to the National Gambling Impact Study Commission* (April 1, 1999, http://cloud9 .norc.uchicago.edu/dlib/ngis.htm) that there is a significant association between lottery availability and the prevalence of at-risk gambling within a state. At-risk gamblers are defined as those who gamble regularly and may be prone to a gambling problem. However, the researchers find that multivisit lottery patrons had the lowest prevalence of pathological and problem gambling among the gambling types examined.

Gerstein et al. also warn that the patron database used in their analysis was small, meaning that the findings may not apply universally. They note that lottery players who do have a problem may be less able to recognize it because lottery players tend to undercount their losses. Lottery players generally lose small amounts at a time, even though these small amounts may eventually total a large amount. In other words, a casino gambler who loses thousands of dollars in a day might be more likely to admit having a gambling problem than a lottery player who loses the same amount over a longer period.

In "Underlying Cognitions in the Selection of Lottery Tickets" (*Journal of Clinical Psychology*, vol. 57, no. 6, 2001), Karen K. Hardoon et al. study undergraduate students to examine cognitive misconceptions of lottery gamblers. Sixty students were given the South Oaks Gambling Screen, which is used to determine the probability that a person has a gambling problem. (See Chapter 2.) All the students were shown sixteen lotto tickets, each marked with a different sequence of six numbers. The sequences were random (e.g., 1, 13, 19, 34, 40, 47), pattern (e.g., 5, 10, 15, 20, 25, 30), long sequence (e.g., 1, 2, 3, 4, 5, 6), or nonequilibrated or unbalanced (a series not covering the whole range of possible numbers, usually limited to either high or low numbers, such as 3, 5, 9, 12, 15, 17). The students were then asked to choose the twelve tickets they would most like to play in the lottery and to rank those tickets from best to worst. Random sequences were by far the most popular: more than half of the tickets selected by the students as their first, second, third, and fourth favorite choices contained random sequences. The second most popular choice was the pattern sequence.

The students were also asked to explain the reasoning behind their selections. Randomness was the reason given 78% of the time. The presence of significant numbers (e.g., a birth date) was the second most popular reason (69.5%).

Hardoon et al. point out that all the students' choices were irrational because every ticket has an equal chance of winning. However, those students who regularly played the lottery or participated in other gambling activities were more likely to display bias when choosing their favorite tickets. In other words, they had stronger opinions about what was "winnable" than did infrequent players and those who did not gamble. The probable pathological gamblers were found to have more illusions about control than all other participants. Hardoon et al. conclude that there was "some level of cognitive distortion" demonstrated by all the gamblers in the study.

## THE FUTURE OF U.S. LOTTERIES
### New State Lotteries?

As of August 2008, only eight states did not have lotteries: Alabama, Alaska, Arkansas, Hawaii, Mississippi, Nevada, Utah, and Wyoming. Hawaii and Utah permit no types of gambling and seem unlikely to amend their constitutions. A lottery in Nevada is very unlikely because of the tremendous growth of casino gambling there. Alaskan politicians have shown minimal interest in a lottery. Though many state lottery bills have been introduced in the Alabama and Mississippi legislatures, most of them died in committee and the rest were soundly defeated on the floor. For several years members of the Wyoming legislature have been pushing a bill to allow the sale of Powerball tickets. The latest bill was defeated in the Wyoming House of Representatives in February 2007. In Arkansas lottery supporters sponsored a petition drive in 2008 that enabled a proposed constitutional amendment that would allow a lottery benefiting education to appear on the ballot in the November 4, 2008, general election.

### Jackpot Fatigue

A major problem facing the lottery industry is called "jackpot fatigue." Lottery consumers demand higher and higher jackpots so they can stay excited about lotto games. However, individual states cannot increase jackpot sizes without either greatly increasing sales or decreasing the portion of lottery revenue going to public funds. The first option is difficult to achieve and the second is politically dangerous. Jackpot fatigue has driven increasing membership in multistate lotteries, such as Mega Millions and Powerball.

### Pressure for Increased Revenue

Even as they cope with jackpot fatigue, many lotteries also face pressure to increase the amount of profit going to government programs. Several states are considering decreasing their lottery payout to raise much needed funds. Opponents argue that cutting prize payouts will reduce sales, thereby making it nearly impossible to increase state revenues.

# CHAPTER 8
# SPORTS GAMBLING

Wagering on sporting events is one of the oldest and most popular forms of gambling in the world. The ancient Romans gambled on chariot races, animal fights, and contests between gladiators. The Romans brought sports and gambling to Britain in the first century AD, where they have flourished for hundreds of years. Cockfighting, bear and bull baiting, wrestling, and footraces were popular sporting events for gambling throughout Europe during the sixteenth and seventeenth centuries. Horse races and boxing matches became popular spectator and betting sports during the eighteenth century. During the nineteenth and twentieth centuries, sporting events became more team-oriented and organized as rugby, soccer, and cricket grew in popularity.

Many early colonists who traveled to North America brought their love of sports and gambling with them. Horse racing, in particular, became a part of American culture. However, the morals of the late eighteenth and early nineteenth centuries decreased popular support for legalized sports gambling. By 1910 almost all forms of gambling were illegal in the United States. This did not stop people from gambling on sports, however. The practice continued to flourish, and horse racing, in particular, managed to maintain some legal respectability as a betting sport.

Nevada legalized gambling again in 1931 and permitted sports wagering for two decades. Point-shaving scandals in college basketball and the exposure of the industry's underworld connections during a federal investigation led by Senator Estes Kefauver (1903–1963; D-TN) led to a crackdown during the 1950s. Legal sports gambling did not return to Nevada until 1975, when it was tightly licensed and regulated.

In the twenty-first century, sports gambling in the United States can be broken down into three primary

categories: pari-mutuel betting (in which those who have bet on the top competitors split the pool of winnings), which is legal in forty-three states, on events such as horse and greyhound races and the ball game jai alai; legal betting using a bookmaker, which is permitted only in Nevada; and illegal betting.

## SOCIAL ATTITUDES TOWARD SPORTS GAMBLING

The popularity of sports gambling is attributed to several factors, including a growing acceptance of gambling in general, intense media coverage of sporting events, and emerging technologies that make wagering easier. Americans can view a wide variety of sporting events from around the world via local and cable television stations, networks dedicated solely to sports, satellite services, and even the Internet. The latest scores can be sent directly to cellular phones. Sports bars and restaurants feature multiple television sets tuned in to various sporting events.

Betting on sports is one of the less popular forms of gambling in the United States. Jeffrey M. Jones of the Gallup Organization reports in *One in Six Americans Gamble on Sports* (February 1, 2008, http://www.gallup.com/poll/104086/One-Six-Americans-Gamble-Sports.aspx) that as of December 2007 the percentages of survey respondents who had gambled on sports were near the low end. Only 14% had bet in an office pool in the past twelve months, 7% had bet on a professional sporting event, and 4% had bet on college sports. About 5% said they had bet on a horse race, and 3% had bet on a boxing match. Table 8.1 shows trends over time as reported by the Pew Research Center and the Gallup Organization for professional sports betting and horse racing. Most of the 2008 figures were at twenty-year lows.

According to Paul Taylor, Cary Funk, and Peyton Craighill of the Pew Research Center, in *Gambling: As the Take Rises, So Does Public Concern* (May 23, 2006,

**TABLE 8.1**

**Poll respondents' reported participation in sports gambling, selected years 1989–2006**

| | Yes % | No % | No opinion % |
|---|---|---|---|
| **Bet on a professional sports event such as baseball, basketball, or football** | | | |
| 2006 Feb–Mar | 14 | 86 | * |
| 2003 Dec 11–14 | 10 | 90 | * |
| 1999 Apr 30–May 23 | 13 | 87 | — |
| 1996 Jun 27–30 | 10 | 90 | — |
| 1992 Nov 20–22 | 12 | 88 | — |
| 1990 Feb 15–18 | 21 | 79 | — |
| 1989 Apr 4–9 | 22 | 78 | — |
| **Bet on a college sports event such as basketball or football** | | | |
| 2006 Feb–Mar | 7 | 93 | * |
| 2003 Dec 11–14 | 6 | 94 | * |
| 1999 Apr 30–May 23 | 9 | 91 | — |
| 1996 Jun 27–30 | 7 | 93 | — |
| 1992 Nov 20–22 | 6 | 94 | — |
| 1990 Feb 15–18 | 11 | 89 | — |
| 1989 Apr 4–9 | 14 | 86 | — |
| **Bet on a boxing match** | | | |
| 2006 Feb–Mar | 3 | 97 | * |
| 2003 Dec 11–14 | 2 | 98 | * |
| 1996 Jun 27–30 | 3 | 97 | * |
| 1992 Nov 20–22 | 6 | 94 | — |
| 1990 Feb 15–18 | 5 | 95 | — |
| 1989 Apr 4–9 | 8 | 92 | — |
| **Participated in an office pool on the World Series, Superbowl, or other game** | | | |
| 2006 Feb–Mar | 18 | 82 | * |
| 2003 Dec 11–14 | 15 | 85 | * |
| 1999 Apr 30–May 23 | 25 | 75 | — |
| 1996 Jun 27–30 | 23 | 77 | — |
| 1992 Nov 20–22 | 22 | 78 | — |

*Less than 0.5%

Note: 2006 figures are from Pew Research Center; data from all other years are from the Gallup Organization.

SOURCE: Adapted from Paul Taylor, Cary Funk, and Peyton Craighill, "What Kind of Bet Did You Place This Year?" in *Gambling: As the Take Rises, So Does Public Concern*, Pew Research Center, May 23, 2006, http://pewresearch.org/assets/social/pdf/Gambling.pdf (accessed August 8, 2008). Data from The Gallup Organization. Copyright © 1989 by The Gallup Organization. Reproduced by permission of The Gallup Organization.

**FIGURE 8.1**

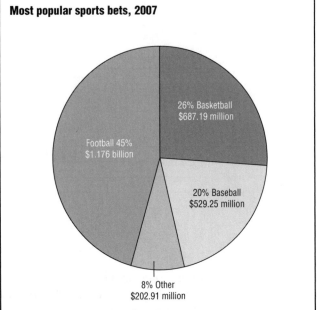

**Most popular sports bets, 2007**

- Football 45% $1.176 billion
- 26% Basketball $687.19 million
- 20% Baseball $529.25 million
- 8% Other $202.91 million

SOURCE: "What Sports Are the Most Popular Bets?" in *2008 State of the States: The AGA Survey of Casino Entertainment*, American Gaming Association, 2008, http://www.americangaming.org/assets/files/aga_2008_sos.pdf (accessed August 1, 2008). Reprinted with permission of the American Gaming Association. All rights reserved.

**TABLE 8.2**

**Poll respondents' opinion on sports betting, by level of interest in sports, 2006**

| | All adults | Follow sports news | | |
|---|---|---|---|---|
| | | Very closely | Somewhat closely | Not very/ not at all |
| | % | % | % | % |
| Approve | 42 | 55 | 42 | 38 |
| Disapprove | 54 | 43 | 55 | 58 |
| Don't know | 4 | 2 | 3 | 4 |
| | 100 | 100 | 100 | 100 |
| Number of respondents | 2,250 | 383 | 646 | 1,216 |

SOURCE: Paul Taylor, Cary Funk, and Peyton Craighill, "Sports Fans Back Legalized Betting on Professional Sports," in *Gambling: As the Take Rises, So Does Public Concern*, Pew Research Center, May 23, 2006, http://pewresearch.org/assets/social/pdf/Gambling.pdf (accessed August 8, 2008). Data from The Gallup Organization. Copyright © 1989 by The Gallup Organization. Reproduced by permission of The Gallup Organization.

http://pewresearch.org/assets/social/pdf/Gambling.pdf), the demographic makeup of those who bet on sports between March 2005 and March 2006 was slightly different from the demographic makeup of the average gambler. Whereas 71% of those with some college education gambled, only 23% of them had bet on sports during the previous year. Similarly, 65% of college graduates gambled, but only 25% bet on sports; and 66% of those who had high school diplomas or less had gambled, but only 22% had bet on sports. African-Americans (24%) and whites (23%) were more likely than Hispanics (16%) to have bet on sports. In 2007 football was the most popular sport on which to wager in the legal Nevada sports books; 45% of all wagers were placed on football games, 26% on basketball games, and 20% on baseball games. (See Figure 8.1.)

Taylor, Funk, and Craighill note that 67% of adults approved of legalized gambling in general in 2006; 50% of people approved of legalized off-track betting on horse races, down 4% from 1989. Only 42% approved of legal betting on professional sports. (See Table 8.2.) In fact, this is the only gambling activity that Taylor, Funk, and Craighill's survey respondents did not find acceptable. However, a higher percentage of sports fans approved of legalized betting on professional sports: 55% of adults who claimed to follow sports news very closely in 2006 approved of legalized betting on professional sports, compared to only 38% of those who did not follow sports news very closely or at all.

## PARI-MUTUEL GAMBLING

Pari-mutuel is a French term meaning "mutual stake." In pari-mutuel betting, all wagers on a particular event or race are combined into a pool that is split between the winning bettors, minus a percentage for the management. The larger the pool, the bigger the payoff. In pari-mutuel gambling, patrons bet against each other, not against the house. The principles of the pari-mutuel system were developed in France during the late nineteenth century by Pierre Oller.

The pari-mutuel system has been used for horse races in the United States since about 1875, but it did not really catch on until the 1920s and 1930s, when the totalizator, an automatic odds calculator, came into use. The totalizator took money, printed betting tickets, and continuously calculated odds based on betting volume.

Previously, horse betting had been conducted mostly by bookmakers who were notoriously corrupt. In 1933 California, Michigan, New Hampshire, and Ohio legalized pari-mutuel gambling on horse racing as a means of regulating the industry and gaining some revenue. Dozens of states followed suit over the next decade. Pari-mutuel gambling was also adopted for greyhound racing and jai alai matches. As of 2008, over forty U.S. states allowed pari-mutuel gambling. A handful of states permit pari-mutuel gambling by law but do not have facilities or systems in place to conduct it.

In pari-mutuel gambling the entire amount wagered is called the betting pool, the gross wager, or the handle. The system ensures that event managers receive a share of the betting pool, regardless of who wins a particular race or match. The management's share is called the takeout. The takeout percentage is set by state law and is usually about 20%.

Breakage refers to the odd cents not paid out to winning bettors because payoffs are rounded. For example, the payout on a $2 bet is typically rounded down in $0.10 or $0.20 increments. The cents left over are the breakage. Even though breakage amounts to only pennies per bet, it adds up quickly with high betting volume. For example, the California Horse Racing Board (CHRB) notes in *Thirty-seventh Annual Report of the California Horse Racing Board: A Summary of Fiscal Year 2006–2007 Racing in California* (2007, http://www.chrb.ca.gov/annual_reports/2007_annual_report.pdf) that California horse racetracks accumulated approximately $11.6 million in breakage in fiscal year (FY) 2007. Each state has its own rules about breakage, but usually the funds are split between the state, the track operators, and the winning horse owners. Breakage is subtracted from the betting pool before payouts are made.

Pari-mutuel wagering can be performed in person at the event or, increasingly, at off-track betting (OTB) facilities. The New York legislature approved the state's first OTB operation in 1970. Some states also allow betting by telephone or Internet when an account is set up before bet placement. Many races are broadcast as they occur by televised transmission to in-state and out-of-state locations (including OTB sites). This process, known as simulcasting, allows intertrack wagering to take place. In other words, bettors at one racetrack can place bets on races taking place at another racetrack.

A race book is an establishment (usually a room at a casino or racetrack) in which intertrack wagering takes place on pari-mutuel events such as horse races and greyhound races. A race book typically features many television monitors that show races as they occur. Race books are included in many Nevada and Atlantic City, New Jersey, casinos as well as in some tribal casinos.

According to the American Gaming Association (AGA), in *2008 State of the States: The AGA Survey of Casino Entertainment* (2008, http://www.americangaming.org/assets/files/aga_2008_sos.pdf), racinos (racetracks at which slot machines are available) took in $5.3 billion in gross gaming revenue in 2007. This represented a 45.6% increase over the previous year, mostly because of new racino openings in Pennsylvania, Florida, and New York.

## HORSE RACING

Horse racing has been a popular sport since the time of the ancient Greeks and Romans. It was popularized in western Europe in the Middle Ages, when knights returned from the Crusades with fast Arabian stallions. These horses were bred with sturdy English mares to produce a new line of horses now known as Thoroughbreds. Thoroughbreds are tall, lean horses with long, slender legs. They are renowned for their speed and grace while running.

Thoroughbred racing became popular among the British royalty and aristocrats, earning it the nickname "Sport of Kings." The sport was transplanted to North America during colonial times. In *Thoroughly Thoroughbred* (2006, http://www.jockeyclub.com/pdfs/thoroughly_thoroughbred.pdf), the Jockey Club, the governing body of Thoroughbred horse racing, indicates that races were run on Long Island, New York, as early as 1665. However, the advent of organized Thoroughbred racing in the United States is attributed to Governor Samuel Ogle (1702–1752) of Maryland, who staged a race between pedigreed horses in "the English style" in Annapolis, Maryland, in 1745. The Annapolis Jockey Club, which sponsored the race, later became the Maryland Jockey Club. Among its members were George Washington (1732–1799) and Thomas Jefferson (1743–1826).

Thoroughbred breeding was prominent in Maryland and Virginia until the Civil War (1861–1865), when many operations were moved to Kentucky. Thoroughbred racing had already grown popular throughout the agricultural South. In 1863 the Saratoga racecourse opened in northern New York. It is considered the oldest Thoroughbred flat track in the country. (A flat track is one with no hurdles or other obstacles for a racing horse to jump over.) The Jockey Club, which maintains the official breed registry for Thoroughbred horses in North America, was established in 1894 in New York City.

Horse racing remained popular in the United States until World War II (1939–1945), when it was severely curtailed. The decades since the war have seen a sharp decline in the popularity of horse racing. Three reasons are commonly mentioned:

- Competition increased from other entertainment venues and leisure activities, such as theme parks, shopping malls, and television.

- The horse racing industry avoided television coverage of races during the 1960s for fear it would keep people away from the tracks. (This is now seen as a failure to take advantage of a major marketing tool.)

- The legalization of state lotteries and casinos created competition for gambling dollars.

However, even though attendance declined, the amount of money gambled on horse races increased overall. According to the Jockey Club, in *Fact Book* (2008, http://www.jockeyclub.com/factbook.asp?section_8), the pari-mutuel handle from Thoroughbred horse racing was approximately $15.2 billion in 2003, up from $9.4 billion in 1990. (See Figure 8.2.) It dropped slightly to $14.7 billion in 2007. About 88% of the amount gambled on horse races during 2007 was bet at OTB facilities. Analysts believe attendance at live racing will continue to decline as more OTB opportunities become available.

## Thoroughbred Racetracks and Races

The Daily Racing Form states in "Racing Links: Race Tracks" (2008, http://www.drf.com/racing_links/links _tracks.html) that ninety-two Thoroughbred racetracks of varying sizes operate throughout the country. Some are open seasonally, whereas those in warm climates are open year-round. Some are owned by the government, and some are owned by private and public companies. Thoroughbred horse racing in the United States is controlled by a relatively small group of players. Two publicly traded companies, Churchill Downs and Magna Entertainment, along with the New York City Off-Track Betting Corporation and the New York Racing Association, control much of the business. The New York Racing Association is a not-for-profit group that controls the Belmont, Saratoga, and Aqueduct racetracks. Analysts predict that the industry will continue to undergo consolidation, with corporations taking over most of the business.

The three most prestigious Thoroughbred races in the United States are the Kentucky Derby at the Churchill

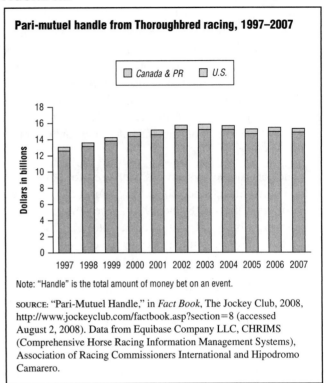

**FIGURE 8.2**

**Pari-mutuel handle from Thoroughbred racing, 1997–2007**

Note: "Handle" is the total amount of money bet on an event.

SOURCE: "Pari-Mutuel Handle," in *Fact Book*, The Jockey Club, 2008, http://www.jockeyclub.com/factbook.asp?section=8 (accessed August 2, 2008). Data from Equibase Company LLC, CHRIMS (Comprehensive Horse Racing Information Management Systems), Association of Racing Commissioners International and Hipodromo Camarero.

Downs track in Kentucky, the Preakness Stakes at Pimlico in Maryland, and the Belmont Stakes at Belmont Park in New York. The races are held over a five-week period during May and June of each year. A horse that wins all three races in one year is said to have won the Triple Crown. Only eleven horses have ever captured the Triple Crown, most recently a horse named Affirmed in 1978.

According to the Jockey Club, in *Fact Book*, there were 51,304 Thoroughbred horse races during 2007. (See Figure 8.3.) California hosted the most events, with 5,055 races, followed by West Virginia (4,357), Pennsylvania (3,748), New York (3,664), and Florida (3,660). The total gross purses amounted to nearly $1.2 billion. The gross purse is the amount awarded to the owners of the winning horses. California racetracks had the highest gross purse of $179.2 million, followed by New York ($142.1 million), Louisiana ($95.3 million), and Kentucky ($81.7 million). The number of Thoroughbred races held each year has steadily declined since the early 1990s. (See Figure 8.4.)

## Non-Thoroughbred Horse Racing

Even though Thoroughbred horse racing is the most popular, other types of horse racing also attract pari-mutuel wagering. In harness racing, specially trained horses trot or pace rather than gallop. Usually, the horse pulls a sulky (two-wheeled cart), which carries a jockey who controls the reins. Sometimes the jockey is seated on the horse rather than in the sulky. Harness racing is performed by standardbred horses, which are shorter,

FIGURE 8.3

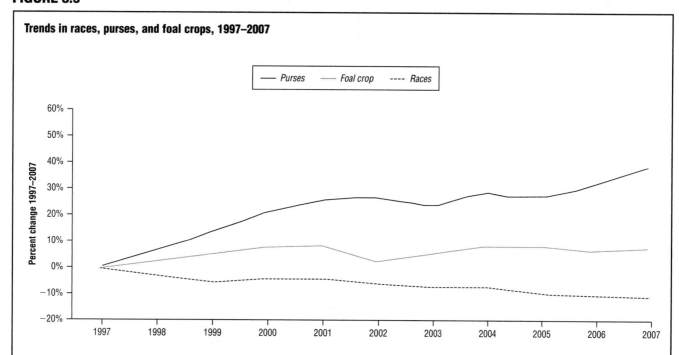

**Trends in races, purses, and foal crops, 1997–2007**

**Relationship of U.S. races, purses and foal crops**

| Year | Total U.S. foal crop | Total U.S. races | Total U.S. purses | Total U.S. starters | Average purse per starter | Average purse per race |
|------|---------------------|------------------|-------------------|---------------------|---------------------------|------------------------|
| 1997 | 32,117 | 57,832 | 851,462,820 | 64,099 | 13,284 | 14,723 |
| 1998 | 32,947 | 55,894 | 904,014,631 | 63,798 | 14,170 | 16,174 |
| 1999 | 33,843 | 54,644 | 962,853,553 | 63,547 | 15,152 | 17,620 |
| 2000 | 34,724 | 55,486 | 1,030,879,290 | 64,443 | 15,997 | 18,579 |
| 2001 | 34,720 | 55,127 | 1,067,490,193 | 65,829 | 16,216 | 19,364 |
| 2002 | 32,984 | 54,304 | 1,074,247,738 | 67,009 | 16,031 | 19,782 |
| 2003 | 33,965 | 53,503 | 1,055,496,849 | 68,249 | 15,465 | 19,728 |
| 2004 | 34,772 | 53,595 | 1,092,085,465 | 68,569 | 15,927 | 20,377 |
| 2005 | 34,932 | 52,257 | 1,085,005,415 | 66,903 | 16,218 | 20,763 |
| 2006 | 34,200* | 51,668 | 1,120,350,012 | 66,733 | 16,789 | 21,684 |
| **2007** | **34,350*** | **51,304** | **1,180,587,881** | **67,261** | **17,552** | **23,012** |

*Estimated figures

SOURCE: Adapted from "Trends in U.S. Races, Purses, and Foal Crops," in *Fact Book*, The Jockey Club, 2008, http://www.jockeyclub.com/factbook.asp?section=12 (accessed August 2, 2008)

more muscled, and longer in body than Thoroughbreds. The National Association of Trotting Horse Breeders in America established the official registry for standardbred horses in 1879. At the time, Thoroughbred horses were the favorite of high society, and standardbred horses were popular among the common folk. In "Track Information" (2008, http://www.ustrotting.com/trackside/track facts/trackfacts.cfm), the U.S. Trotting Association indicates that in 2008 there were forty-six licensed harness racetracks that offered pari-mutuel betting. Harness racing is also an attraction at state and county fairs, although not all allow wagering.

A third type of horse known for racing is the quarter horse, so named because of its high speed over distances of less than a quarter of a mile. Quarter horses were originally bred by North American colonists to be both hardworking and athletic. The American Quarter Horse Association (2008, http://www.aqha.com/aqharacing.com/horsemaninfo/2008USRaceDates.pdf) reports that in 2008 races were conducted at eighty-two separate meets, which lasted from a mere two days of racing at some local fairs to two hundred race days offered at the Los Alamitos Race Course in Los Alamitos, California.

Arabian horses are considered the only purebred horses in the race circuit. In "Arabian Racing in the US: 2007 Summary" (2007, http://www.arabianracing.org/upload/Microsoft_Word_-_Arabian_Racing_in_the_US__Summary_2007.pdf), the Arabian Jockey Club indicates that they raced at seventeen tracks in the United States that held sixty-three stake races in 2007.

**Betting on Horse Races**

The betting pool for a particular horse race depends on how much is wagered by bettors on that race. Each

FIGURE 8.4

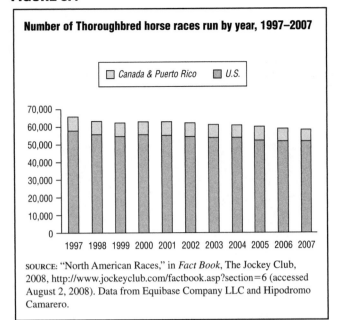

**Number of Thoroughbred horse races run by year, 1997–2007**

SOURCE: "North American Races," in *Fact Book*, The Jockey Club, 2008, http://www.jockeyclub.com/factbook.asp?section=6 (accessed August 2, 2008). Data from Equibase Company LLC and Hipodromo Camarero.

FIGURE 8.5

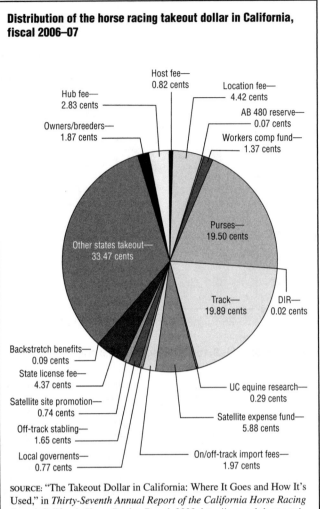

**Distribution of the horse racing takeout dollar in California, fiscal 2006–07**

SOURCE: "The Takeout Dollar in California: Where It Goes and How It's Used," in *Thirty-Seventh Annual Report of the California Horse Racing Board*, California Horse Racing Board, 2008, http://www.chrb.ca.gov/vvannual_reports/2007_annual_report.pdf (accessed August 2, 2008)

wager affects the odds. The more money bet on a horse, the lower that horse's odds and the potential payoff become. The payout for winning tickets is determined by the amount of money bet on the winner in relation to the amount bet on all the other horses in that particular race.

First, the takeout is subtracted from the betting pool. This money goes toward track expenses, taxes, and the purse. Most states also require that a portion of the takeout be put into breeder incentive funds to encourage horse breeding and health in the state. Figure 8.5 shows the breakdown of each takeout dollar in California. (Note: In this graphic, "other states takeout" refers to wagering fees that are paid to betting facilities in other states that take bets on California races.) After the takeout and the breakage are subtracted from the betting pool, the remaining money is divided by the number of bettors to determine the payoff, or return, on each wager.

The odds on a particular horse winning first, second, or third place are estimated on the morning of a race and then are constantly recalculated by computer during the betting period before the race. The odds are posted on a tote board and on television screens throughout the betting area. The tote board also tallies the total amount paid into each pool. Bettors can wager that a particular horse will win (come in first), place (come in first or second), or show (come in first, second, or third). The payoff for a win is higher than payoffs for place or show, because the latter two pools have to be split more ways. For example, the show pool must be split between all bettors who selected win, place, or show.

Betting on horse races is considered more a game of skill than a game of chance. Professional racing bettors spend many hours observing individual horses and con-

sider previous race experience when they make their picks. This gives them some advantage over bettors who pick a horse based on whim—for example, because they like its name. Even though bettors do not play directly against each other, an individual bettor's skill does affect other bettors because the odds are based on the bets of all gamblers.

## Horse Racing in California

California led the nation in 2007 in terms of the number of races held and the purses paid to winning horses. The state has allowed pari-mutuel gambling on horse races since 1933, when a constitutional amendment was passed by the voters. California has six privately owned racetracks and nine racing fairs. Racing fairs are county and state fairs—often held at racetracks—where wagering on horse races is one of many fair events. The fairs usually last only a week or two and are conducted several times a year. Gamblers can also bet on horse races at twenty simulcast facilities in the state.

FIGURE 8.6

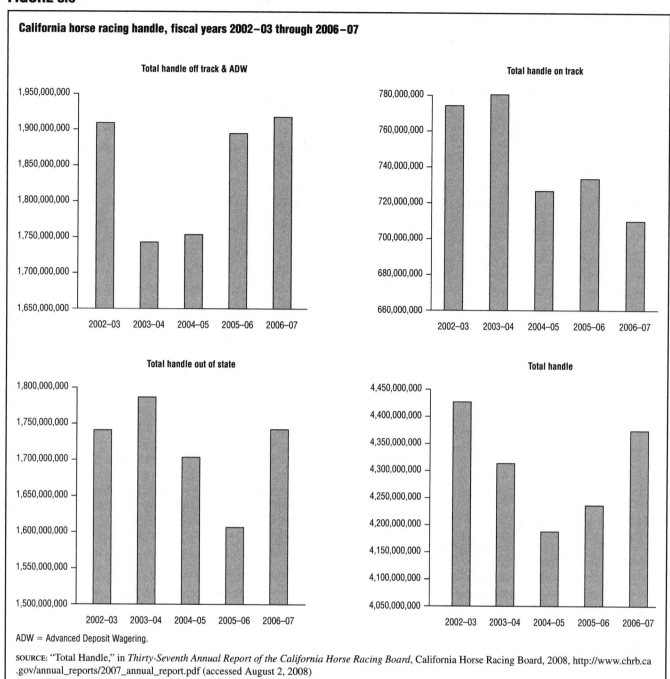

**California horse racing handle, fiscal years 2002–03 through 2006–07**

ADW = Advanced Deposit Wagering.

SOURCE: "Total Handle," in *Thirty-Seventh Annual Report of the California Horse Racing Board*, California Horse Racing Board, 2008, http://www.chrb.ca.gov/annual_reports/2007_annual_report.pdf (accessed August 2, 2008)

The CHRB states in *Thirty-seventh Annual Report of the California Horse Racing Board* that the industry grossed $4.4 billion during FY 2007, the highest of any state in the country. Figure 8.6 shows the handle broken down by on-track, off-track, and out-of-state wagers. Only 16.2% ($709 million) of all wagers occurred at the track during 2007. The vast majority of wagers were placed at off-track locations. Winning bettors received 80.1% of the betting pool. The state received revenues of $38 million.

### The Economic Effects of Horse Racing

The industry provides direct income to horse owners, trainers, and jockeys through purses. In *Fact Book*, the Jockey Club notes that in 2007 California tracks paid out the highest gross purse for the year ($179.2 million), followed by New York ($142.1 million) and Louisiana ($95.3 million). The largest portion of a Thoroughbred race purse (typically 60%) goes to the owner of the first-place horse. The owner is responsible for paying the horse's trainer and jockey. The owners of the horses finishing second and third typically receive around 20% and 12%, respectively, of a race purse.

The racing industry also supports a large business in horse breeding. In 1962 Maryland was the first state to establish a program to encourage breeders within the state through direct money payments. The practice spread quickly to other states involved in horse racing.

In *Economic Impact of Horse Racing in Maryland* (January 20, 1999), University of Maryland researchers at the College of Agriculture and Natural Resources provide a flow chart to show the economic impact of horse racing. (See Figure 8.7.) The researchers determine that the sport's main impact is not the cash flow between the wagering public, the racetracks and OTBs, the horse owners, jockeys, breeders, and trainers, and the regulatory government agencies. Rather, they suggest that the true economic effects of the sport occur outside the industry from expenditures on goods and services.

Racetrack and OTB operators spend money on land, labor, and other goods and services from various businesses. Horse owners, breeders, and trainers spend money on land, labor, veterinary care, and horse feed and supplies. All these pump money into the general economy. In *Fact Book*, the Jockey Club estimates that the horse racing industry creates the equivalent of 1.4 million jobs both directly and indirectly in the United States.

Unlike the casino industry, the horse racing industry has only a minor impact on tourism. Most racetracks are not typical tourist destinations that attract overnight visitors who spend money on lodging, food, and other entertainment. The exceptions are the races held as part of the Triple Crown. These racing events attract visitors from all over the world and bring a significant number of tourist dollars to local businesses.

### Horse Fatalities and Injuries

Horse racing does have a price in terms of horse fatalities and injuries. For example, in *Thirty-seventh Annual Report of the California Horse Racing Board*, the CHRB notes that California had 301 racehorse fatalities between November 2006 and November 2007. Nearly half (147) of the deaths occurred during races, and another 97 deaths occurred during training. The remainder occurred during other activities.

The horse racing industry has invested millions of dollars in veterinary research on injuries and illnesses that affect racehorses. The Grayson-Jockey Club Research Foundation, the leading private source of funding for research into horse health issues, was founded in 1940. The foundation reports in *2007 Annual Report* (2008, http://www.grayson-jockeyclub.org/resources/2007%20 Annual%20Report.pdf) that in 2007 it allocated over $1.1 million toward twenty-one projects at universities that conduct equine research.

Two horse health issues of major concern are mare reproductive loss syndrome (MRLS) and exercise-induced pulmonary hemorrhage (EIPH). In "Eastern Tent Caterpillars Now Wandering, Populations up Sharply from 2007" (May 9, 2008, http://www.ca.uky.edu/gluck/mrls/2008/050

908ETCupdate.htm), the University of Kentucky's College of Agriculture reports that MRLS is an illness that killed 30% of Kentucky foals (horses less than one year old) between 2001 and 2002. Since then, scientists have determined that MRLS is caused by eastern tent caterpillars, which can find their way into horse food. Manu M. Sebastian et al. estimate in "Review Paper: Mare Reproductive Loss Syndrome" (*Veterinary Pathology*, vol. 45, no. 5, September 2008) that MRLS has had an economic impact on the horse racing industry of approximately $500 million.

EIPH is a common condition in racehorses: they bleed from the lungs during strenuous exercise, probably because increased blood pressure ruptures tiny blood vessels in their lungs. Up to 80% of racehorses are affected. Horses that experience EIPH can be temporarily or permanently barred from racing, depending on state regulations and the severity of the problem.

## GREYHOUND RACING

Greyhounds are mentioned in many ancient documents. English noblemen used greyhounds to hunt rabbits, a sport known as coursing. Greyhound racing was given the nickname the "Sport of Queens" because Queen Elizabeth I (1533–1603) of England established the first formal rules for greyhound coursing during the 1500s. Greyhounds were brought to the United States during the late 1800s to help control the jackrabbit population on farms in the Midwest. Eventually, farmers began holding local races, using live rabbits to lure the dogs to race. In the early 1900s Owen Patrick Smith (1867–1927) invented a mechanical lure for this purpose. The first circular greyhound track opened in Emeryville, California, in 1919.

Three major organizations manage greyhound racing in the United States: the National Greyhound Association (NGA), which represents greyhound owners and is the official registry for racing greyhounds; the American Greyhound Track Operators Association (AGTOA); and the American Greyhound Council (AGC), a joint effort of the NGA and AGTOA, which manages the industry's animal welfare programs, including farm inspections and adoptions.

Wagering on greyhounds is similar to wagering on horse races. However, greyhound racing is not nearly as popular as horse racing, and its popularity has declined dramatically in the past few decades. According to the Humane Society of the United States (HSUS), in "Greyhound Racing Facts" (2008, http://www.hsus.org/pets/issues _affecting_our_pets/running_for_their_lives_the_realities_of _greyhound_racing/greyhound_racing_facts.html), the handle from greyhound racing declined by 45% during the 1990s, leading to the closure or cessation of live racing at sixteen tracks across the country. In addition, seven states specifically banned live greyhound racing during that decade: Idaho, Maine, Nevada, North Carolina, Vermont, Virginia, and Washington. Pennsylvania became the

**FIGURE 8.7**

**Maryland horse racing industry flow chart**

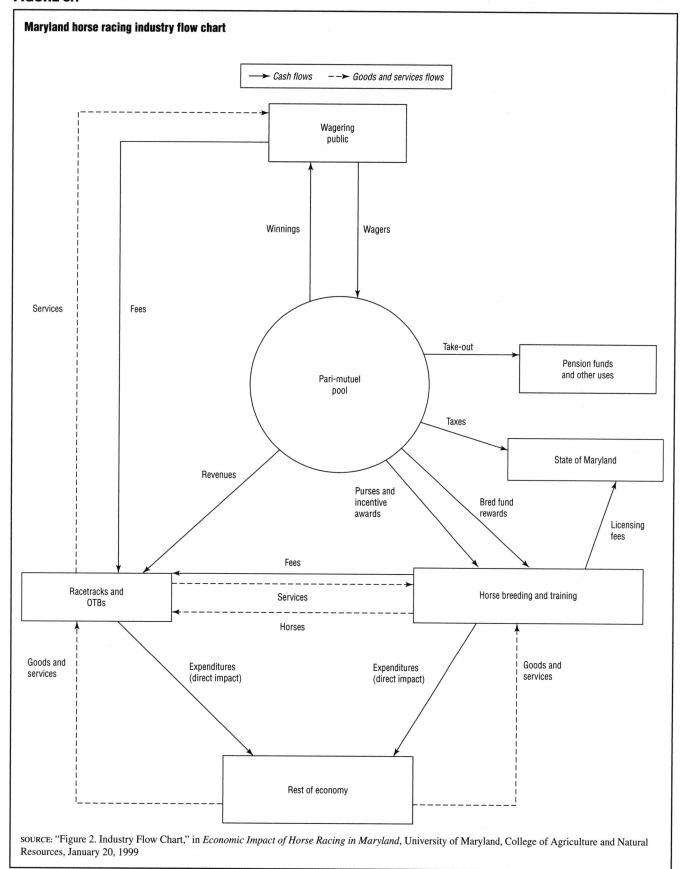

SOURCE: "Figure 2. Industry Flow Chart," in *Economic Impact of Horse Racing in Maryland*, University of Maryland, College of Agriculture and Natural Resources, January 20, 1999

eighth state to ban greyhound racing in 2004, and Massachusetts placed an initiative to ban greyhound racing on the November 2008 ballot.

In "U.S. Greyhound Racing Fact Sheet" (April 2007, http://www.rescuedgreyhounds.com/home/GPL-One_Page _Fact_Sheet.pdf), the Greyhound Protection League states that in 2007 greyhounds raced at thirty-eight racetracks in thirteen states: Alabama, Arizona, Arkansas, Colorado, Florida, Iowa, Kansas, Massachusetts, New Hampshire, Rhode Island, Texas, West Virginia, and Wisconsin. Florida had the most number of racetracks: fifteen.

### Florida's Greyhound-Racing Industry

According to the Florida Department of Business and Professional Regulation's Division of Pari-mutuel Wagering, in *76th Annual Report: Fiscal Year 2006–2007* (January 2008, http://www.myflorida.com/dbpr/pmw/documents/ AnnualReport2006-2007.pdf), greyhound races were the most attended pari-mutuel event in Florida in FY 2007, attracting 1.7 million visitors, up 14% from the previous year. There were 4,896 greyhound races in that year, up 9% from the previous year. (See Figure 8.8.) The greyhound-racing handle in FY 2007 was $465.3

million, a 3% decrease from the previous fiscal year, despite the increase in track attendance. (See Figure 8.9.) This decrease was due to a reduction of the simulcast handle from outside the state of 73% over the previous year, reflecting the increasing condemnation of greyhound racing outside of Florida. Purses totaled $30.7 million.

**FIGURE 8.8**

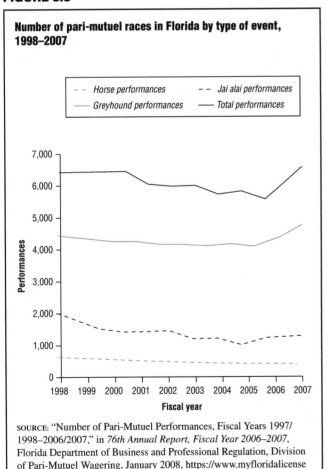

Number of pari-mutuel races in Florida by type of event, 1998–2007

SOURCE: "Number of Pari-Mutuel Performances, Fiscal Years 1997/ 1998–2006/2007," in *76th Annual Report, Fiscal Year 2006–2007*, Florida Department of Business and Professional Regulation, Division of Pari-Mutuel Wagering, January 2008, https://www.myfloridalicense .com/dbpr/pmw/documents/AnnualReport2006–2007.pdf (accessed August 8, 2008)

**FIGURE 8.9**

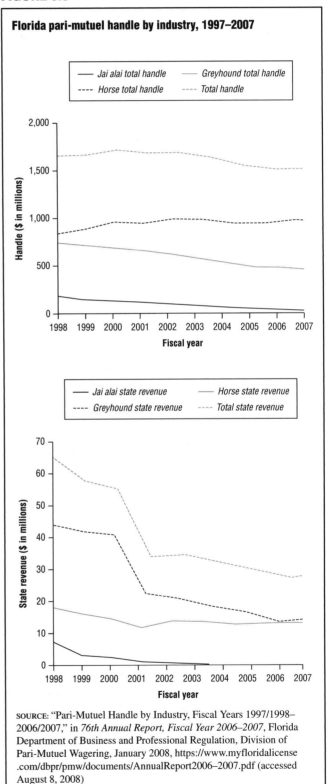

Florida pari-mutuel handle by industry, 1997–2007

SOURCE: "Pari-Mutuel Handle by Industry, Fiscal Years 1997/1998– 2006/2007," in *76th Annual Report, Fiscal Year 2006–2007*, Florida Department of Business and Professional Regulation, Division of Pari-Mutuel Wagering, January 2008, https://www.myfloridalicense .com/dbpr/pmw/documents/AnnualReport2006–2007.pdf (accessed August 8, 2008)

Greyhound racetracks paid $14 million to the state during FY 2007, accounting for 51% of the state's revenue from pari-mutuel gambling. The taxes paid to the state increased by 1% over the previous year.

## The Economic Effects of Greyhound Racing

The American Greyhound Council, a pro-racing group, reports in "Racing in the U.S.: Economic Impact" (2008, http://www.agcouncil.com/racing.cfm?page=3) that breeding farms and racing kennels invest more than $150 million in land, buildings, and equipment and contribute $96 million into local economies each year. The council states that the nation's racing greyhounds are worth over $200 million. In addition, greyhound tracks around the country employ fourteen thousand people, pay $150 million in wages, and pay nearly $100 million per year in state tax revenue. The tracks are credited with donating about $11.7 million per year to charities and community causes.

## Concerns about Greyhound Welfare

The Greyhound Protection League (November 2004, http://www.greyhounds.org/gpl/contents/PDFs/abuse_cases_11-04.pdf) explains that during the 1990s there were dozens of well-documented cases of cruelty and abuse in the greyhound industry involving thousands of dogs that were shot, starved, abandoned, or sold to research laboratories. Because of the work of animal rights groups such as the HSUS, the cruelty of the greyhound industry was revealed to the American public. Many greyhound racing organizations changed the way they treated greyhounds and initiated adoption programs for dogs that were too old to race.

However, the practice of killing unsuccessful greyhounds is still very much alive. In "U.S. Greyhound Racing Fact Sheet," the Greyhound Protection League compiles statistics on what it states are the number of greyhounds bred, adopted, and killed each year. The league claims that more than 600,000 greyhound puppies and adult dogs were killed by the industry between 1986 and 2006, including 186,221 puppies. During this same period, 179,000 greyhounds were adopted. The organization alleges that the racing industry overbreeds greyhounds in the hopes of producing winners, leading to the destruction of thousands of unwanted puppies each year. A racing greyhound's career is typically over at the age of four years, well below its average lifespan of twelve years, meaning that thousands of adult dogs are also destroyed each year when they are no longer able to race.

According to the Division of Pari-mutuel Wagering, in *76th Annual Report*, almost all of Florida's greyhound tracks actively sponsor greyhound adoption programs, and many have on-site adoption booths. The tracks are required to pay 10% of the credit they receive for uncashed winning tickets to organizations that promote or encourage greyhound adoptions. These mandatory contributions amounted to $194,897 during FY 2007.

## JAI ALAI

Jai alai is a court game in which players bounce a ball against a wall and catch it using a *cesta* (a long curved basket) that is strapped to the wrist. The term *jai alai* comes from the Spanish Basque phrase for "merry festival." The first permanent jai alai arena, called a *fronton*, was built in Florida in 1924.

The game's scoring system has been adjusted over the years to make it more attractive to gamblers. Typical games include eight players, with two players competing for a point at one time. The game continues until one player obtains seven points. Win, place, and show positions are winning bets, just as in horse racing.

The Division of Pari-mutuel Wagering notes in *76th Annual Report* that only six frontons in Florida offered pari-mutuel gambling on jai alai in 2007. (Other frontons in the United States—in Connecticut and Rhode Island—had closed by 2003.) Paid attendance in Florida was 337,246 at 1,363 events in FY 2007. Attendance was up 14% from the year before. The state received $659,001 in taxes and fees from the jai alai industry in 2007.

Jai alai peaked in popularity during the early 1980s, when more than $600 million was wagered on the sport. By fiscal 2007 the total handle had declined to $81.4 million. (See Figure 8.9.)

## THE FUTURE OF PARI-MUTUEL GAMBLING
### Decreasing Popularity and Income

Pari-mutuel gambling is decreasing in popularity as it faces increasing competition from other gambling options, particularly casinos. The horse racing industry experienced a 40% decline in attendance during the 1990s. As a result, racetracks found it increasingly difficult to attract a large enough betting pool to afford to run races. According to the Jockey Club, in *Fact Book*, the number of Thoroughbred races run each year in the United States fell from 74,071 in 1989 to 51,304 in 2007, a decrease of 31%. Figure 8.4 illustrates the decline from 1995 to 2007.

### Attempts to Attract New Gamblers

Gambling industry analysts suggest that horse races have a relatively small hard-core group of attendees, most of whom are older people. The industry is trying to attract a larger and younger fan base (twenty-five to forty-five years old) with a disposable income. Some racetracks have tried to become entertainment venues by offering food courts, malls, and music concerts. Even though these attractions may increase attendance, the newcomers do not necessarily gamble. Meanwhile, devoted race fans complain that such promotions are too distracting and draw attention away from the racing.

Increasingly, pari-mutuel facilities are offering other gambling choices to patrons. The AGA indicates in *2008 State of the States* that eleven states had slot machines and/or video lottery terminals at their racetracks in 2007: Delaware, Florida, Iowa, Louisiana, Maine, New Mexico, New York, Oklahoma, Pennsylvania, Rhode Island, and West Virginia. Racinos have been a huge success. Consumer spending at racinos rose from $2 billion in 2002 to $5.3 billion in 2007, an increase of 163%. (See Figure 8.10.)

In 2007 gamblers in Pennsylvania wagered nearly $1.1 billion, or 20 percent of the revenue brought in by racinos nationwide. (See Figure 8.11.) Many new properties opened in 2006 and 2007, including in Pennsylvania, New York, and Florida. The top racino market in 2007 was Charles Town, West Virginia, which took in $463.4 million in revenue. (See Table 8.3.)

Most of Florida's racetracks and jai alai frontons have card rooms in which gamblers wager on card games, mainly poker. In *76th Annual Report*, the Division of Pari-mutuel Wagering notes that the gross revenue in the state's card rooms was $54.2 million in FY 2007, an increase of 18% from the previous year. The number of card rooms had increased from 457 in FY 2006 to 469 in FY 2007. The card rooms contributed $5.7 million in taxes and fees to state and local governments in FY 2007.

**FIGURE 8.10**

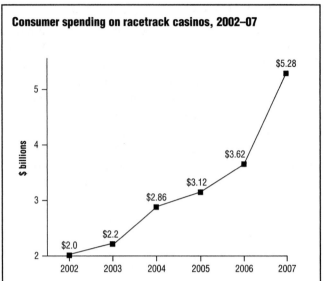

Consumer spending on racetrack casinos, 2002–07

**FIGURE 8.11**

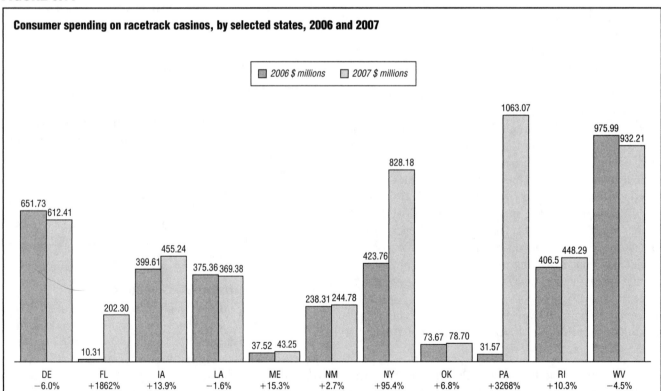

Consumer spending on racetrack casinos, by selected states, 2006 and 2007

**TABLE 8.3**

**Top 10 racetrack casino markets, 2007**

| | Location | Revenue |
|---|---|---|
| 1 | Charles Town, W.Va. | $463.37 million |
| 2 | Yonkers, N.Y. | $394.33 million |
| 3 | Providence, R.I. | $375.38 million |
| 4 | Dover/Harrington, Del. | $339.79 million |
| 5 | Delaware Park/Wilmington, Del. | $272.62 million |
| 6 | Chester, Pa. | $272.48 million |
| 7 | Bensalem, Pa. | $262.80 million |
| 8 | Chester, W.Va. | $228.21 million |
| 9 | Broward County, Fla. | $202.52 million |
| 10 | Wheeling, W.Va. | $200.98 million |

Note: New Mexico does not report revenue by individual facility.

SOURCE: "Top 10 U.S. Racetrack Casino Markets, 2007," in *2008 State of the States: The AGA Survey of Casino Entertainment*, American Gaming Association, 2008, http://www.americangaming.org/assets/files/aga_2008_sos.pdf (accessed August 1, 2008). Data from The Innovation Group. Reprinted with permission of the American Gaming Association. All rights reserved.

## LEGAL SPORTS GAMBLING

Besides the sports involved in pari-mutuel gambling, legal sports gambling is extremely limited in the United States. Only one state, Nevada, allows high-stakes gambling on sports such as football, basketball, and baseball.

In 1992 Congress passed the Professional and Amateur Sports Protection Act, which banned sports betting in all states except those that already allowed it in some form (Delaware, Montana, Nevada, New Mexico, Oregon, and Washington).

### Sports and Race Books in Nevada

Sports books are establishments that accept and pay off bets on sporting events. They are legal only in Nevada. Bettors must be over age twenty-one and physically present in the state.

According to the Nevada Gaming Control Board (October 1, 2008, http://gaming.nv.gov/documents/pdf/race_sports.pdf), 201 locations in the state were licensed to operate sports books and/or race books in 2008. More than half of them were in Las Vegas, and most were operated by casinos. The typical casino book is a large room with many television monitors showing races and games from around the world. Most casinos have combined race/sports books, although the betting formats are usually different. Race book betting is mostly of the pari-mutuel type, whereas sports book betting is by bookmaking.

### Bookmaking

Bookmaking is the common term for the act of determining odds and receiving and paying off bets. The person performing the service is called the bookmaker or bookie. Bookmaking has its own lingo, which can be confusing to those who are not familiar with it. For example, a dollar bet is actually a $100 bet, a nickel bet is a $500 bet, and a dime bet is a $1,000 bet. To place a bet with a bookmaker, the bettor lays down (pays) a particular amount of money to win a particular payoff.

Bookmakers make money by charging a commission called "vigorish." Even though the exact origins of the word are not known, *Merriam-Webster's Collegiate Dictionary* (2003) suggests that the term *vigorish* may be derived from the Ukrainian word *vygrash* or the Russian word *vyigrysh*, both of which mean "winnings" or "profit." In any event, vigorish is an important yet misunderstood concept by most bettors.

Most gambling literature describes vigorish as a 4.55% commission that a bookie earns from losers' bets. In "A Crash Course in Vigorish...and It's Not 4.55%" (September 10, 2008, http://www.professionalgambler.com/vigorish.html), J. R. Martin, a sports handicapper (a person who analyzes betting odds and gives advice to bettors), provides a different interpretation of vigorish. Statistically, only bettors who win exactly half of their bets pay exactly 4.55% in vigorish. Other bettors pay different percentages. Martin explains that a bettor must win 53% of all equally sized bets to break even. However, this bettor would wind up paying a vigorish of at least 4.82%.

Some sports bets are simple wagers based on yes or no logic. Examples include under and over bets, in which a bettor wagers that a particular game's final score will be under or over a specific number of points.

Most sports bets are based on a line set by the bookmaker. For example, the line for a National Football League (NFL) football game between the Miami Dolphins and the Tennessee Titans might say that the Dolphins are picked by seven points. A bettor picking the Dolphins to win the game wins money only if the Dolphins win the game by more than seven points.

The line does not reflect a sport expert's assessment of the number of points by which a team will win. Rather, it is a concept designed to even up betting and to ensure that the bookmaker gets bets on both sides. This reduces the bookie's financial risk. Bookmakers will change lines if one side receives more betting action than the other. The skill of sports gambling comes in recognizing the accuracy of the line. Experienced bettors choose games in which they believe the posted lines do not accurately reflect the expected outcomes. This gives them an edge.

The odds for most licensed sports books in Nevada are set by Las Vegas Sports Consultants, Inc. Formerly owned by SportsLine.com, Inc., the company was purchased in November 2003 by a group of private investors in Las Vegas.

## Developments in Legal Sports Gambling in Nevada

Nevada legalized gambling during the Great Depression (1929–1939) as a means of raising revenue. During that time, Charles K. McNeil (?–1981), a Chicago securities analyst, developed the handicapping system, in which bookmakers establish the betting line. The new system provided incentive for gamblers to bet on the underdog in a contest and made gambling more appealing. During the 1940s the Nevada legislature legalized off-track betting on horses, and sports and race books were popular in the state's casinos.

Then in 1950 and 1951 a series of U.S. Senate hearings led by Senator Kefauver investigated the role of organized crime in the gambling industry. The televised hearings focused the nation's attention on gangsters, corrupt politicians, and legal and illegal gambling. One of the results was the passage of a 10% federal excise tax on "any wager with respect to a sports event or a contest." Because of the tax, the casino sports books, which were making only a small profit, were forced to shut down.

In 1974 the federal excise tax was reduced to 2%, and the sports books slowly made a comeback. Frank "Lefty" Rosenthal (1929–), a renowned handicapper, is credited with popularizing the sports book in Las Vegas during the 1970s. The 1980s were boom years for the sports and race books: in 1983 the federal excise tax was reduced to 0.25%. Jimmy "the Greek" Snyder (1919–1996) brought some legitimacy to sports gambling through his appearances on televised sports shows. The amount of money wagered in the Nevada sports books increased dramatically until the mid-1990s, when it began to level off.

### Money and Games

Nevada's sports books had a betting handle of $2.6 billion in 2007. (See Figure 8.12.) This was up from $2.4 billion in 2006. The profit made on sports betting is actually quite low. In 2007 the sports books had a revenue of only $168 million, down from the previous year's high of $192 million.

According to the AGA, in *2008 State of the States*, football wagers accounted for 45% of Nevada's sports book wagering during 2007. The Super Bowl alone generated $92.1 million in wagers in 2007. (See Figure 8.13.) However, Nevada's sports books lost money on Super Bowl betting in that year.

Industry experts estimate that one-third of the bets placed in the Nevada sports books are on college sporting events. Wagering is not allowed on high school sporting events or Olympic events. Nevada law also restricts the sports books to wagering on events that are athletic contests: betting is not allowed on related events, such as who will win most valuable player awards.

**FIGURE 8.12**

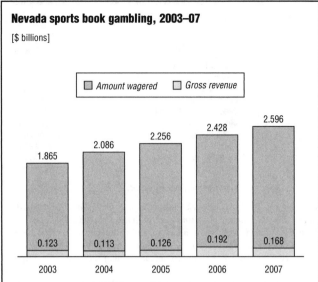

**Nevada sports book gambling, 2003–07**

[$ billions]

**FIGURE 8.13**

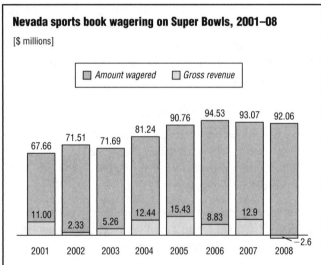

**Nevada sports book wagering on Super Bowls, 2001–08**

[$ millions]

### Options Outside Nevada

**OREGON.** In the 1990s Oregon operated two sports betting games as part of its lottery. The Oregon Lottery (2008, http://www.oregonlottery.org/sports/program.php) explains that proceeds from the Sports Action game went to the state's Intercollegiate Athletic and Academic Scholarship Fund. The game earned more than $30 million for the fund. The betting was conducted only during the football season on selected professional football games. Because professional football leagues restrict the use of their trademarked names, lottery officials referred to teams by location only (e.g., Denver versus Miami). In a second lottery game, Scoreboard, bettors won money if they correctly picked a number that matched the last digit of the scores from selected professional football games. The state passed a law in 2005 that eliminated both the Sports Action and Scoreboard lottery games.

DELAWARE. Delaware tried a sports lottery in 1976 based on NFL games. The league sued for trademark violation but eventually lost the case. The sports lottery, which was called Scorecard, proved to be unpopular with bettors and unprofitable for the state. It was abandoned after only one football season. A task force was set up in 2002 to investigate the feasibility of reinstating a sports lottery game. The group's report to the Delaware General Assembly in 2003 estimated that a legal sports lottery could raise approximately $13 million for the state. In 2005 legislation was introduced to give the state lottery permission to create a pari-mutuel betting game. The bill was soundly defeated. In addition, Governor Ruth Ann Minner (1935–) was opposed to expanded gambling in Delaware, making it unlikely that a sports lottery would be initiated while she was in office. The expansion of sports betting is also opposed by the NFL, the National Basketball Association, the National Hockey League, Major League Baseball, and the National Collegiate Athletic Association (NCAA).

MONTANA. Montana allows five types of sports gambling: sports pools, Calcutta pools, fantasy sports leagues, sports tab games, and fishing derbies.

Calcutta pools operate much like pari-mutuel betting: all the money wagered on a sporting event is pooled together. In a Calcutta pool, an auction is held before a sporting event, and bettors bid for the opportunity to bet on a particular player. For example, before a golf tournament, the pool participants bid against each other for the right to bet on a particular golfer. The money collected during the auction becomes the wagering pool. It is divided among the "owners" of the best finishing players and the pool sponsor. Calcutta pools are most often associated with rodeos and golf tournaments.

Fantasy sports leagues are games in which the participants create fictitious teams composed of actual professional athletes. Each team wins points based on its performance against other teams in the league over a designated period. Team performance is based on the actual performance of the selected athletes during real sporting events. The points collected by each participant in the league can be exchanged for cash or merchandise paid for by membership fees collected from each participant. In Montana, licensed Sports Action retailers can conduct fantasy sports wagering. Profits benefit the Montana Board of Horse Racing.

A sports tab game is one in which players purchase a numbered tab from a game card containing one hundred tabs with different number combinations. Bettors win money or prizes if their numbers match those associated with a sporting event—for example, digits in the winning team's final score. The cost of a sports tab is limited by law to less than $5. Operators of sports tab games (except charities) are allowed to take no more than 10% of the total amount wagered to cover their expenses (charities are allowed to take 50%). Sports tab sellers must obtain a license from the state and pay licensing fees and gaming taxes.

OTHER STATES. Other states that offer limited sports gambling are Washington, which permits $1 bets on race cars, and New Mexico, where small bets on bicycle races are legal. Office pools on sporting events are legal in a few states as long as the operator does not take a commission. Despite these examples of sports betting in other parts of the United States, the big money in legal sports gambling is in Nevada.

## ILLEGAL SPORTS GAMBLING

The AGA estimates in the fact sheet "Sports Wagering" (2008, http://www.americangaming.org/Industry/factsheets/issues_detail.cfv?id=16) that in 2007 Nevada sports books accounted for less than 4% of all sports gambling in the country, and that the vast majority of sports bets were illegal. This makes it difficult to assess exactly how much money is involved.

Illegal sports gambling encompasses a wide variety of activities. Most illegal bets on sporting events have been placed with bookies, although Internet gambling and office pools have also been popular. In addition, some "sporting" events, illegal in themselves, are popularly associated with gambling—for example, cockfighting and dog fighting.

### The Link to the Nevada Sports Books

Most illegal books use the odds posted by the Nevada sports books because these are well publicized. Nevada sports books also provide illegal bookies with a means for spreading the risk on bets: illegal bookies who get a lot of action on one side of a bet often bet the other side with the Nevada sports books to even out the betting.

Transmitting gambling information across state lines for the purpose of placing or taking bets is illegal. News items about point spreads (the predicted scoring difference between two opponents) can be reported for informational and entertainment purposes only, but betting lines are still published by many U.S. newspapers. The Newspaper Association of America, which represented nearly 90% of daily circulation papers in the country in

2008, defends the practice as free speech protected under the First Amendment of the U.S. Constitution. The association claims that readers want to see the lines for informational purposes—to learn which teams are favored to win—and not necessarily for betting purposes. Even though the NCAA has argued that a ban on all college sports wagering would pressure newspapers to stop publishing point spreads, the AGA has countered that betting lines would still be accessible through independent sports analysts, offshore Internet gambling sites, and other outlets.

## The Link to Organized Crime

Illegal sports gambling has long been associated with organized crime in the United States. During the 1920s and early 1930s mobsters set up organized bookmaking systems across the country, including two illegal wire services, Continental Wire Service and Trans America Wire, which operated under the direction of the gangster Al Capone (1899–1947). The legal wire service, Western Union, was prohibited by law from transmitting race results until races were officially declared over. Sometimes this declaration did not take place for several minutes after the race finish, so mobsters reported the winners on the illegal wire services to prevent bettors from taking advantage of these delays by posting winning bets before the official results were wired.

During the 1950s the federal government cracked down on organized crime and eventually drove mobsters out of the Nevada casino industry. As the casinos were taken over by corporations, organized crime strengthened its hold on illegal bookmaking. Even though law enforcement officials acknowledge that many "independent" bookies operate throughout the country, the big money in illegal sports gambling is still controlled by organized crime.

## ANIMAL FIGHTING

Gambling on animal fights has a long history in the United States, despite its unsavory reputation. Most staged animal fights involve cocks (roosters) or dogs specially bred and trained. Even though such fighting is usually associated with rural areas, urban police reports about cockfighting and dog fighting have increased in recent years as the "sport" has become popular among street gangs. Animal fights are of particular concern to law enforcement authorities because large amounts of cash and weapons are usually present.

No official national statistics are available on animal fighting. However, Pet-Abuse.com, a Web site operated by a nonprofit organization in New York, collects and documents information about animal abuse cases. As of October 2006 the Web site's database included 1,210 documented cases of animal fighting; 127 of them had occurred in 2008.

## Cockfighting

In the wild, cocks fight and peck one another to establish a hierarchy within their social order. These altercations rarely lead to serious injury. By contrast, fighting cocks are specially bred and trained by humans to be as aggressive as possible. They are given stimulants, steroids, and other drugs to heighten their fighting nature. Sharp spikes, called gaffs, are attached to their legs. The cocks are thrown into a pit from which they cannot escape. They slash and peck at one another, often until death. Spectators wager on the outcome of these fights. Cockfighting was banned by most states during the 1800s.

According to the HSUS, in "Cockfighting Fact Sheet" (2008, http://www.hsus.org/acf/fighting/cockfight/cockfighting_fact_sheet.html), cockfighting was illegal in all fifty states in 2008. In "Cracking down on Cockfighting: Why the Bloodsport Remains a Thriving Industry" (*Newsweek*, March 24, 2008), Winston Ross notes that Louisiana was the last state to ban the practice in 2007. Cockfighting was a felony in thirty-seven states and a misdemeanor offense in thirteen others, although states differ in their treatment of cockfight spectators and those caught in possession of birds for fighting. The federal Animal Welfare Act prohibits the interstate transport of birds for cockfighting.

As of October 2008, Pet-Abuse.com listed 376 documented cases of cockfighting in the United States. For example, in June 2005 in Sevierville, Tennessee, the Federal Bureau of Investigation broke up a cockfighting ring, known as the Del Rio, one of the oldest and largest in the country. About three hundred birds and more than seven hundred spectators were discovered in the raid. Individual bets were said to be as high as $30,000. According to officials, it was common to have 250 fights per night at that location, resulting in dozens of dead chickens; 143 people were charged in the incident.

In January 2008 California officials discovered a cockfighting ring in Livermore. After arriving at the scene, police found a cockfight in progress. More than fifteen hundred birds associated with the ring had to be euthanized. Seven people discovered watching the fight were arrested and charged.

## Dog Fighting

Spectators huddle around pits or small, boarded arenas to watch dog fights. They place bets on the outcome of the contests, which can go on for hours, sometimes to the death.

Dogs are specially bred and trained for such fights— the American pit bull terrier is the most common breed because of its powerful jaws. Authorities report that the dogs are often draped in heavy chains to build muscle mass and systematically deprived of food and water. Stolen and stray pet dogs and cats are commonly used as bait to train the fighters. The smaller animals are stabbed or sliced open and thrown to the fighting dogs to enhance their blood lust. Dogs are often drugged to increase their aggressiveness.

Dog fighting is a felony in all fifty states. Dog fighting rings are often intermingled with other criminal activities. For example, Pet-Abuse.com notes that in May 2005 Louisiana authorities broke up one of the larger dog fighting rings in the state. Police said more than 140 dogs were seized from 2 kennels in the rural towns of Church Point and Franklinton. The owners of the kennels had been under investigation for money laundering (the act of engaging in transactions designed to hide or obscure the origin of illegally obtained money) and drug dealing when authorities uncovered the dog fighting ring. Four people were arrested.

Dog fighting is not limited to southern states and rural areas. According to T. J. Pignataro, in "Betting on Cruelty" (*Buffalo News*, February 2004), drug and weapons raids by police accidentally uncovered well-organized dog fighting operations around Buffalo, New York. Authorities reported that thousands of dollars in cash and other valuables, such as car titles, guns, and drugs, were commonly wagered at the dog fights. Authorities also described gruesome scenes in which owners chopped off the heads of dogs that disgraced them by losing or backing down during a fight. Trash bags full of mangled pit bulls have also been found by city authorities in vacant fields or along city streets.

One of the highest profile cases of dog fighting is that of Michael Vick (1980–), a first-round pick in the NFL's 2001 draft and a quarterback for the Atlanta Falcons. In July 2007 Vick was indicted on charges linked to dog fighting, including federal conspiracy charges involving crossing state lines to participate in illegal activity and buying and sponsoring pit bulls in fighting ventures. Vick and his associates were charged with having bought property in Virginia on which to stage dog fights; the dogs were fought over a six-year period. Dogs who performed poorly were killed violently by the dog fighting ring. Vick himself admitted to killing several dogs. He pleaded guilty and was sentenced to twenty-three months in prison. When Vick is released from prison in July 2009, Virginia authorities said he will be tried on state charges.

## THE EFFECTS OF ILLEGAL SPORTS GAMBLING ON SOCIETY
### Money and Crime

Because the vast majority of sports gambling that occurs in this country is illegal, it is difficult to determine its economic effects. However, the only people definitely benefiting from illegal sports gambling are the bookmakers. Large bookmaking operations overseen by organized crime groups take in billions of dollars each year. The betting stakes are high and the consequences for nonpay-

ment can be violent. Small independent bookies typically operate as entrepreneurs, taking bets only from local people they know well. Illegal bookmaking cases reported in the media range from multimillion-dollar enterprises to small operations run by one person.

### Sports Tampering

In *National Incident-Based Reporting System—Volume 1: Data Collection Guidelines* (August 2000, http://www.fbi.gov/ucr/nibrs/manuals/v1all.pdf), the Federal Bureau of Investigation defines sports tampering as "to unlawfully alter, meddle in, or otherwise interfere with a sporting contest or event for the purpose of gaining a gambling advantage." The most common form is point shaving, which occurs when a player deliberately limits the number of points scored by his or her team in exchange for payment of some sort. For example, if a basketball player purposely misses a free throw in exchange for a fee, that player is participating in a point-shaving scheme.

Gambling has led to some famous sports scandals, mostly in college basketball games. However, any link between an athlete and gambling gives rise to suspicions about the integrity of the games in which that athlete participates.

The professional baseball player Pete Rose (1941–) is an example. On September 11, 1985, at Riverfront Stadium in Cincinnati, Ohio, Rose broke Ty Cobb's (1886–1961) all-time hit record. Before the end of the decade, however, Rose was under investigation by the Major League Baseball commissioner and by federal prosecutors for betting on sporting events and associating with known bookies. He agreed to leave baseball, and the case was dropped. At the time, Rose denied ever betting on baseball games. However, in January 2004 he admitted that he had bet on baseball games while he managed the Cincinnati Reds during the late 1980s.

**THE INTEGRITY OF COLLEGE SPORTS.** The popularity of sports gambling among college students leads to suspicions that athletes, coaches, and officials associated with collegiate sports could be wagering on the very games in which they are participating. In May 2004 the extent of gambling among college athletes was examined in "Pushing the Limits: Gambling among NCAA Athletes" (*The Wager*, vol. 9, no. 21, May 26, 2004). The article summarizes the findings of two major studies: *2003 NCAA National Study on Collegiate Sports Wagering and Associated Health Risks* (December 2004, http://www.ncaa.org/wps/wcm/connect/resources/file/eb8b854c219ea54/2003_sports_wagering_study.pdf?MOD=AJPERES) by the NCAA and "Correlates of College Student Gambling in the United States" (*Journal of American College Health*, vol. 52, no. 2, September–October 2003) by Richard A. LaBrie et al. of the Harvard School of Public Health.

Table 8.4 compares the findings of the studies. The NCAA examined gambling activities by students during the previous twelve months, and LaBrie et al. asked students about gambling during the current school year. The results indicate that approximately one-quarter of the male student athletes had gambled on college sporting events.

The NCAA opposes both legal and illegal sports gambling in the United States. Bylaw 10.3 of the NCAA prohibits staff members and student athletes from engaging in gambling activities related to college and professional sporting events. It also forbids them from providing any information about collegiate sports events to people involved in organized gambling activities.

The NCAA opposes sports gambling for the following reasons:

- It attracts organized crime.

- The profits fund other illegal activities, such as drug sales and loan-sharking (loaning money at an excessive rate of interest).

**TABLE 8.4**

**Comparison of statistics from the National Collegiate Athletic Association (NCAA) and the Harvard School of Public Health College Alcohol Study (CAS) on gambling by student athletes, 2004**

| Study | Student athletes who gamble on anything | | Student athletes who gamble on any sport | | Student athletes who gamble on college sports | | Student athletes who gamble on the Internet | |
|---|---|---|---|---|---|---|---|---|
| | Women | Men | Women | Men | Women | Men | Women | Men |
| NCAA | 47% | 69% | 10% | 35% | 6% | 21% | 2% | 6% |
| CAS* | 33% | 57% | 10% | 33% | 6% | 26% | 2% | 5% |

*CAS student athletes self-reported that they played or practiced intercollegiate sports.

SOURCE: "Table 1. Comparison between NCAA and CAS Statistics on Student Athletes Who Gamble," in "Pushing the Limits: Gambling among NCAA Athletes," in *The Wager*, vol. 9, no. 21, May 26, 2004. Data from Harvard School of Public Health College Alcohol Study (CAS), Harvard School of Public Health, Boston, MA, 2004, and Executive Summary for the National Study on Collegiate Sports Wagering and Associated Health Risks, National Collegiate Athletic Association, Indianapolis, IN, 2004.

- Student athletes who become involved can become indebted to bookies, leading to point-shaving schemes.

# CHAPTER 9
# INTERNET GAMBLING

Internet gambling is a relatively new phenomenon. The first gambling Web sites launched in the mid-1990s and soared in popularity, particularly in the United States. Millions of Americans have gambled online, even though the practice is illegal. Christiansen Capital Advisors (January 9, 2006, http://www.cca-i.com/Primary%20Navigation/ Online%20Data%20Store/internet_gambling_data.htm), which provides gambling analysis and management services, estimates that Internet gambling generated $21 billion worldwide in 2008, up from just $3.1 billion in 2001.

Exact figures on Internet gambling revenue are not known because the sites are not permitted to operate within the United States and because most of the countries that do allow them to operate do not collect or report revenue statistics. According to David Stewart, in *An Analysis of Internet Gambling and Its Policy Implications* (2006, http:// www.americangaming.org/assets/files/studies/wpaper_inter net_0531.pdf), two-thirds of Internet gambling operations are located in small Caribbean and Central American countries that provide little or no government oversight of the industry.

Many Internet gambling sites either do not pay taxes to their home countries or pay lower taxes than land-based gambling establishments. For example, Stewart notes that in March 2005 the tiny island of Antigua in the Caribbean was the headquarters for 536 gambling sites, the most of any country. The sites were only required to pay 3% of their gambling revenues (winnings after payout to customers) to the government of Antigua with a ceiling of $50,000 per month. Other popular locations included Central and South America, Canadian Native American reservations, and the British Isles.

Unlike most land-based casinos, the vast majority of Internet gambling sites are operated by small, virtually unknown companies. A land-based casino costs several hundred million dollars to build and operate and requires hundreds of employees, whereas an online casino is set up and operated by a handful of people for an initial investment of a few million dollars. The relatively low setup and operating costs make the businesses extremely profitable and allow them to offer higher payoffs to winners than land-based casinos.

The future of Internet gambling in the United States remains uncertain. Under the Unlawful Internet Gambling Enforcement Act (UIGEA) of 2006 banks and credit card companies are committing a crime if they transfer Americans' money to Internet gambling sites. Though serious Internet gamblers will likely find ways of transferring funds to online casinos and card rooms, lawmakers hope the law will turn casual gamblers away. As of late 2006, many of the larger, publicly traded Internet gambling companies, such as PartyPoker, had stopped accepting American customers altogether to avoid any conflicts with the U.S. government. However, the legality of Internet gaming remains somewhat uncertain. The law does not resolve whether the horseracing industry or Native American tribes are exempt from the ban on online gambling.

## THE DEVELOPMENT OF INTERNET GAMBLING

No consensus exists on when the first Internet casino began operating and who started it. However, it is generally agreed that the first online casinos began operating sometime in 1995 or 1996. Among the first was Intercasino, based in Antigua, which has positioned itself as one of the leaders in Internet gambling. In 1996 the country legalized and licensed online gambling sites. The companies that operate these Web sites are trade-zone corporations— that is, foreign-owned corporations operating in specific areas of the country as if they were on foreign soil. In Antigua, trade-zone corporations cannot produce products for domestic consumption, so Antiguans are not allowed to participate in online gambling with any trade-zone companies located there.

Various agencies and private entities have attempted to estimate the extent of the online gambling industry, including the National Gambling Impact Study Commission (NGISC), the U.S. Department of Justice, and industry researchers such as Christiansen Capital Advisors and Bear Stearns & Co. Even though their estimates differ, these analysts agree that the growth of online gambling has been phenomenal. In 1997 there were fifty to sixty Internet casinos in operation, most based in the Caribbean, which earned approximately $300 million to $350 million. By 2000 an estimated six hundred to seven hundred sites were operating and revenues approached $2 billion. By 2007 the American Gaming Association (AGA) estimates in the fact sheet "Internet Gambling" (2007, http://www.americangaming.org/Industry/factsheets/issues_detail.cfv?id=17) that about two thousand online casinos were estimated to exist.

## ONLINE GAMES

Stewart indicates that sports book betting constituted roughly one-third (35%) of all Internet gambling in 2005, totaling $4 billion. Casino games made up about 25% of the online gambling market. Online poker accounted for 18% of all online gambling revenue in 2005. Poker is growing in popularity at a faster rate than any other type of online gambling. In 2000 online poker sites, such as PartyPoker, racked up $82 million in revenue. By 2005 poker sites worldwide were thought to have revenues of $2 billion. The rest of online gaming revenue came from the sale of lottery tickets, pari-mutuel race betting (in which those who bet on the top competitors share the total amount bet and the house gets a percentage), and other games.

Casino sites offer many of the same games available in land-based casinos, such as poker, blackjack, roulette, and slot machines. Bet denominations range from pennies to thousands of dollars. Poker Web sites have card rooms where players compete against each other rather than against the house. This is an example of person-to-person betting. To make a profit on these sites, the casino operators take a small percentage of the winning hand.

Online casino games operate in much the same way as the electronic games found in actual casinos. Both depend on random number generators: real slot machines have a computer chip built in; online games have random number generators written into their programming. Even though slot machine payoff percentages at actual casinos are dictated by the state in which they are located, online payoffs are not. However, online providers who never have winners would not have return customers, so their programs are designed to pay out a particular percentage. Online games are particularly appealing to people who enjoy card games because the betting limits are much lower than they are in actual casinos. For example, an online gambler can play blackjack for $1 per hand, whereas many land-based casinos set a $10- or $25-per-hand minimum.

Some sites require players to download software onto their personal computer. The software still runs through a program at the Web site, so the user must be online to play. Other games are played right at the Web site. Many use high-technology software that allows players to gamble in virtual reality: they can "look" around the table or around the casino room. Players can even "chat" with each other via online messaging during a game. Both of these effects make online gambling more interactive for the user.

Many sites offer free play to introduce visitors to the types of games offered and to give them a chance to practice. Visitors who decide to play for money must register, open an account, and deposit money into that account. This requires input of personal information, including name and address. The user usually sets up a user name and password for future access. Money is transferred to the gambling site via credit or debit card, through an account with an online bank or payment service, or via electronic check or wire transfer.

Most online sites offer bonuses of 5% to 20% of the amount of the initial deposit. These bonuses usually require that the gambler wager an amount two to three times the size of the bonus. Other sites offer prizes, such as trips, for repeat business. Winnings are typically deposited into the user's online account or paid via a certified check mailed to the winner.

## ONLINE GAMBLERS

Paul Taylor, Cary Funk, and Peyton Craighill of the Pew Research Center note in *Gambling: As the Take Rises, So Does Public Concern* (May 23, 2006, http://pewresearch.org/assets/social/pdf/Gambling.pdf) that few American adults have gambled for money on the Internet: only 2% of adults polled had participated in online gambling in the previous twelve months. Though this number is small, Taylor, Funk, and Craighill explain that the number of people who gambled online doubled from 1996, when a Gallup poll reported that only 1% of Americans gambled online. Perhaps more significantly, in *One in Six Americans Gamble on Sports* (February 1, 2008, http://www.gallup.com/poll/104086/One-Six-Americans-Gamble-Sports.aspx), Jeffrey M. Jones of the Gallup Organization reports that the percentage of Americans who gambled on the Internet in 2007, after the UIGEA went into effect, remained steady at 2%.

In "Small Percentages of U.S. and British Online Adults Admit to Gambling Online" (February 22, 2006, http://www.harrisinteractive.com/harris_poll/index.asp?PID=641), Harris Interactive notes that in 2006 it interviewed 2,985 adults in the United States and 2,074 adults in Great Britain and asked them about their online gambling habits. The Harris poll reveals that most people who gambled online did it frequently. Some 2% of those surveyed in the United States played online poker once a month, as opposed to 1% who played online poker once a year. In addition, 1% gambled at an online casino once a month. Fewer than 0.5% reported gambling at an online casino only once a year.

Peter D. Hart Research Associates and Luntz Maslansky Strategic Research conducted a more extensive poll of online gaming habits in the United States in 2005, which was presented by the AGA in *2006 State of the States: The AGA Survey of Casino Entertainment* (2006, http://www.americangaming.org/assets/files/2006_Survey_for_Web.pdf). The poll found that nearly 4% of Americans gambled online in 2005, which was twice the percentage of those who had gambled online in 2004. Online gamblers were much more likely than the average casino customer to be male, under the age of thirty, and have a college degree. (See Figure 9.1, Figure 9.2, and Figure 9.3.) Of casino gamblers, 53% were male. Only 9% were twenty-one to twenty-nine, and 28% had four-year college degrees. Of online gamblers, 68% were male, 43% were between the ages of twenty-one and twenty-nine, and 35% had four-year college degrees. In addition, 24% had an income of between $75,000 and $99,999 and 17% had an income of more than $100,000. (See Figure 9.4.)

The AGA indicates that 38% of those who gambled online in 2005 had started betting online a year before, and 32% said they had started one to two years before. The largest number of online gamblers (80%) reported playing poker against other people in the previous year. Nearly as many online gamblers (78%) played casino games for money, and far fewer people (56%) placed bets on sports online. Out of those people who played poker online, nearly two-thirds (65%) said that Texas Hold 'Em was their favorite game, followed by seven-card stud (13%), five-card draw (13%), and Omaha (8%). For online casino gamblers, people reported playing blackjack (78%) most often, followed by video poker (65%), slot machines (60%), roulette (37%), and craps (29%).

Robert T. Wood, Robert J. Williams, and Paul K. Lawton examine in "Why Do Internet Gamblers Prefer Online versus Land-Based Venues? Some Preliminary Findings and Implications" (*Journal of Gambling Issues*, no. 20, June 2007) why gamblers patronize Internet gambling sites. The researchers find that gamblers' top reasons for betting on the Internet rather than at a casino involved convenience (12.9%), ease (12.2%), and comfort (11.7%). (See Table 9.1.) One out of ten (10%) gamblers surveyed said they gambled online because of their distance from a casino or because they wanted privacy (9.8%). Other rea-

FIGURE 9.1

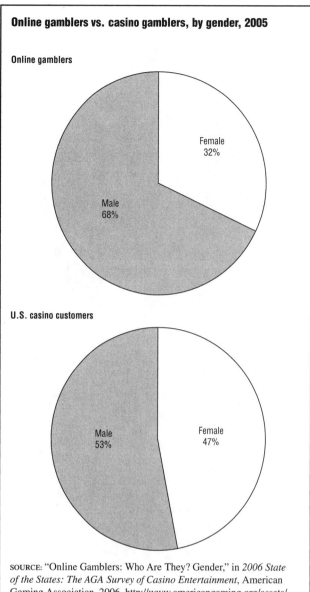

**Online gamblers vs. casino gamblers, by gender, 2005**

Online gamblers

Female 32%

Male 68%

U.S. casino customers

Male 53%

Female 47%

SOURCE: "Online Gamblers: Who Are They? Gender," in *2006 State of the States: The AGA Survey of Casino Entertainment*, American Gaming Association, 2006, http://www.americangaming.org/assets/files/2006_Survey_for_Web.pdf (accessed September 6, 2006). Reprinted with permission from the American Gaming Association. All rights reserved. Data from Peter D. Hart Research Associates, Inc., and Luntz, Maslansky Strategic Research.

sons given included dislike of casino clientele, crowds, noise, or cigarette smoke.

## THE LEGAL ISSUES

Regulating any activity on the Internet has turned out to be a political and legal headache for authorities. Every country wants jurisdiction (the authority to enforce its own laws) over content that its citizens can access over the Internet. This has proved to be difficult, however, because the Internet has no boundaries. A business based on a host computer might be legal in the country in which it is physically located but illegal in other countries where it can be accessed over the Internet.

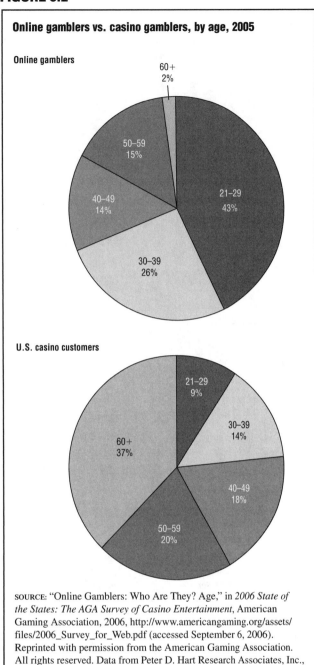

**FIGURE 9.2**

**Online gamblers vs. casino gamblers, by age, 2005**

Online gamblers

- 60+ 2%
- 50–59 15%
- 40–49 14%
- 21–29 43%
- 30–39 26%

U.S. casino customers

- 21–29 9%
- 30–39 14%
- 40–49 18%
- 50–59 20%
- 60+ 37%

SOURCE: "Online Gamblers: Who Are They? Age," in *2006 State of the States: The AGA Survey of Casino Entertainment*, American Gaming Association, 2006, http://www.americangaming.org/assets/files/2006_Survey_for_Web.pdf (accessed September 6, 2006). Reprinted with permission from the American Gaming Association. All rights reserved. Data from Peter D. Hart Research Associates, Inc., and Luntz, Maslansky Strategic Research.

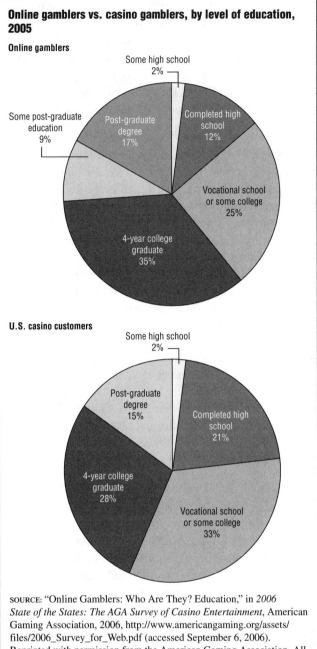

**FIGURE 9.3**

**Online gamblers vs. casino gamblers, by level of education, 2005**

Online gamblers

- Some high school 2%
- Completed high school 12%
- Post-graduate degree 17%
- Some post-graduate education 9%
- Vocational school or some college 25%
- 4-year college graduate 35%

U.S. casino customers

- Some high school 2%
- Completed high school 21%
- Post-graduate degree 15%
- 4-year college graduate 28%
- Vocational school or some college 33%

SOURCE: "Online Gamblers: Who Are They? Education," in *2006 State of the States: The AGA Survey of Casino Entertainment*, American Gaming Association, 2006, http://www.americangaming.org/assets/files/2006_Survey_for_Web.pdf (accessed September 6, 2006). Reprinted with permission from the American Gaming Association. All rights reserved. Data from Peter D. Hart Research Associates, Inc., and Luntz, Maslansky Strategic Research.

Most countries restrict gambling activity much less than the United States does, but in the United States the individual states and not the federal government regulate gambling. Even though there are federal antigambling laws, they defer to the Tenth Amendment of the U.S. Constitution, which guarantees the rights of the states to govern their own affairs. Every state allows or disallows different forms of gambling. For example, Utah and Hawaii prohibit all types of gambling. Commercial casino gambling is legal in eleven states. Pari-mutuel wagering on horse or dog races is legal in more than forty states. Gambling on sporting events through a book-maker is legal only in Nevada. Internet gambling, however, is not subject to state boundaries. A user in any state can access online gambling sites operated from countries around the world where gambling is legal.

Determining jurisdiction is a major problem for authorities. Does online gambling occur at the location where the Web site is hosted or at the location where the gambler is located? The Department of Justice states that gambling occurs in both places. The problem grows even more complicated when one or the other is not on U.S. soil. Even though an international treaty with extradition rights could

FIGURE 9.4

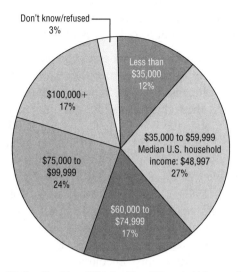

**Household income of online gamblers, 2005**

- Don't know/refused 3%
- Less than $35,000 12%
- $100,000+ 17%
- $75,000 to $99,999 24%
- $35,000 to $59,999 Median U.S. household income: $48,997 27%
- $60,000 to $74,999 17%

SOURCE: "Online Gamblers: Who Are They? Household Income," in *2006 State of the States: The AGA Survey of Casino Entertainment*, American Gaming Association, 2006, http://www.americangaming.org/assets/files/2006_Survey_for_Web.pdf (accessed September 6, 2006). Reprinted with permission from the American Gaming Association. All rights reserved. Data from Peter D. Hart Research Associates, Inc., and Luntz, Maslansky Strategic Research.

**TABLE 9.1**

**Reasons for preferring Internet gambling, 2003–04**

| Reason | Percentage of all reasons given by respondents* |
|---|---|
| Convenience | 12.9% |
| Ease | 12.2% |
| Comfort | 11.7% |
| Distance from casino | 10.0% |
| Privacy | 9.8% |
| Dislike land-based clientele | 5.1% |
| Dislike crowds | 4.7% |
| Dislike noise | 4.1% |
| Dislike smoke | 3.9% |
| High speed of game play | 3.8% |
| Leisurely pace of game play | 3.1% |
| Lower overall expenditure | 3.0% |
| More fun | 3.0% |
| Preference for Internet interface | 2.5% |
| Higher potential wins | 1.8% |
| Safety concerns | 1.6% |
| Lower secondary costs | 1.0% |
| Aversion to casino atmosphere | 0.7% |
| Land-based gambling illegal | 0.5% |
| Disability | 0.4% |
| Other | 4.3% |

*Respondents could offer multiple reasons.

SOURCE: Robert T. Wood, Robert J. Williams, and Paul K. Lawton, "Table 1. Reasons for Preferring Internet Gambling versus Gambling at a Land-Based Venue," in "Why Do Internet Gamblers Prefer Online Versus Land-Based Venues? Some Preliminary Findings and Implications," *Journal of Gambling Issues*, no. 20, June 2007, http://www.camh.net/egambling/issue20/pdfs/issue20.pdf (accessed August 8, 2008)

settle such matters, it is unlikely that one would be written and signed.

Various forms of gambling are legal in many parts of Europe, Central and South America, the Caribbean, Australia, and New Zealand. Most of those areas have set up regulatory measures that are similar to the laws regulating land-based casinos in the United States. For example, in June 2001 the Australian senate passed the Interactive Gambling Act, which prohibits online casinos in the country from taking bets from Australians. The law has provisions allowing interactive sports gambling and wagering services. Foreign residents can gamble at the Australian-based online casinos unless their governments sign up to be excluded from the program. In 2005 the parliament of the United Kingdom passed the Gaming Act, which set up regulations and licensing procedures for online casinos. Though online casinos in Britain were required to pay higher taxes than such companies pay in Caribbean countries, many analysts believe Internet casino operations will flock to Great Britain because of the advanced communications infrastructure, the stable political environment, and the educated workforce.

**The Interstate Wire Act**

In 1961 President John F. Kennedy (1917–1963) signed the Interstate Wire Act—widely known as the Wire Act—which makes it a crime to use telephone lines (wire communication) in interstate or foreign commerce for the placement of sports bets or even to transmit information assisting in the placement of bets on sporting events. The act applies only to the gambling business, not to gamblers themselves.

The article "Gambling on the Internet: Crossing the Interstate Wire" (*The Wager*, vol. 6, no. 6, February 7, 2001) examines the legal issues involved in Internet gambling, particularly criticisms of the Wire Act. It finds that many legal experts say the law does not directly apply or is too ambiguous to apply to offshore Internet gambling sites because:

- The Internet did not exist when the act was made law.

- Gambling Web sites maintained on offshore computers are not under U.S. jurisdiction.

- Internet service providers do not fall under the definition of wire communications facilities (particularly those associated with satellite and mobile-phone transmissions).

- The law specifically mentions only sports betting, not casino games.

- Prosecutors cannot prove that online gambling sites "knowingly" transmit bets from U.S. citizens, because the physical location of online gamblers cannot be determined.

The states have interpreted the Wire Act to mean that online wagering is illegal if it occurs in any state in which gambling is illegal. In 1999 the issue was addressed by the New York Supreme Court in *People v. World Interactive Gaming Corporation* (No. 404428/98 [1999]). The state of New York brought suit against the World Interactive Gaming Corporation (WIGC) and the Golden Chips Casino for offering online gambling to New York residents. The Golden Chips Casino operated a legal land-based casino in Antigua. The company was wholly owned by the WIGC, a Delaware-based corporation with corporate offices in New York. The suit alleged that the casino had installed interactive software on its computer servers in Antigua that allowed Internet users around the world to gamble. The online casino was advertised on various Internet sites and in U.S. gambling magazines, both of which were accessible to New York residents.

Users had to wire money to a bank account in Antigua and type in their permanent address before play. Only users who entered addresses within states that permitted land-based gambling, such as Nevada, were allowed to play, so a user who entered a New York address was not granted permission. However, the suit alleged that the barrier was easily overcome by typing in an out-of-state address, because the software had no way of checking the physical location of the user. The state did not consider this a "good faith effort" to keep New Yorkers from gambling, as required by law.

The WIGC argued that the federal and state laws in question did not apply to an offshore casino operated in full compliance with the law in the country in which it was located. The court ruled in favor of the state, saying that the act of entering the bet and transmitting the betting information originated in New York and constituted illegal gambling activity. The legality of gambling in Antigua was not an issue.

Furthermore, the court said the gambling activity violated three federal laws: the Wire Act; the Foreign Travel or Transportation in Aid of Racketeering Enterprising Act (U.S. Code §1952), known as "the Travel Act"; and the Interstate Transportation of Wagering Paraphernalia Act (U.S. Code §1953), known as "the Paraphernalia Act." According to the court, "the Travel Act prohibits the use of 'any facility in interstate or foreign commerce' with intent to promote any unlawful activity." The Paraphernalia Act is specific to gambling activity, prohibiting the interstate or foreign transmission of any item for use "in (a) bookmaking; or (b) wagering pools with respect to a sporting event or (c) in a numbers, policy, bolita, or similar game." The court ruled the WIGC violated this law because it had used the U.S. mail to send literature to potential investors and to send computers to the Antigua operations.

One issue was still not settled yet: Which types of gambling sites were covered by the Wire Act? The Wire

Act only states that people cannot make sports bets over communication lines. In 2002 the Appeals Court for the Fifth Circuit ruled in *In regarding MasterCard International, Inc.* (313 F.3d 257) that the Wire Act applies specifically to online sports gambling (also known as sports books) and not to online casinos or poker sites.

During the late 1990s federal prosecutors went after the operators of offshore sports books that had taken bets from U.S. citizens via the Internet and telephone. In March 1998 they charged twenty-one people with conspiring to violate the Wire Act. Ten pleaded guilty to that charge, and three pleaded guilty to related misdemeanor charges. Seven could not be apprehended and are considered fugitives. The last defendant, a U.S. citizen named Jay Cohen (1968–), decided to stand trial. Cohen operated a sports book called World Sports Exchange in Antigua. The prosecution in the case argued that Cohen solicited U.S. customers through U.S. newspaper and magazine advertisements, encouraging them to contact World Sports Exchange via a toll-free telephone number and Internet site to place sports bets. On February 28, 2000, Cohen was convicted of conspiracy to violate the Wire Act and seven substantive violations of the Wire Act. He was sentenced to twenty-one months in prison and assessed a $5,000 fine.

In 2001 U.S. agents arrested Jeff D'Ambrosia (1959–) and Duane Pede (1949–), who were the principle owners of Gold Medal Sports, a sports book Web site that operated out of Curaçao. Both pleaded guilty to violating the Wire Act by accepting bets online from people on U.S. soil. They were sentenced to five years in jail and were forced to pay $1.4 million in back taxes.

Despite these arrests, many online sports books operating outside the United States continued to openly market their Web sites to Americans and allow Americans to place bets. In 2006 the Department of Justice cracked down once again on the owners of Internet sports book sites when it arrested David Carruthers (1957–), who was the chief executive officer of the Costa Rican–based BetOnSports. Federal agents arrested Carruthers when he changed planes in Dallas. He was charged with violating the Wire Act, committing mail fraud, and a host of other felonies. Carruthers, who is a British citizen, was awaiting trial as of October 2008. After the arrest, BetOnSports shut down the division of its operations that took bets from U.S. gamblers and fired Carruthers. Other arrests were made of BetOnSports executives, but Carruthers was the most high profile. He remains an outspoken opponent of U.S. federal legislation designed to eliminate online gambling.

Jacob Sullum reports in "Some Bets Are Off" (*Reason*, June 2008) that in 2003 Antigua and Barbuda claimed that the stance the United States took on online gambling was in violation of several free trade agreements laid down by the World Trade Organization (WTO), a multinational trading organization with limited power that sets up and enforces trading agreements between its members. When they appealed to the WTO in an effort to end U.S. restrictions, Antigua and Barbuda maintained that thousands of jobs in their nation depended on online gambling and that the United States was harming their economy by attempting to restrict access by U.S. citizens. The WTO ruled against the United States in 2004, claiming that several U.S. laws regarding online gambling violated WTO free trade agreements. After two years of talks, the United States refused to change its position on online gambling. Antigua and Barbuda approached the WTO again, and in July 2006 the WTO convened a panel to further investigate U.S. laws regarding online gambling. On February 15, 2007, the panel found that the United States was in violation of international trade agreements. The judge presiding over Carruthers's case subsequently ruled that the WTO ruling could be used as part of his defense. As of 2008, the European Union was considering filing a complaint of its own with the WTO, arguing that the United States is treating foreign businesses like criminals.

## The UIGEA

Politicians have long recognized the shortcomings of the Wire Act to address modern gambling technologies. In *Final Report* (June 1999, http://govinfo.library.unt.edu/ ngisc/reports/fullrpt.html), the NGISC recommended that Congress enact federal legislation that prohibits wire transfers from U.S. banks to online gambling sites or their banks.

Some form of Internet gambling legislation has been circulating around Congress since 1995, when Senator Jon L. Kyl (1942–; R-AZ) introduced a bill to amend the Wire Act to specifically prohibit online gambling via the Internet and satellite technologies. It would have allowed individual states to permit online forms of gambling already legal in their states (such as lotteries and casino games), while prohibiting forms that were not (chiefly sports gambling). Considered by many to be virtually impossible to enforce, it did not gain popular support. It failed to pass in 1997 and 1999 as well.

In following years other legislation was proposed in the U.S. House of Representatives by Jim Leach (1942–; R-IA), Robert W. Goodlatte (1952–; R-VA), Michael G. Oxley (1944–; R-OH), and John J. LaFalce (1939–; D-NY) and in the U.S. Senate by Richard C. Shelby (1934–; R-AL) and Dianne Feinstein (1933–; D-CA). In an effort to address the concerns raised by earlier attempts to regulate online gambling, most of the later bills' focus had shifted to outlawing the use of credit cards or electronic payment services to pay for online gambling. The UIGEA, which was signed into law in October 2006, did just that. Rather than regulate the behavior of individuals,

it was intended to prohibit credit card companies from making transactions with online gambling establishments and to authorize the U.S. secretary of the treasury to prohibit any future, unforeseen payment methods that might be used for online gambling.

Michael Blankenship notes in "The Unlawful Internet Gambling Enforcement Act: A Bad Gambling Act? You Betcha!" (*Rutgers Law Review*, vol. 60, no. 2, 2008) that even after the UIGEA became law, many questions remained about how it would be enforced. It was clear that banks and credit card companies could no longer transfer money directly to online casinos or poker sites, such as PartyPoker—it would be a crime to do so. However, whether banks and credit card companies could transfer money for gambling to online payment processors, such as NETeller, was considerably murkier. Many online gamblers set up accounts with payment processors, which function as online banks, and then transfer money in and out of online casinos. Even though the new law would prohibit U.S. banks and credit card companies from sending money to payment processors that deal exclusively with casinos, the law is less clear about payment processors that cater to a wide array of businesses and to payment processors or casinos that are in other countries or are privately held: foreign businesses are not regulated by U.S. law, and privately held companies are not required by law to divulge publicly how they make money. According to Blankenship, many people believe that those who are determined to gamble online will find a way, probably by going to foreign, private payment processors and casinos.

In 2007 several bills were introduced in Congress that sought to regulate, rather than outlaw, Internet gambling. In April 2007 the Internet Gambling Regulation and Enforcement Act (H.R. 2046) was introduced in the House of Representatives. This act would license and regulate Internet gambling sites. The bill was referred to the Subcommittee on Commerce, Trade, and Consumer Protection. In June 2007 the Internet Gambling Regulation and Tax Enforcement Act was introduced to amend the Internal Revenue Code to establish licensing requirements and fees for Internet gambling sites. This bill was referred to the House Committee on Ways and Means. The bill was reintroduced in March 2008 and again referred to the House committee.

## State Laws

Both Hawaii and Utah outlaw any acts of gambling within state borders, which by default includes Internet gambling. According to the AGA, in "Internet Gambling," attorneys general in Florida, Kansas, Minnesota, Oklahoma, and Texas maintained the position in 2007 that online wagering is illegal in their states and in violation of existing laws. In New Jersey the courts ruled that online gambling violates state laws. Massachusetts had a law on the books that specifically forbids gambling transactions over phone lines, which has been interpreted to include online gambling. Six states have enacted laws specifically prohibiting aspects of Internet gambling:

- Illinois prohibits anyone from establishing, maintaining, or operating an Internet gambling site and prohibits making a wager by means of the Internet.

- Louisiana prohibits the operation of an Internet gambling business and providing computer services to Web sites primarily engaged in gambling businesses.

- Oregon law forbids the collection of Internet gambling debts through credit card payments, checks, or electronic fund transfers. Credit card providers are not held liable for debts incurred by Internet gamblers.

- South Dakota prohibits anyone engaged in a gambling business from using the Internet to take bets and prohibits anyone from establishing an Internet gambling business in the state. The law does not apply to the state's licensed casinos.

- Indiana's law states that anyone who operates a gambling Web site or who assists in the operation of such a site commits a felony.

- Washington had the toughest state law against online gambling. Anyone caught gambling online in Washington can be convicted of committing a class C felony, which means that Internet gambling is legally as egregious an offense as possessing child pornography.

## Credit Cards

In 1997 and 1998 a California woman named Cynthia Haines charged more than $70,000 in online gambling losses to her credit cards. Providian National Bank, which issued the cards, sued her for nonpayment. In June 1998 Haines countersued the bank, claiming that it had engaged in unfair business practices by making profits from illegal gambling activities. At that time all casino gambling was illegal in California. Haines's lawyers argued that her debt was void because it arose from an illegal contract. Providian ultimately settled out of court, forgave her debt, and paid $225,000 of her attorney's fees. The company decided to no longer accept online gambling transactions.

The settlement caught the attention of other major credit card issuers. Nonpayment of outstanding credit card charges results in serious losses, called charge-offs in the industry. Faced with the potential for massive charge-offs and legal uncertainties, many card issuers—including Bank of America, Capital One Bank, Chase Manhattan, Citibank, Direct Merchants, Fleet, and MBNA—stopped accepting financial transactions from online gambling sites. Issuers that do accept online gambling transactions

generally delay payment of part or all the money to the online sites for several months in case the user decides to dispute the charges.

The U.S. Government Accounting Office (now the U.S. Government Accountability Office) explains in *Internet Gambling: An Overview of the Issues* (December 2002, http://www.gao.gov/new.items/d0389.pdf) that all the major credit card companies (Discover, American Express, Visa, and MasterCard) have enacted measures to restrict the use of their cards for Internet gambling. Discover and American Express do so primarily by preventing Internet gambling sites from becoming merchants in the first place. All potential merchants are screened, and existing merchants are spot-checked to make sure they are not engaged in online gambling. Visa and MasterCard are issued by a large network of financial institutions that have credit card associations, which set policies for member institutions and provide the computer systems used to process financial transactions. The associations have a coding system that merchants must use to distinguish the different types of transactions. It was refined in 1998 so that online gambling sites have to enter a special two-part code that tells the issuer the nature of their business and gives the issuer a chance to deny authorization. Figure 9.5 shows how an online gambling transaction can be blocked at various points.

However, the coding system does not distinguish between legal and illegal transactions. For example, Americans visiting countries in which online gambling is legal may find their credit cards rejected there when they try to gamble over the Internet. The coding system has also been tricked by unscrupulous merchants who entered the wrong code for their businesses, according to the credit card associations.

Because credit card transactions were blocked at online gambling sites, merchants and gamblers turned to alternative payment systems, called online payment providers. These services allow customers to transfer money from their credit cards into accounts that can then be debited to pay for a variety of online goods and services, including gambling. Money going to and from these intermediary accounts is not easily traced. Online payment providers include PayPal, Neteller, FirePay, and ECash. Some credit card associations are refusing to do business with online payment providers unless they receive assurances that money will not be transferred to Internet gambling sites.

In 2002 and 2003 the online payment network PayPal paid millions of dollars to settle allegations that the company violated the Uniting and Strengthening America by Providing Appropriate Tools Required to Intercept and Obstruct Terrorism Act of 2001 (also called the Patriot Act) during 2001 and early 2002 by processing online gambling transactions from U.S. citizens. The Patriot Act forbids the electronic transmission of funds

FIGURE 9.5

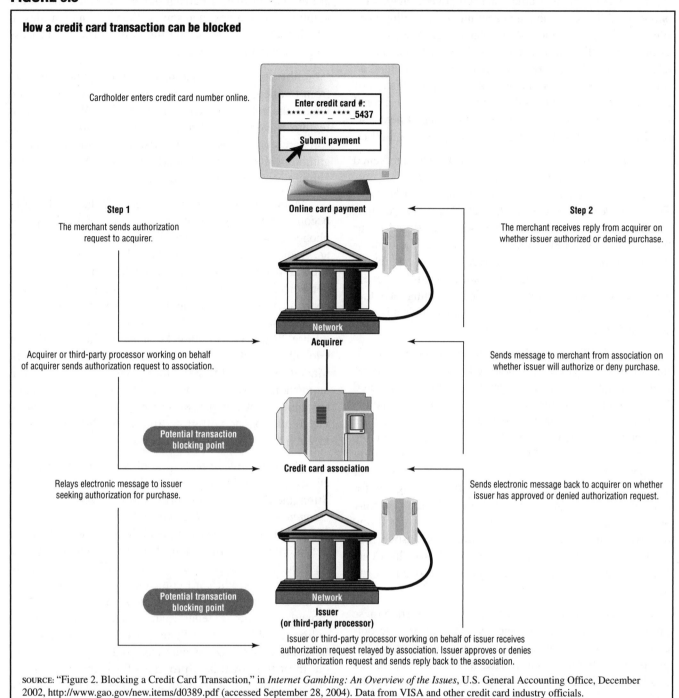

**How a credit card transaction can be blocked**

Cardholder enters credit card number online.

Enter credit card #:
**** _ **** _ **** _5437

Submit payment

**Online card payment**

**Step 1**
The merchant sends authorization request to acquirer.

**Step 2**
The merchant receives reply from acquirer on whether issuer authorized or denied purchase.

Network
**Acquirer**

Acquirer or third-party processor working on behalf of acquirer sends authorization request to association.

Sends message to merchant from association on whether issuer will authorize or deny purchase.

Potential transaction blocking point

**Credit card association**

Relays electronic message to issuer seeking authorization for purchase.

Sends electronic message back to acquirer on whether issuer has approved or denied authorization request.

Potential transaction blocking point

Network
**Issuer**
**(or third-party processor)**

Issuer or third-party processor working on behalf of issuer receives authorization request relayed by association. Issuer approves or denies authorization request and sends reply back to the association.

SOURCE: "Figure 2. Blocking a Credit Card Transaction," in *Internet Gambling: An Overview of the Issues*, U.S. General Accounting Office, December 2002, http://www.gao.gov/new.items/d0389.pdf (accessed September 28, 2004). Data from VISA and other credit card industry officials.

known to be associated with criminal acts. PayPal stopped handling online gambling transactions in November 2002. Neteller processed these funds until January 2007, when its Canadian founders were arrested in the United States on charges of conspiracy and money laundering (the act of engaging in transactions designed to hide or obscure the origin of illegally obtained money).

In 2006 the UIGEA forbade banks and credit card companies from transferring money to both Internet gambling sites and online payment processors strongly associated with virtual casinos. However, identifying pay-

ment processors that deal primarily with casinos is not a simple task. This is especially true if the payment provider is a private corporation with no financial transparency. Even if all such payment providers are identified, large European banks could offer credit cards to Americans, opening Internet gambling services once again to people in the United States.

## Federal Crackdown on Advertising

Under the Wire Act, advertisements for online gaming are illegal in the United States. According to the Department of Justice, media outlets that run advertisements for online gambling are aiding and abetting the gambling Web sites, yet online gambling companies have advertised extensively online, in magazines and newspapers, and on television. In 2003 the Department of Justice mounted an offense against the U.S. media to stop the proliferation of such advertisements. One salvo was a letter to the National Association of Broadcasters in which the department outlined its views on advertising for online gambling outfits.

Then in 2004 the Department of Justice intervened when Discovery Communications agreed to run $3.9 million in ads for Paradise Poker, mostly during *World Poker Tour* episodes on the Travel Channel. Discovery Communications aired $600,000 worth of ads and refused to air the rest. Before Paradise Poker could recover the remainder of the balance paid to Discovery for the ads (about $3.3 million), the Department of Justice seized the money. The obvious message was that online gambling sites that advertised in the United States could have their ads canceled and their assets seized.

In April 2004 major Internet search engines, including Yahoo and Google, announced that they would no longer display ads for online gambling sites that targeted U.S. citizens. The companies reportedly acted to head off plans by the Department of Justice to pursue legal action against them. Many other Web sites did not heed the department's warning. For example, in 2005 the parent company of *The Sporting News* was forced to surrender $4.2 million in advertising revenue after running ads for several online gambling sites. Furthermore, the company agreed to spend $3 million to create and run antigambling advertisements online. The Department of Justice also intervened in 2005 when *Esquire* ran ads for the Costa Rican poker site Bodog.com. *Esquire* agreed not to run any more online casino ads.

One way Internet gambling sites have subverted these prohibitions is to create dot-net sites that mirror the dot-com sites, except that users play with fake money. For example, PartyPoker.com created a site, PartyPoker.net, that bills itself as the "world's largest poker school." Media outlets have accepted advertising for these dot-net sites.

## THE EFFECTS OF ONLINE GAMBLING

Because the Internet gambling medium is relatively new, a limited number of studies have been conducted to determine its effects on people and their gambling habits. Economic factors are also difficult to assess because most online gambling sites operate in foreign countries with little government oversight.

### Economics

Unlike traditional casinos, online gambling sites are not licensed or taxed by state governments. Therefore, they provide no revenue for social and educational programs. The primary financial beneficiaries are the online gambling companies themselves, the foreign countries in which they are located, and the companies that process their financial transactions.

Other businesses that benefit directly or indirectly from online gambling include Internet service providers, phone and cable companies, nongambling Web sites that feature advertisements for online gambling sites, and software companies. Major software providers to online gambling sites include WagerLogic, Boss Media, Microgaming Systems, and World Gaming.

Mobile phone companies expect cellular gambling to become commonplace in the future, particularly for phones with video streaming. Ladbrokes and William Hill are traditional British bookmakers that accept wagers via cellular phones using wireless application protocol. The company Eurobet launched wireless betting in 2000. Other companies, such as Slotland.com, allow people to play slots and win jackpots on their mobile phones. In the press release "Mobile Gambling Forecast to Top $16 Billion Globally by 2011, Despite Bleak Prospects for U.S. Market" (January 15, 2007, http://www.juniperresearch.com/shop/viewpressrelease.php?id=21&pr=42), industry analysts at Juniper Research predict that gambling via cellular phone will grow from a $1.4 billion business in 2006 to a $16.6 billion business by 2011.

The economic effects of online gambling are discussed by Ryan D. Hammer in "Does Internet Gambling Strengthen the U.S. Economy? Don't Bet on It" (*Federal Communications Law Journal*, vol. 54, no. 1, December 2001). Hammer argues that people who do not gamble on the Internet suffer financially from online gambling. The high costs of litigation and unpaid bills, he notes, are passed on by credit card companies to other consumers in the form of higher interest rates and fees. Taxpayer money also funds federal and state lawsuits against online gambling sites. State governments receive no licensing fees or tax revenue from online gambling sites but must fund treatment programs for pathological gamblers, a growing number of whom are online gamblers. The federal government collects income taxes from the big winners of lotteries and traditional casino games, but no taxes are collected from online gambling winners.

### Money Laundering

Law enforcement agencies are concerned about the possible use of online gambling businesses for money laundering. In his testimony before the U.S. Senate Committee on Banking, Housing, and Urban Affairs Committee, the U.S. deputy assistant attorney general John G. Malcolm (March 18, 2003, http://banking.senate.gov/03_03hrg/031803/malcolm.htm) explained that once the money has been stashed with an online casino, criminals can use the games themselves to transfer money to their associates. Some criminals set up private tables at online casino sites and then intentionally lose their money to business associates at the table. In other instances, the casino is part of the crime organization, so all the criminal has to do is lose money to the casino.

The factors that make online gambling susceptible to money laundering, officials say, include the speed and anonymity with which financial transactions take place and the offshore locations of the gambling companies. Many financial analysts believe the risk is low when credit cards are used, because credit card transactions are closely monitored and recorded. Now that credit card use is illegal in online gambling, other, less traceable payment methods may become popular.

## Compulsive Gambling

Experts suggest that the fast pace and instant gratification associated with online gambling make it more addictive than other types of gambling. Online gambling is quite different from traditional casino gambling, because it is a solitary and anonymous activity. By contrast, casino gambling is a social activity, usually conducted in the company of family or friends. The Council on Compulsive Gaming of New Jersey estimates that a large percentage of online gamblers gamble alone. Online gamblers who contact the organization for help are usually younger than traditional gamblers and have built up large amounts of debt in a shorter time than traditional gamblers.

George T. Ladd and Nancy M. Petry of the University of Connecticut conducted a study of Internet gamblers and published their results in "Disordered Gambling among University-Based Medical and Dental Patients: A Focus on Internet Gambling" (*Psychology of Addictive Behaviors*, vol. 16, no. 1, March 2002). Between August 1999 and September 2000 the researchers surveyed patients seeking free or reduced-cost services at the university's health and dental clinics. All the 389 patients who completed the questionnaires in full reported gambling at some point in their life. About 90% had gambled in the previous year and 42% had gambled in the previous week. Some 8.1% had gambled online during their lifetime and 4% gambled online weekly. The younger respondents were more likely to have Internet gambling experience than the older respondents: the median age of the online gamblers was 31.7 years, compared to 43.5 years for traditional gamblers. Ethnicity also made a difference. Non-whites made up only 15.8% of the total group surveyed but 38.7% of the Internet gamblers.

All participants were given the South Oaks Gambling Screen (SOGS), a standard series of questions used to determine the probability that a person has a gambling problem. Results showed that the mean SOGS score of online gamblers was 7.8, compared to 1.8 for those who had no online gambling experience. Researchers catego-rized all respondents into levels depending on their SOGS scores. Level 1 gamblers had SOGS scores of 0 to 2 and were considered not to have a gambling problem. Level 2 gamblers had SOGS scores of 3 to 4 and were considered probable problem gamblers. Level 3 gamblers had SOGS scores of 5 or greater and were considered probable patho-logical gamblers.

Internet gamblers were much more likely to have gambling problems than non-Internet gamblers. Slightly more than 74% of Internet gamblers were rated at Levels 2 or 3, compared to 21.6% of the traditional gamblers.

Nancy M. Petry reports the results of a follow-up study in "Internet Gambling: An Emerging Concern in Family Practice Medicine" (*Family Practice*, vol. 23, no. 4, August 2006). In this study, 1,414 adults in health clinic waiting areas were given the SOGS test. Some 6.9% of adults reported ever gambling on the Internet, and 2.8% said they gambled online frequently. Of those who gambled frequently, nearly two-thirds (65.9%) were cate-gorized as problem gamblers, as compared to 29.8% of those who reported ever gambling on the Internet and 7.6% of those who were classified as non-Internet gam-blers. The researchers then retrieved the medical records for those who participated in the study, finding that Internet gamblers had poorer mental and physical health than those who did not.

In detailing their study, Ladd and Petry write that "the availability of Internet gambling may draw individ-uals who seek out isolated and anonymous contexts for their gambling behaviors." Even though problem gam-blers are able to resist traveling to another state to casi-nos, they find online gambling more difficult to avoid because Internet sites are always open and accessible.

## Underage Gambling

In January 2001 the American Psychiatric Associa-tion was already warning the public about Internet gam-bling. In a public health advisory, it noted that because online sites are not regulated, no measures were being taken to prevent underage gamblers from participating. It considered children and teenagers, who already play non-gambling games on the Internet, at significant risk of being lured to gambling sites. It also noted that few safeguards were in place to ensure the fairness of the Internet games or to establish exactly who had responsi-bility for operating them.

In "FTC Warns Consumers about Online Gambling and Children" (June 26, 2002, http://www.ftc.gov/opa/2002/06/onlinegambling.shtm), the U.S. Federal Trade Commission (FTC) also warns parents about children and online gambling. The FTC states it is too easy for kids, particularly teenagers, to access online gambling sites. It complains that many nongambling game-playing sites pop-ular with kids contain links to gambling sites. The agency had examined one hundred Internet gambling sites and finds that 20% had no warnings at all to children and many lacked measures to block minors from gambling.

Each year the Annenberg Public Policy Center at the University of Pennsylvania releases the National Annenberg Risk Survey of Youth. In "More than 1 Million Young People Use Internet Gambling Sites Each Month" (October 2, 2006, http://www.annenbergpublicpolicycenter.org/NewsDetails.aspx?myId=32), the center finds that the weekly use of Internet gambling sites had increased from 2.3% in 2005 to 5.8% in 2006 among males aged eighteen to twenty-two. By the next year, however, the center notes in "Card Playing down among College-Age Youth; Internet Gambling Also Declines" (October 18, 2007, http://www.annenbergpublicpolicycenter.org/NewsDetails.aspx?myId=242) that after the passage of the UIGEA, weekly use of the Internet for gambling had dropped to 1.5%.

# IMPORTANT NAMES
# AND ADDRESSES

**American Gaming Association**
1299 Pennsylvania Ave. NW, Ste. 1175
Washington, DC 20004
(202) 552-2675
FAX: (202) 552-2676
E-mail: info@americangaming.org
URL: http://www.americangaming.org/

**Annenberg Public Policy Center**
3535 Market St., Ste. 200
Philadelphia, PA 19104-3309
(215) 898-9400
FAX: (215) 898-7116
URL: http://www.annenbergpublic
policycenter.org/

**Arizona Department of Racing**
1110 W. Washington, Ste. 260
Phoenix, AZ 85007
(602) 364-1700
FAX: (602) 364-1703
E-mail: ador@azracing.gov
URL: http://www.azracing.gov/

**Arizona Lottery**
PO Box 2913
Phoenix, AZ 85062-2913
(480) 921-4400
URL: http://www.arizonalottery.com/

**Arkansas Racing Commission**
PO Box 3076
Little Rock, AR 72203
(501) 682-1467
URL: http://www.arkansas.gov/dfa/racing/

**Birmingham Racing Commission**
1000 John Rogers Dr., Ste. 102
Birmingham, AL 35210
(205) 838-7470
URL: http://www.birminghamracing
commission.com/

**Boyd Gaming**
3883 Howard Hughes Pkwy, Ninth Floor
Las Vegas, NV 89169

(702) 792-7200
URL: http://www.boydgaming.com/

**California Horse Racing Board**
1010 Hurley Way, Ste. 300
Sacramento, CA 95825
(916) 263-6000
FAX: (916) 263-6042
URL: http://www.chrb.ca.gov/

**California Lottery**
600 N. Tenth St.
Sacramento, CA 95814
(916) 323-7095
URL: http://www.calottery.com/

**Christiansen Capital Advisors**
170 Sawyer Rd.
New Gloucester, ME 04260
(207) 688-4500
E-mail: cca-ny@verizon.net
URL: http://www.cca-i.com/

**Colorado Division of Gaming**
1881 Pierce St., Ste. 112
Lakewood, CO 80214-1496
(303) 205-1355
FAX: (303) 205-1342
URL: http://www.revenue.state.co.us/
Gaming/home.asp

**Colorado Lottery**
212 W. Third St., Ste. 210
Pueblo, CO 81003
(719) 546-2400
FAX: (719) 546-5208
URL: http://www.coloradolottery.com/

**Connecticut Division of Special Revenue**
555 Russell Rd.
Newington, CT 06111-1523
(860) 594-0500
FAX: (860) 594-0509
E-mail: dosr@po.state.ct.us
URL: http://www.ct.gov/dosr/site/
default.asp

**Connecticut Lottery Corporation**
777 Brook St.
Rocky Hill, CT 06067
(860) 713-2805
FAX: (860) 713-2600
E-mail: ctlottery@po.state.ct.us
URL: http://www.ctlottery.org/

**DC Lottery and Charitable Games
Control Board**
2101 Martin Luther King Jr. Ave. SE
Washington, DC 20020
(202) 645-8000
URL: http://lottery.dc.gov/lottery/site/
default.asp

**Delaware Lottery**
1575 McKee Rd., Ste. 102
Dover, DE 19904
(302) 739-5291
FAX: (302) 739-6706
URL: http://lottery.state.de.us/

**Florida Department of Business and
Professional Regulation, Division of
Pari-mutuel Wagering**
1940 N. Monroe St.
Tallahassee, FL 32399
(850) 487-1395
E-mail: Call.Center@dbpr.state.fl.us
URL: http://www.myflorida.com/dbpr/pmw/
index.shtml

**Florida Lottery**
250 Marriott Dr.
Tallahassee, FL 32301
(850) 487-7725
FAX: (850) 488-8049
E-mail: asklott@flalottery.com
URL: http://www.flalottery.com/

**Gamblers Anonymous**
PO Box 17173
Los Angeles, CA 90017
(213) 386-8789
FAX: (213) 386-0030

E-mail: isomain@gamblersanonymous.org
URL: http://www.gamblersanonymous.org/

**Georgia Lottery Corporation**
250 Williams St., Ste. 3000
Atlanta, GA 30303
(404) 215-5000
URL: http://www.galottery.com/

**Greyhound Protection League**
PO Box 669
Penn Valley, CA 95946
1-800-446-8637
URL: http://www.greyhounds.org/

**Hoosier Lottery**
Pan Am Plaza
201 S. Capitol Ave., Ste. 1100
Indianapolis, IN 46225
1-800-955-6886
E-mail: playersupport@hoosierlottery.com
URL: http://www.in.gov/hoosierlottery/

**Humane Society of the United States**
2100 L St. NW
Washington, DC 20037
(301) 258-8276
FAX: (301) 258-3078
URL: http://www.hsus.org/

**Idaho Lottery**
1199 Shoreline Ln., Ste. 100
Boise, ID 83702
(208) 334-2600
E-mail: info@idaholottery.com
URL: http://www.idaholottery.com/

**Idaho State Police Racing Commission**
PO Box 700
Meridian, ID 83680-0700
(208) 884-7080
FAX: (208) 884-7098
URL: http://www.isp.state.id.us/race/
index.html

**Illinois Gaming Board**
160 N. LaSalle, Ste. 300
Chicago, IL 60601
(312) 814-4700
URL: http://www.igb.state.il.us/

**Illinois Lottery**
101 W. Jefferson St.
Springfield, IL 62702
1-800-252-1775
E-mail: Rev.LotteryInfo@illinois.gov
URL: http://www.illinoislottery.com/

**Illinois Racing Board**
100 W. Randolph, Ste. 7-701
Chicago, IL 60601
(312) 814-2600
E-mail: IRB.Info@illinois.gov
URL: http://www.state.il.us/agency/irb/

**Indiana Gaming Commission**
East Tower, Ste. 1600
101 W. Washington St.
Indianapolis, IN 46204
(317) 233-0046
FAX: (317) 233-0047
URL: http://www.in.gov/gaming/

**Indiana Horse Racing Commission**
ISTA Center, Ste. 530
150 W. Market St.
Indianapolis, IN 46204
(317) 233-3119
URL: http://www.in.gov/hrc/

**Institute for Problem Gambling**
955 S. Main St.
Middletown, CT 06457
(860) 343-5500, ext. 2125
FAX: (860) 347-3183
E-mail: herb@theconnectioninc.org
URL: http://www.gamblingproblem.net/

**Institute for the Study of Gambling and Commercial Gaming**
College of Business Administration
University of Nevada
Reno, NV 89557-0025
(775) 784-1442
FAX: (775) 784-1057
URL: http://www.unr.edu/gaming/index.asp

**Iowa Lottery**
2323 Grand Ave.
Des Moines, IA 50312-5307
(515) 725-7900
URL: http://www.ialottery.com/

**Iowa Racing and Gaming Commission**
717 E. Court, Ste. B
Des Moines, IA 50309
(515) 281-7352
FAX: (515) 242-6560
E-mail: irgc@iowa.gov
URL: http://www.state.ia.us/irgc/

**Jockey Club**
40 E. Fifty-second St.
New York, NY 10022
(212) 371-5970
FAX: (212) 371-6123
URL: http://www.jockeyclub.com/

**Kansas Lottery**
128 N. Kansas Ave.
Topeka, KS 66603
(785) 296-5700
E-mail: lotteryinfo@kslottery.net
URL: http://www.kslottery.com/

**Kansas Racing and Gaming Commission**
700 SW Harrison, Ste. 420
Topeka, KS 66603-3754
(785) 296-5800
FAX: (785) 296-0900
E-mail: krgc@ksracing.org
URL: http://www.ksracing.org/

**Kentucky Horse Racing Commission**
4063 Ironworks Pkwy., Bldg. B
Lexington, KY 40511
(859) 246-2040
FAX: (859) 246-2039
E-mail: lisa.underwood@ky.gov
URL: http://www.khrc.ky.gov/

**Kentucky Lottery**
1011 W. Main St.
Louisville, KY 40202
(502) 560-1500
URL: http://www.kylottery.com/

**Louisiana Gaming Control Board**
9100 Bluebonnet Centre Blvd., Ste. 500
Baton Rouge, LA 70809
(225) 295-8450
FAX: (225) 295-8479
URL: http://www.dps.state.la.us/lgcb/

**Louisiana Lottery Corporation**
555 Laurel St.
Baton Rouge, LA 70801-1813
(225) 297-2000
URL: http://www.louisianalottery.com/

**Maine Harness Racing Promotion Board**
State House Station 28
Augusta, ME 04333
(207) 287-3221
E-mail: info@maineharnessracing.com
URL: http://www.maineharnessracing.com/

**Maine State Lottery Commission**
Eight State House Station
Augusta, ME 04333
(207) 287-3721
1-800-452-8777
URL: http://www.mainelottery.com/

**Maryland Racing Commission**
300 E. Towsontowne Blvd.
Towson, MD 21286
(410) 296-9682
FAX: (410) 296-9687
E-mail: racing@dllr.state.md.us
URL: http://www.dllr.state.md.us/racing/

**Maryland State Lottery Agency**
1800 Washington Blvd., Ste. 330
Baltimore, MD 21230
(410) 230-8800
E-mail: paffairs@msla.state.md.us
URL: http://www.mdlottery.com/

**Massachusetts State Lottery Commission**
60 Columbian St.
Braintree, MA 02184
(781) 849-5555
FAX: (781) 849-5509
URL: http://www.masslottery.com/

**Massachusetts State Racing Commission**
One Ashburton Pl., Rm. 1313
Boston, MA 02108
(617) 727-2581
FAX: (617) 277-6062

E-mail: racing.commission@state.ma.us
URL: http://www.state.ma.us/src/

**Michigan Gaming Control Board**
3062 W. Grand Blvd., L-700
Detroit, MI 48202-6062
(313) 456-4100
FAX: (313) 456-4200
URL: http://www.michigan.gov/mgcb

**Michigan Lottery**
101 E. Hillsdale
Lansing, MI 48933
URL: http://www.michigan.gov/lottery

**Michigan Office of the Racing
Commissioner**
Constitution Hall
525 W. Allegan St.
Lansing, MI 48909
(517) 335-1420
FAX: (517) 241-3018
URL: http://www.michigan.gov/horseracing

**Minnesota Gambling Control Board**
1711 W. County Road B, Ste. 300B
Roseville, MN 55113
(651) 639-4000
URL: http://www.gcb.state.mn.us/

**Minnesota Racing Commission**
1100 Canterbury Rd.
Shakopee, MN 55379
(952) 496-7950
FAX: (952) 496-7954
URL: http://www.mnrace.commission.state
.mn.us/

**Minnesota State Lottery**
2645 Long Lake Rd.
Roseville, MN 55113
(651) 635-8273
E-mail: lottery@mnlottery.com
URL: http://www.lottery.state.mn.us/

**Mississippi Gaming Commission**
620 North St., Ste. 200
Jackson, MS 39225-3577
(601) 576-3800
1-800-504-7529
FAX: (601) 576-3929
E-mail: info@mgc.state.ms.us
URL: http://www.mgc.state.ms.us/

**Missouri Gaming Commission**
3417 Knipp Dr.
Jefferson City, MO 65102
(573) 526-4080
FAX: (573) 526-1999
E-mail: PublicRelation@mgc.dps.mo.gov
URL: http://www.mgc.dps.mo.gov/

**Missouri Lottery**
1823 Southridge Dr.
Jefferson City, MO 65109-1603
(573) 751-4050
FAX: (573) 751-5188
URL: http://www.molottery.com/

**Montana Department of Livestock,
Board of Horse Racing**
PO Box 200512
Helena, MT 59620
(406) 444-4287
E-mail: livemail@mt.gov
URL: http://liv.mt.gov/liv/HR/index.asp

**Montana Gambling Control Division**
2550 Prospect Ave.
PO Box 201424
Helena, MT 59620-1424
(406) 444-1971
E-mail: gcd@mt.gov
URL: http://www.doj.mt.gov/gaming/

**Montana Lottery**
2525 N. Montana Ave.
Helena, MT 59601-0598
(406) 444-5825
E-mail: montanalottery@mail.com
URL: http://www.montanalottery.com/

**Multi-state Lottery Association**
4400 NW Urbandale Dr.
Urbandale, IA 50322
(515) 453-1400
URL: http://www.musl.com/

**National Association of Fundraising
Ticket Manufacturers**
1360 Energy Park Dr., Ste. 210
St. Paul, MN 55108
(651) 644-4710
URL: http://www.naftm.org/

**National Center for Responsible Gaming**
1299 Pennsylvania Ave. NW, Ste. 1175
Washington, DC 20004
(202) 552-2689
FAX: (202) 552-2676
E-mail: contact@ncrg.org/
URL: http://www.ncrg.org/

**National Coalition against Legalized
Gambling**
100 Maryland Ave. NE, Rm. 311
Washington, DC 20002
1-800-664-2680
E-mail: ncalg@ncalg.com
URL: http://www.ncalg.org/

**National Council on Problem Gambling**
730 Eleventh St., NW, Ste. 601
Washington, DC 20001
(202) 547-9204
1-800-522-4700
FAX: (202) 547-9206
E-mail: ncpg@ncpgambling.org
URL: http://www.ncpgambling.org/

**National Indian Gaming Association**
224 Second St. SE
Washington, DC 20003
(202) 546-7711
FAX: (202) 546-1755
E-mail: info@indiangaming.org
URL: http://www.indiangaming.org/

**National Indian Gaming Commission**
1441 L St. NW, Ste. 9100
Washington, DC 20005
(202) 632-7003
FAX: (202) 632-7066
E-mail: info@nigc.gov
URL: http://www.nigc.gov/

**Nebraska Lottery**
1800 O St., Ste. 101
Lincoln, NE 68509
(402) 471-6100
E-mail: lottery@nelottery.com
URL: http://www.nelottery.com/

**Nebraska State Racing Commission**
301 Centennial Mall South, Sixth Fl.
Lincoln, NE 68509-5014
(402) 471-4155
FAX: (402) 471-2339
URL: http://www.horseracing.state.ne.us/

**Nevada Gaming Commission and State
Gaming Control Board**
1919 College Pkwy
Carson City, NV 89706
(775) 684-7750
FAX: (775) 687-5817
URL: http://gaming.nv.gov/

**New Hampshire Lottery Commission**
14 Integra Dr.
Concord, NH 03301
(603) 271-3391
1-800-852-3324
FAX: (603) 271-1160
E-mail: webmaster@lottery.nh.gov
URL: http://www.nhlottery.org/

**New Hampshire Racing and Charitable
Gaming Commission**
57 Regional Dr., Unit 3
Concord, NH 03301-8518
(603) 271-2158
FAX: (603) 271-3381
URL: http://www.racing.nh.gov/

**New Jersey Casino Control Commission**
Arcade Bldg.
Tennessee Avenue and Boardwalk
Atlantic City, NJ 08401
(609) 441-3799
URL: http://www.state.nj.us/casinos/

**New Jersey Lottery**
PO Box 041
Trenton, NJ 08625-0041
(609) 599-5800
FAX: (609) 599-5935
E-mail: publicinfo@lottery.state.nj.us
URL: http://www.state.nj.us/lottery/

**New Jersey Racing Commission**
140 E. Front St., Fourth Fl.
Trenton, NJ 08625
(609) 292-0613
FAX: (609) 599-1785
URL: http://www.nj.gov/oag/racing/index.html

**New Mexico Gaming Control Board**
4900 Alameda Blvd. NE
Albuquerque, NM 87113
(505) 841-9700
FAX: (505) 841-9725
URL: http://www.nmgcb.org/

**New Mexico Lottery**
PO Box 93130
Albuquerque, NM 87199-3130
(505) 342-7600
E-mail: custservice@nmlottery.com
URL: http://www.nmlottery.com/

**New Mexico Racing Commission**
4900 Alameda NE, Ste. A
Albuquerque, NM 87113
(505) 222-0700
FAX: (505) 222-0713
E-mail: rosemary.leeder@state.nm.us
URL: http://nmrc.state.nm.us/

**New York City Off-Track Betting**
Times Square Station
PO Box 7777
New York, NY 10108
(212) 221-5200
1-800-682-8118
URL: http://www.nycotb.com/newnycotb/
Default.aspx

**New York Lottery**
PO Box 7500
Schenectady, NY 12301-7500
(518) 388-3300
URL: http://www.nylottery.org/index.php

**New York State Racing and Wagering
Board**
One Broadway Center, Ste. 600
Schenectady, NY 12305-2553
(518) 395-5400
FAX: (518) 347-1250
E-mail: info@racing.state.ny.us
URL: http://www.racing.state.ny.us/

**North American Association of State and
Provincial Lotteries**
6 N. Broadway
Geneva, OH 44041
(440) 466-5630
FAX: (440) 466-5649
E-mail: info@nasplhq.org
URL: http://www.naspl.org/

**North Carolina Department of Crime
Control and Public Safety, Alcohol Law
Enforcement Division, Bingo Licensing
Section**
4704 Mail Service Center
Raleigh, NC 27699-4701
(919) 733-2126
URL: http://www.nccrimecontrol.org/

**North Carolina Education Lottery**
2100 Yonkers Rd.
Raleigh, NC 27604
(919) 715-6886

FAX: (919) 715-8833
URL: http://www.nc-educationlottery.org/

**North Dakota Lottery**
600 E. Boulevard Ave., Dept. 125
Bismarck, ND 58505
(701) 328-1574
E-mail: ndlottery@nd.gov
URL: http://www.ndlottery.org/

**North Dakota Office of Attorney General,
Gaming Division**
600 E. Boulevard Ave., Dept. 125
Bismarck, ND 58505
(701) 328-4848
URL: http://www.ag.state.nd.us/Gaming/
Gaming.htm

**Ohio Lottery Commission**
615 W. Superior Ave.
Cleveland, OH 44113
1-800-686-4208
E-mail: olcwebmail@olc.state.oh.us
URL: http://www.ohiolottery.com/

**Ohio State Racing Commission**
77 S. High St., Eighteenth Fl.
Columbus, OH 43215-6108
(614) 466-2757
FAX: (614) 466-1900
URL: http://www.racing.ohio.gov/

**Oklahoma Horse Racing Commission**
Shepherd Mall
2401 NW Twenty-third St., Ste. 78
Oklahoma City, OK 73107
(405) 943-6472
FAX: (405) 943-6474
E-mail: ohrc@socket.net
URL: http://www.ohrc.org/

**Oregon Lottery**
500 Airport Rd. SE
Salem, OR 97309
(503) 540-1000
FAX: (503) 540-1001
E-mail: lottery.webcenter@state.or.us
URL: http://www.oregonlottery.org/

**Oregon Racing Commission**
800 NE Oregon St., Ste. 310
Portland, OR 97232
(971) 673-0207
FAX: (971) 673-0213
URL: http://racing.oregon.gov/

**Penn National Gaming**
825 Berkshire Blvd., Ste. 200
Wyomissing, PA 19610
(610) 373-2400
FAX: (610) 373-4966
E-mail: corporate@pngaming.com
URL: http://www.pngaming.com/

**Pennsylvania Lottery**
1200 Fulling Mill Rd., Ste. 1
Middletown, PA 17057
(717) 702-8000

1-800-692-7481
FAX: (717) 702-8024
URL: http://www.palottery.state.pa.us/

**Pennsylvania State Horse Racing
Commission**
2301 N. Cameron St.
Agriculture Bldg., Rm. 304
Harrisburg, PA 17110
(717) 787-1942
FAX: (717) 346-1546
URL: http://www.agriculture.state.pa.us/
agriculture/cwp/view.asp?a=3&q=128999

**Pet-Abuse.com**
PO Box 5
Southfields, NY 10975-0005
1-888-523-7387
E-mail: info@pet-abuse.com
URL: http://www.pet-abuse.com/

**Pew Research Center**
1615 L St. NW, Ste. 700
Washington, DC 20036
(202) 419-4300
FAX: (202) 419-4349
E-mail: info@pewresearch.org
URL: http://www.pewresearch.org/

**Rhode Island Department of Business
Regulation, Division of Racing and
Athletics**
1511 Pontiac Ave.
Cranston, RI 02920
(401) 462-9525
FAX: (401) 462-9645
E-mail: RacingAthleticsInquiry@dbr.state
.ri.us
URL: http://www.dbr.state.ri.us/divisions/
commlicensing/

**Rhode Island Lottery**
1425 Pontiac Ave.
Cranston, RI 02920
(401) 463-6500
FAX: (401) 463-5669
URL: http://www.rilot.com/

**South Carolina Education Lottery**
PO Box 11949
Columbia, SC 29211-1949
(803) 737-2091
FAX: (803) 737-2316
URL: http://www.sceducationlottery.com/

**South Dakota Commission on Gaming**
1320 E. Sioux Ave.
Pierre, SD 57501
(605) 773-6050
FAX: (605) 773-6053
URL: http://www.state.sd.us/drr2/reg/
gaming/

**South Dakota Lottery**
207 E. Capitol Ave.
Pierre, SD 57501
(605) 773-5770
FAX: (605) 773-5786

E-mail: lottery@state.sd.us
URL: http://www.sdlottery.org/

**Tennessee Lottery**
Plaza Tower Metro Center
200 Athens Way, Ste. 200
Nashville, TN 37228
(615) 324-6500
URL: http://www.tnlottery.com/

**Texas Lottery Commission**
611 E. Sixth St.
Austin, TX 78701
(512) 344-5000
1-800-375-6886
FAX: (512) 344-5080
E-mail: customer.service@lottery.state.tx.us
URL: http://www.txlottery.org/

**Texas Racing Commission**
8505 Cross Park Dr., Ste. 110
Austin, TX 78754
(512) 833-6699
FAX: (512) 833-6907
URL: http://www.txrc.state.tx.us/

**U.S. Trotting Association**
750 Michigan Ave.
Columbus, OH 43215
(614) 224-2291
1-877-800-8782
FAX: (614) 228-1385
E-mail: customerservice@ustrotting.com
URL: http://www.ustrotting.com/

**Vermont Lottery Commission**
1311 U.S. Rte. 302, Ste. 100
Barre, VT 05641
(802) 479-5686
1-800-322-8800
FAX: (802) 479-4294
E-mail: vlc@state.vt.us
URL: http://www.vtlottery.com/

**Virginia Department of Charitable Gaming**
101 N. Fourteenth St., Seventeenth Fl.
Richmond, VA 23219
(804) 786-1681
FAX: (804) 786-1079
E-mail: webmaster@DCG.Virginia.gov
URL: http://www.dcg.state.va.us/

**Virginia Lottery**
900 E. Main St.
Richmond, VA 23219
(804) 692-7000
FAX: (804) 692-7102
URL: http://www.valottery.com/

**Virginia Racing Commission**
10700 Horsemen's Rd.
New Kent, VA 23124
(804) 966-7400
FAX: (804) 966-7418
URL: http://www.vrc.virginia.gov/

**Washington Horse Racing Commission**
6326 Martin Way, Ste. 209
Olympia, WA 98516
(360) 459-6462
FAX: (360) 459-6461
E-mail: whrc@whrc.state.wa.us
URL: http://www.whrc.wa.gov/

**Washington's Lottery**
814 Fourth Avenue East
Olympia, WA 98504-3000
(360) 664-4720
FAX: (360) 664-2630
E-mail: director's_office@walottery.com
URL: http://www.walottery.com/

**Washington State Gambling Commission**
4565 Seventh Ave. SE
Olympia, WA 98503

(360) 486-3440
1-800-345-2529
FAX: (360) 486-3629
URL: http://www.wsgc.wa.gov/

**West Virginia Lottery**
312 MacCorkle Ave. SE
Charleston, WV 25327
(304) 558-0500
1-800-982-2274
FAX: (304) 558-3321
E-mail: mail@wvlottery.com
URL: http://www.wvlottery.com/

**West Virginia Racing Commission**
106 Dee Dr.
Charleston, WV 25134
(304) 558-2150
FAX: (304) 558-6319
URL: http://www.wvf.state.wv.us/
racing/

**Wisconsin Division of Gaming**
3319 W. Beltline Hwy., First Fl.
Madison, WI 53713
(608) 270-2555
FAX: (608) 270-2564
URL: http://www.doa.state.wi.us/gaming/
index.asp

**Wisconsin Lottery**
PO Box 8941
Madison, WI 53708-8941
(608) 261-4916
URL: http://www.wilottery.com/

**Wyoming Pari-mutuel Commission**
Hansen Bldg.
2515 Warren Ave., Ste. 301
Cheyenne, WY 82002
(307) 777-5928
FAX: (307) 777-3681
URL: http://parimutuel.state.wy.us/

# RESOURCES

Several resources useful to this book were published by companies and organizations within the gambling industry. Most notable are *Profile of the American Casino Gambler: Harrah's Survey 2006* (June 2006) by Harrah's Entertainment; *Charity Gaming in North America Annual Report 2006* (2007) by the National Association of Fundraising Ticket Manufacturers; and *2008 State of the States: The AGA Survey of Casino Entertainment* (2008) and *An Analysis of Internet Gambling and Its Policy Implications* (2006, David O. Stewart) by the American Gaming Association. The National Indian Gaming Association (NIGA) published *The Economic Impact of Indian Gaming in 2006* (2007). The NIGA's resource library also provided excellent information about tribal gambling.

Informative resources from industry analysts include publications from Christiansen Capital Advisors, including *Past as Prologue. E-gambling: What Does the Future Hold?* (2005) by Sebastian Sinclair and *The Gross Annual Wager of the United States: 2003* (2004) by Eugene Martin Christiansen and Sebastian Sinclair. The Pew Research Center provided valuable insight into the industry in *Gambling: As the Take Rises, So Does Public Concern* (May 2006, Paul Taylor, Cary Funk, and Peyton Craighill).

I. Nelson Rose of Whittier Law School maintains the Web site Gambling and the Law (http://www.gamblingandthelaw.com/), which is a valuable resource for historical and legal information on gambling. Gambling Law US (http://www.gambling-law-us.com/) is maintained by the attorney Chuck Humphrey; it provides a detailed listing of all the state and federal gambling laws as well as those laws that affect gambling indirectly. The National Council against Legalized Gambling (http://www.ncalg.org/) provides the latest news updates on gambling and politics around the United States.

Several publications of the U.S. Government Accountability Office, the investigative arm of Congress, were used in preparation of this book, including *Indian Issues: Improvements Needed in Tribal Recognition Process* (November 2001) and *Internet Gambling: An Overview of the Issues* (December 2002). The National Indian Gaming Commission issues a quarterly newsletter that was also helpful in preparing Chapter 5.

Each state that allows gambling issues a quarterly or annual report describing revenues, employment, tax payments, and more. Reports helpful for this book included *Casino Gross Gaming Revenues* (2008) by the Mississippi State Tax Commission; *2007 Annual Report* (2008) by the State of New Jersey Casino Control Commission; *State of Nevada Gaming Revenue Report: Year Ended December 31, 2007* (2008) by the Nevada State Gaming Control Board; *2007 Annual Report to Governor Mitch Daniels* (2007) by the Indiana Gaming Commission; *2007 Annual Report* (2008) by the Illinois Gaming Board; *Iowa Racing and Gaming Commission: Gaming Revenue by Fiscal Year* (2002–2007) by the Iowa Racing and Gaming Commission; *Gaming in Colorado: Fact Book and 2007 Abstract* (2008) by the Colorado Division of Gaming; *Annual Report, Fiscal Year 2007* (2007) by the South Dakota Commission on Gaming; *Annual Report to the Governor, Calendar Year 2007* (2007) by the Michigan Gaming Control Board; *Thirty-seventh Annual Report of the California Horse Racing Board: A Summary of Fiscal Year 2006–2007 Racing in California* (2007) by the California Horse Racing Board; and *76th Annual Report: Fiscal Year 2006–2007* (January 2008) by the Florida Department of Business and Professional Regulation's Division of Pari-mutuel Wagering.

The Bureau of Labor Statistics published *Occupational Outlook Handbook, 2008–09 Edition* (2008), which provided information on career opportunities in the gaming industry. Information on gambling policy and legislation is available from the National Conference of State Legislatures. The Legislative Analyst's Office, which provides fiscal and policy advice to the California legislature, has published information papers on gambling on tribal lands.

The Greyhound Protection League and the Humane Society of the United States provided important information on the history and status of animal racing and fighting in this country. Additional statistics on animal fighting were obtained from Pet-abuse.com. With regard to the horse racing industry, the Jockey Club and the U.S. Trotting Association issue informative materials.

The Gallup Organization and Harris Interactive provide valuable results from recent polls regarding gambling in the United States. Another helpful resource is *Illegal Sports Bookmakers* (2003, http://www.unc.edu/~cigar/papers/Bookie4b.pdf) by Koleman S. Strumpf of the University of North Carolina, Chapel Hill. The Society for Human Resource Management and the report "Employees Placing Their Bets" (February 28, 2006) by Vault .com provided valuable information about gambling in the workplace. The Annenberg Public Policy Center of the University of Pennsylvania compiles information each year detailing the gambling habits of young people in their teens and twenties. *Demographic Survey of Texas Lottery Players 2007* (December 2007) from the Center for Public Policy at the University of Houston provided helpful information on lottery players.

Scientific and educational publications devoted to problem gambling were invaluable to this book. They include *The Wager*, which is published by Harvard Medical School and the Massachusetts Council on Compulsive Gambling, and *Journal of Gambling Issues*, which is published by the Centre for Addiction and Mental Health in Toronto, Ontario, Canada. Other scholarly journals referenced for this publication include *American Journal on Addictions, American Journal of Geriatric Psychiatry, American Journal of Psychiatry, Behaviour Research and Therapy, Family Practice, Federal Communications Law Journal, Federal Register, Journal of American College Health, Journal of Behavioral Decision Making, Journal of Clinical Psychology, Journal of Gambling Issues, Journal of Hispanic Higher Education, Journal of Technology Law and Policy, National Tax Journal, Progress in Neuro-Psychopharmacology and Biological Psychiatry, Psychology of Addictive Behaviors, Review of Economics and Statistics, Rutgers Law Review, Southern Medical Journal, Suicide and Life-Threatening Behavior,* and *Veterinary Pathology.*

Organizations devoted to problem gambling that provided helpful data and information include Gamblers Anonymous, the National Center for Responsible Gaming, and the National Council on Problem Gambling. Some states run their own programs to address problem gambling. One helpful report is the Iowa Department of Public Health's *Iowa Gambling Treatment Program Historical Summary* (June 2007).

*Final Report* (June 1999) by the National Gambling Impact Study Commission is a critical reference for information about the effects of gambling on society. The report is based on information submitted by many researchers.

# INDEX

*Page references in italics refer to photographs. References with the letter* t *following them indicate the presence of a table. The letter* f *indicates a figure. If more than one table or figure appears on a particular page, the exact item number for the table or figure being referenced is provided.*

## A

Abramoff, Jack, 63

Addiction. *See* Compulsive gambling

Addiction treatment centers, 20

Addresses/names, of organizations, 109–113

Admissions
    for Illinois casinos, 38
    for Indiana casinos, 37
    for Louisiana casinos, 36

Adoption, of greyhounds, 89

Advertisements, for online gambling, 105–106

Affirmed (horse), 82

African-Americans, 75–76

"After Months of Steady Growth, U.S. Online Gambling Shows Decline in October" (Nielsen/NetRatings), 5

AGA. *See* American Gaming Association

AGC (American Greyhound Council), 86, 89

Age
    of casino gamblers, 24, 25, 25(*f*3.3)
    gambling by senior citizens, 16
    gambling by young people, 17
    of Internet gamblers, 107
    of Las Vegas visitors, 29
    of lottery players, 69
    of online gamblers, 99
    online gamblers *vs.* casino gamblers, by age, 100(*f*9.2)
    of problem gamblers, 17
    public opinion on gambling and, 7
    underage gambling, 61–62, 62(*t*6.7)
    underage Internet gambling, 107–108

AGTOA (American Greyhound Track Operators Association), 86

Agua Caliente Band of Cahuilla Indians, 50

Alabama, 77

Alaska, 5, 77

Allen, Jeff, 20

American Express, 104

American Gaming Association (AGA)
    on casino acceptability, 22–23, 23*f*
    on casino gamblers, 24–25
    on casinos, 21–22
    on charitable gambling, 13
    on commercial casinos, 29, 43, 47
    on compulsive gambling, 60
    contact information, 109
    on direct government revenue, 53–55
    education on responsible gambling, 61
    on employment at commercial casinos, 57
    on gaming revenue, 9
    on Internet gambling, 12, 98, 103–104
    on Nevada's commercial casinos, 30
    online gambling poll, 99
    on poker, 26
    on public opinion about casinos, 51
    on racetrack casinos, 81, 90
    on sports gambling, 92
    on tourism and casinos, 57
    on underage gambling, 61–62

American Greyhound Council (AGC), 86, 89

American Greyhound Track Operators Association (AGTOA), 86

*The American Indians on Reservations: A Datebook of Socioeconomic Change between the 1990 and 2000 Censuses* (Taylor & Kalt), 52

American Psychiatric Association (APA)
    Internet gambling warning of, 107
    recognition of pathological gambling, 6, 18

American Quarter Horse Association, 83

Americans with Disabilities Act of 1990, 57

*An Analysis of Internet Gambling and Its Policy Implications* (Stewart), 12, 97

*An Analysis of the Economic Impact of Indian Gaming in 2005* (NIGA)
    on money spent on regulation, 45
    on revenue from tribal casinos, 43
    on taxes, 55
    tribal casinos, effects of, 52

Animal fighting, 94–95

Anne, Queen of England, 2

Annenberg Public Policy Center
    on card playing by young people, 17
    contact information, 109
    on underage Internet gambling, 108

*Annual Report, Fiscal Year 2007* (South Dakota Commission on Gaming), 41

*Annual Report of Harrah's Entertainment, Inc., to the United States Securities and Exchange Commission*, 10

*Annual Report of Penn National Gaming, Inc., to the United States Securities and Exchange Commission*, 11

*Annual Report of the Minnesota Gambling Control Board: Fiscal Year 2007*, 14

*Annual Report to the General Assembly: Fiscal Year 2006* (Missouri Gaming Commission), 59, 59*t*

*Annual Report to the Governor: Calendar Year 2007* (Michigan Gaming and Control Board), 39

*Annual Report to the Security Exchange Commission* (Station Casinos), 11

Antidepressant drugs, 20

Antigua, Caribbean, 97, 102–103

Antze, Paul, 19

APA. *See* American Psychiatric Association

Arabian horses, 83

Arabian Jockey Club, 83

"Arabian Racing in the US: 2007 Summary" (Arabian Jockey Club), 83